*Behn*

***Sir Patient Fancy*** by Aphra Behn
From the first professional woman author in English history,
this comedy about an old man and
a young wife is both witty and risqué.

***The Spanish Wives*** by Mary Griffith Pix
More ardently feminist than some of her peers, Pix
humorously mocks the importance of virginity
and male fears of cuckoldry.

***A Bold Stroke for a Wife*** by Susanna Centlivre
Successful, prolific, and popular, Centlivre excelled at
comedies of manners and intrigue, and here
introduces the famous character "Simon Pure."

***The Group*** by Mercy Otis Warren
An American patriot, Warren satirizes British and American
Tories . . . and men's willingness to bully and sacrifice
women for political causes.

***The Witlings*** by Frances Burney
From the master of the novel of manners, this unproduced
play takes place in a millinery shop
where pretensions abound in a woman's
microcosm of the world.

***The Belle's Stratagem*** by Hannah Cowley
Deferring to traditional notions of propriety,
Cowley earned enthusiastic audiences with this mild farce
featuring a clever young woman
determined to win a man's heart.

KATHARINE M. ROGERS is the editor of *The Meridian Anthology of 18th and 19th Century British Drama*, *The Meridian Anthology of Early Women Writers: British Literary Women from Aphra Behn to Maria Edgeworth, 1600–1800*, and *The Meridian Anthology of Early American Women Writers: From Anne Bradstreet to Louisa May Alcott, 1650–1865*. Her most recent book is *Frances Burney: The World of*

The Meridian Anthology of

# Restoration and Eighteenth-Century Plays by Women

Katharine M. Rogers, Editor

A MERIDIAN BOOK

MERIDIAN
Published by the Penguin Group
Penguin Books USA Inc., 375 Hudson Street,
New York, New York 10014, U.S.A.
Penguin Books Ltd, 27 Wrights Lane,
London W8 5TZ, England
Penguin Books Australia Ltd, Ringwood,
Victoria, Australia
Penguin Books Canada Ltd, 10 Alcorn Avenue,
Toronto, Ontario, Canada M4V 3B2
Penguin Books (N.Z.) Ltd, 182–190 Wairau Road,
Auckland 10, New Zealand

Penguin Books Ltd, Registered Offices:
Harmondsworth, Middlesex, England

First published by Meridian,
an imprint of Dutton Signet,
a division of Penguin Books USA Inc.

First Printing, July, 1994
10  9  8  7  6  5  4  3  2

Permission to reprint Fanny Burney's *The Witlings* granted by
Henry W. and Albert A. Berg Collection, The New York Public Library,
Aster, Lenox and Tilden Foundations.

 REGISTERED TRADEMARK—MARCA REGISTRADA

LIBRARY OF CONGRESS CATALOGING-IN-PUBLICATION DATA:
The Meridian anthology of Restoration and Eighteenth-century plays by
women / Katharine M. Rogers, editor.
    p.  cm.
  ISBN 0-452-01110-8
  1. English drama—Restoration, 1660-1700. 2. English drama—Women authors.
3. English drama—18th century. I. Rogers, Katharine M. II. Title: Restoration
and Eighteenth-century plays by women.
PR1266.M47   1994
822.008'09287—dc20                                                93-39368
                                                                      CIP

Printed in the United States of America
Set in Stempel Garamond Aud Sabon
Designed by Julian Hamer

# Contents

# Introduction

I n 1660, when theaters in England reopened after eighteen years of Puritan repression, there was a startling innovation: actresses first appeared on the English stage. Before the decade was out, a few plays by women had appeared as well—two translations of French classical tragedies by the refined amateur Katherine Philips, called "the matchless Orinda," and an original tragedy by the otherwise unknown Frances Boothby.[1] In 1670, the production of *The Forced Marriage* initiated the career of Aphra Behn, the first English woman to become a professional author—to support herself by her writing and to compete on equal terms with men. Behn then averaged over a play a year until her death in 1689, with two plays produced posthumously.

But her example did not inspire other women to emulate her until the season of 1695–1696, when three female playwrights burst upon the scene. Catharine Trotter's tragedy *Agnes de Castro* was produced in December 1695; Delarivier Manley's comedy *The Lost Lover* in March 1696 and her tragedy *The Royal Mischief* in April; and Mary Pix's tragedy *Ibrahim, the Thirteenth Emperor of the Turks* in May or June and her farce *The Spanish Wives* in August. These women may have profited from an increasing demand for new plays, as a group of insurgent actors had opened a second theater in London in April 1695. And they were probably encouraged by a wave of feminist assertion at the end of the seventeenth century: Sarah Fyge Egerton's *Female Advocate* (1686); Mary Astell's *Serious Proposal to the Ladies* (1694) and *Some Reflections upon Marriage* (1700); Judith Drake's (?) *Essay in Defence of the Female Sex* (1696); and Lady Mary Chudleigh's *Ladies' Defence* (1700). Trotter, Manley, and Pix made much of their sex as women writers and displayed notable female solidarity, in contrast to Behn, who presented herself more as an individual who had the ability to write even though she was female. Manley claimed in commendatory verses that Trotter's first play challenged the sway of "Aspiring Man." When *The Royal Mischief* opened, Pix addressed Manley as "Pride of our sex, and glory of the stage" and associated her with Sappho, Behn, and Orinda; and Trotter hailed Manley's success as a triumph for women: "Well you've maintained our equal right in fame, / To which vain man had quite engrossed the claim."

Predictably, their success prompted a lampoon, *The Female Wits* (produced probably in the fall of 1696), whose anonymous author followed misogynistic stereotype by representing them as jealous rivals. Marsilia (Manley) proclaims herself, Calista (Trotter), and Mrs. Wellfed (Pix) "the Female Triumvirate" and asserts their superiority to male authors; but in fact the women miss no opportunity to run one another down. Marsilia, the principal object of attack, displays the strident egotism attributed to any woman who published her work. She is self-centered, demanding, arrogant, and vain, of both her person and her worthless plays. She is shown rehearsing her tragedy, a parody of *The Royal Mischief*, full of fustian and lawless love, and wrangling with the actors. Calista, the intellectual, is conceited and pedantic, although Mrs. Wellfed is merely overfond of food and drink.

Manley turned to profitable scandal chronicles and political pamphleteering, but Pix and Trotter continued to produce plays regularly for the next four years, and sporadically thereafter. The next thoroughgoing professional woman playwright was Susanna Centlivre, who produced nineteen plays between 1700 and 1724, three of which—*The Busy Body* (1709), *The Wonder* (1714), and *A Bold Stroke for a Wife* (1718)—held the stage well into the nineteenth century. In the eighteenth century, however, women were increasingly apt to turn to fiction. *The London Stage* lists fifty women who had at least one play produced in London during the 1700s; but many of them, like Charlotte Lennox or Frances Sheridan, were novelists who wrote a play or two in the intervals of their careers.[2]

Only later in the century were successful plays more profitable than novels. Hannah More made 750 pounds from her dull tragedy *Percy* (1775), although only because her close friend the actor and manager David Garrick shepherded it through production. After the sensational success of her novel *Evelina* (1778), Frances Burney was strongly advised to write a play in order to make real money by her talents, although for various reasons she never did get a comedy produced. Two women in particular took advantage of the more favorable climate for women dramatists: Hannah Cowley and Elizabeth Inchbald each left a substantial body of good plays. Inchbald's *British Theatre* (1806–09), a collection of the 125 most commonly acted plays of the time, includes eleven plays by women: five by Inchbald, three by Centlivre, two by Cowley, and Joanna Baillie's untheatrical but highly acclaimed tragedy *De Monfort* (1798).

Although women proved their ability to succeed in the theater on the same terms as men, their sex was never forgotten. In the earlier period, their work was automatically suspect, and women who put themselves forward laid themselves open to personal attack. Behn, Pix, and Centlivre all started off trying to capitalize on their sex, on the whole successfully; then each met with a setback and occasionally at least found it necessary to conceal her gender. In the prologue and epilogue to her first play, Behn coquettishly appealed to the audience to be kind to a woman's work. But when her third play (1673) got a hostile reception, she attributed it to prejudice against a female author. The prologues to her *Rover* (1677) and *Feigned Courtesans* (1679) refer to the author as male, although she went on to publish the latter play with a signed dedication. About half her plays appeared with signed dedications, and three have combative prefaces defending a woman's ability to write and insisting that her work should be judged on the same basis as a man's. Pix made feminine appeals to her audience in the prologues to her first six plays (1696–1699) and published them under her own name. But the prologue to her *Beau Defeated* (1700) refers to the author as male, and she published her last four plays anonymously.

Centlivre advertised her sex in the prologue to her first play and mentioned it in her second prologue, but referred to herself as a man in her third. Her first play was printed with her name on the title page, but succeeding ones appeared anonymously or "by the author of *The Gamester.*" In 1707, she declared that the most promising play would be blighted if discovered to be a woman's work; it would fall immediately in the opinion of those who had praised it before and in the price the publisher would offer for it (dedication to *The Platonic Lady*). After her marriage and the success of *The Busy Body,* she began to publish her plays under her own name. Still, in her dedication to *Marplot* (1710) she felt it necessary to apologize that because women are debarred from a learned education, their writing must necessarily be artless, offering mere observation of human nature rather than wit or general knowledge. Thus she accepted the traditional assumption that conventional higher education was important to creative writing (an argument constantly thrown at women writers, and demolished by Behn in her preface to *The Dutch Lover,* 1673) and disparaged the one qualification she claimed for women.

Playwriting by women retained a dubious aura even after it had become entirely respectable for them to publish in other forms. While novels and poems could be marketed privately, the dramatist had to deal with managers and actors in the loose-living, rough-and-tumble world of the theater. Some conspicuous early woman playwrights, such as Behn and Manley, were disreputable; and even respectable women wrote or accepted crudely flirtatious prologues to their plays. In her prologue to *The Spanish Wives,* Pix explicitly compares herself as author to a prostitute:

> As for you spruce gallants, pray be n't too nice,
> But show you can oblige a woman twice.
> The first time she was grave, as well she might,
> For women will be damned sullen the first night;
> But faith, they'll quickly mend, so be n't uneasy:
> Tonight she's brisk, and tries new tricks to please ye.

Hannah Cowley also capitalizes on her sex in the prologue to her first play, *The Runaway* (1776), but in a radically different way: she appeals to the audience's favor as a mother. Her comedy is playful rather than witty, because her Comic Muse is "a little blue-eyed maid" and her Apollo a romping boy, and she devised her plot and characters in her nursery: "A mother's pencil gave the light and shades, / A mother's eye through each soft scene pervades." She hopes her audience will approve the play, so that "Tom shall have his kite, and Fan new dollies."

Unlike her predecessors, Cowley did not find it necessary to conceal her authorship: all her plays after the first were published with her name. The woman author, even the playwright, was now respectable (although it is true that Frances Burney's prudish mentors scared her away from offering *The Witlings* for production in 1779). But she paid a price, in the form of deference to the ideal of feminine propriety. Cowley protected herself by a humble tone in her dedication to *The Runaway,* a play that required no apology: she attributed the play's enthusiastic reception to her sex, acknowledged that its "thousand faults" would have been castigated in a man's work, and paid tribute to "the gallantry of the English nation," which pitied the difficulties of "a *woman* tracing with feeble steps the borders of the Parnassian Mount" and "placed her *high* above her level." How different from Behn's claim (admittedly, coming after many successful plays) that she had written "as many good comedies, as any one man that has writ in our age" and her avowal that she wrote for ego satisfaction as well as need—"I value fame as much as if I had been born a *hero*" (preface to *The Lucky Chance,* 1686).

The change in status of women playwrights is indicated also by the difference in our biographical knowledge about them. We do not know the maiden names of Behn and Centlivre and cannot be sure that Mr. Behn and Mr. Carroll (Centlivre's first husband) existed, or whether Behn went to Surinam in her youth and in what capacity, or whether Centlivre ran away from home in her teens and was picked up by an undergraduate and lived with him in Cambridge. We do not know what happened to Mary Pix's husband and have only indirect evidence of when she died. For the writers of the 1770s and 1780s, on the other hand, we have quite complete biographical information, known during their lives and preserved shortly after their deaths. We have reliable accounts of their family backgrounds, education, marriages and children, means of support, and social lives. Because these playwrights were esteemed, people wanted to know the facts about them; because their careers were accepted as normal, people were not tempted to make them into colorful adventuresses.

The plays in this book reflect the changes in English drama from 1678 to 1787—toward increasing decorum, stricter morality, warmer human interest. Behn's *Sir Patient Fancy* (1678) is typical of Restoration comedy in its assumption that an old man who marries a young woman deserves to be cuckolded and will be, its acceptance of unlicensed as well as matrimonial love, its brutally forthright language, and its explicit bedroom scenes. In Pix's *Spanish Wives* (1696), on the other hand, the old Governor and his young wife are both portrayed sympathetically. The Governor's Lady is tempted to cuckold him with a young colonel, but she is prevented just in time; and the married couple's mutual affection is sufficient to reunite them. The Governor loves his wife without doting, and in the end he accepts her assurances of future constancy. There is no question of cuckolding in Centlivre's *Bold Stroke for a Wife* (1718), where Ann Lovely and Fainwell aim straightforwardly at marriage from the beginning. Ann shows good sense rather than the wit of her Restoration predecessors and does not share their delight in making fun of fools, and she must be rescued by the hero from her confining situation, although she is capable of feigning when necessary.

Although *A Bold Stroke for a Wife* seems innocent, Inchbald declared it immoral in her preface to the play in *The British Theatre,* presumably because the action involves fooling the older generation and the language is not sufficiently chastened. She went on to prescribe a special standard for woman writers: because "the virtue of fortitude is expected from a female, when delicacy is the object which tries it," Centlivre "should have laid down her pen, and taken, in exchange, the meanest implement of labor, rather than have imitated the licentious example given her by the renowned [male] poets of those days."

Cowley's *Belle's Stratagem* (1780) comes much closer to Inchbald's standards for proper female authorship, but she nevertheless preferred the Touchwood subplot to the Letitia Hardy main plot as "more refined and more natural, though neither so bold nor so brilliant." Letitia is a properly modest young lady of the late eighteenth century, but she is as witty, resourceful, and enterprising as a Restoration belle. Her goal is significantly different, however: not merely to marry a desirable young man but to win his wholehearted devotion in marriage—a sentimental ideal that would not have been recognized by a Restoration heroine. Doricourt, her young man, has the tastes of a Restoration rake but is corrected of them; Mrs. Racket and Flutter are delightful but chastened versions of the Restoration fop and coquette. The mutual plotting of the heroine's party and the hero's is as exuberantly enjoyed as that which took place in Restoration comedy, but more amiable.

Burney's *The Witlings* (1779) and Inchbald's *Such Things Are* (1787) depend for their comic effects on pretentious illiteracy, inept social manipulation, and vulgar manners, rather than misadventures in courtship and sexuality, the staples of Restoration comedy; thus they are not constrained by contemporary notions of sexual propriety. Fortunately, the authors pursued their themes without deferring to the standard of gentility that equally flattened contemporary comedy, although Inchbald herself was later to deplore the "incorrectness of language, and meanness, bordering on vulgarity" of her Sir Luke and Lady Tremor (remarks on the play for *The British Theatre*). The Tremors enliven the scene with their squabbles and mortifying secrets, and Burney sets off her overbearing nonstop talker Lady Smatter with lower-middle-class Mrs. Voluble. Inchbald's representation of Elvirus and the Female Captive does reveal the contemporary taste for tears and high-flown emotions, but at least her outstanding example of virtue in the play is a genuine hero, the prison reformer John Howard. In general, women's plays show less sentimentality than men's, perhaps because women recognized its potential to demean them when it went to extremes: amiable women in sentimental comedy were apt to be reduced to pathetic, helpless victims (like Richard Steele's Indiana in *The Conscious Lovers,* 1722) or idealized into self-sacrificing martyrs who throw everything they have at the feet of some man (like Edward Moore's Mrs. Beverley in *The Gamester,* 1753).[3]

However, these women's plays show less evidence of feminine sensibility or feminist awareness than the novels of their contemporaries. Plays written for the stage had to be more respectful of conventional views than other forms of literature, because they had to be accepted by managers and actors in order to be produced, and to be accepted promptly by a popular audience in order to survive. As Inchbald explained in her preface to George Colman the younger's *John Bull* (1808), a playwright must "know the temper of the times with accuracy," because a stage play must please the public "at first sight, or never be seen more." Therefore, "he must direct his force against the weakness, as well as the strength, of his jury. He must address their habits, passions, and prejudices, as the only means to gain this sudden conquest of their minds and hearts."

Cowley protested against this constraint in her prefatory address to *A School for Greybeards* (1786). This comedy, more closely based on Behn's *Lucky Chance* than she cared to admit, had exposed her to criticism for indelicate language; and she vigorously defended herself, as Behn had.[4] Protesting that vulgar characters cannot converse in elegant language, she also hints at the inhibiting effect of involving the personal lives of women writers, more than men's, in evaluation of their work: "the point to be considered, is not whether that *dotard,* or that *pretender,* or that *coquet,* would have so given their feelings, but whether Mrs. *Cowley* ought so to have expressed herself." "The novelist may use the boldest tints," she goes on, drawing characters from every rank of society and displaying "them in their strongest colors," and thus "snatch immortality both for them, and for herself! I, on the contrary, feel encompassed with chains when I write, which check me in my happiest flights, and force me continually to reflect, not, whether *this is just?* but, whether, *this is safe?*"

If women playwrights deviated from convention to express a distinctively female point of view, they took care to do it incidentally or indirectly. Behn, who described her literary talent as "my masculine part" (preface to *The Lucky Chance),* modeled her plays on the successful comedies of her male contemporaries. The most convincing evidence of female outlook in her work is her sympathetic presentations of mature, unconventional women who would have been pilloried by the men. The Restoration stage was filled with imitations of Molière's *Les Femmes savantes* that exposed learned ladies in order to show that women are incapable of intellectual achievement and obnoxious if they attempt it. Lady Knowell in *Sir Patient Fancy* is conceited and garrulous, as they are, but she is not ignorant: she genuinely knows the classics and finds true delight in reading the epigrams of Martial (admittedly, in the company of an attractive young man). She facilitates the love affairs of the young people, in contrast to Sir Patient, the other representative of the older generation, who dismisses love as irrelevant to marriage. His detestation of well-read, talkative, opinionated women is the main object of satire, rather than her intellectual claims.

Two of the plays in this volume raise the problem of jealous, repressive husbands, a painfully important one in a society where husbands had almost unlimited power, divorce was virtually impossible, and the crime of adultery by a wife was obsessively emphasized—so much so that men might debar their wives from innocent pleasure and friendship to prevent the minutest possibility of its occurring, and feel justified in doing so. Through the parallel marriages in *The Spanish Wives,* Pix humorously but radically challenges the assumptions on which such conjugal oppression was based. She suggests, first, that a wife's fidelity or lack thereof is just not important enough to be anyone's main concern in life; and second, that a lapse in constancy is about the same in a wife as in a husband. The Governor allows his young wife a great deal of freedom, because he is not haunted by the fear of being cuckolded. His trust does not prevent her from being tempted, which would be unrealistic; but it causes her to feel remorseful, and thus disposed to mend her ways, and allows him to forgive her, so that their reconciliation is plausible and we may hope for a satisfactory marriage thereafter. Thus Pix reverses the conventional plot in which a wife forgives her erring husband, found, for example, in Colley Cibber's *Love's Last Shift* (1696). In Cibber's edifying picture of the restoration of harmony in a troubled marriage, an impeccably virtuous wife reclaims her profligate husband by demonstrating her inextinguishable love for him. Pix's plot suggests a sort of equality, since the wife learns to appreciate her husband despite his deficiency in physical attractions and he chooses to overlook her deficiency in constancy. In Cibber's play, where the innocent wife is overwhelmed with gratitude when her total self-sacrifice is rewarded with a promise of minimally decent behavior, the disproportion between the concessions of husband and wife indicates her inferiority.

In the contrasting marriage in *The Spanish Wives,* the Marquess confines his wife because he is pathologically jealous, behavior that was often condoned in this period as evidence of intense love. Pix makes his sadism clear, and she compassionately extricates the poor woman so that she can marry her true lover, who is not disturbed by the fact that she has been living with another man in an invalid marriage; Pix's devaluation of the importance of physical virginity is as unconventional as her mockery of fears of cuckoldry.

Cowley's Sir George Touchwood, a more subtle character than the Marquess, believes that he wholeheartedly loves his wife, but in fact he wishes to possess her as completely as he would the priceless jewel he compares her to. He prides himself on his idealistic view of marriage as a total union of minds, meaning, of course, that if she loves him, she will have no will separate from his. Because he loves her so much, he expects her to place "her whole delight" in him, without seeking any other society. Cowley uses her other characters to expose his selfishness. Mrs. Racket, for example, gleefully derides his pathetic surprise when his wife declares that she would rather see the sights of London with two women than stay home with him. In the end, he is persuaded that a wife can be loving and constant without focusing every thought upon her husband.

Neither Cowley nor Pix, however, unequivocally discredits the selfish possessiveness that often passed for husbandly love in their patriarchal society. Pix's Marquess is so odious that no one could take him for a loving husband; he even avows that he is more interested in his wife's fortune than in her person. Sir George is a basically decent and sensible man, capable, with minor corrections, of being a good husband who deserves his wife's love.[5] Cowley more convincingly chastises several other male characters who assume their right to order up women to suit their specifications: Doricourt spends his first scene listing his requirements of a woman who can please him, and in the end has to eat his words while everyone laughs.

*The Witlings* opens with women talking about women's concerns in the female world of a millinery shop. Mr. Censor despises the shop as silly and trivial, but it is vitally important to the working women, who must support themselves, and the upper-class women, who must dress properly in order to be married and socially accepted. Burney vividly creates the scene, showing detailed knowledge of sewing, fashion, and trade practices; and throughout the play, the millinery business stands for the real world, before which the Witlings act out their inane games.[6]

Mercy Otis Warren's dramatic satire *The Group,* the only one of our plays written in America, necessarily presents a male world, since even a politically active eighteenth-century woman would see politics in terms of masculine values. The female speaker who concludes the play assumes it is right to fight for political liberty if that is the only way to preserve it. Nevertheless, Warren makes a point of showing how men sacrifice women to their pursuit of political gain. Two of her Tory villains boast of bullying their wives into cooperation; Simple Sapling confesses

that his Sylvia weeps, "as my ambition beggars all her babes."
The only rational, virtuous speaker in the play is the woman (Sylvia?) who concludes it by deploring the unnecessary bloodshed
that is to come.

All of the playwrights in this book put something of their distinctively female perceptions and experience into their plays, but
their more significant achievement was in pioneering and finally
legitimating the profession of playwriting for women. Burney was
primarily a novelist and Warren a political writer, but the other
five women were successful professional playwrights, each of
whom produced a substantial quantity and quality of work, fully
equal to that of most of their male contemporaries. It was a showing not to be matched until contemporary times.[7]

# Notes to Introduction

1. Several Renaissance noblewomen had written closet drama, a tradi-
   tion continued in the later seventeenth century by Margaret Caven-
   dish, Duchess of Newcastle, and Anne Finch, Countess of
   Winchilsea. Philips was also an amateur, who needed vigorous en-
   couragement to allow her work to be produced on the public stage.
2. Exceptions are Eliza Haywood, with three plays; Elizabeth Griffith,
   with five; and Frances Brooke, whose comic operas *Rosina* (1782)
   and *Marian* (1788) were extremely popular. None of these plays,
   however, is artistically significant.
3. Inchbald bitingly exposed the irrationality of such behavior in her
   comments on *The Gamester* in *The British Theatre*.
4. Needless to say, Cowley had already toned down Behn's bawdy to a
   level that seems totally innocuous today.
5. Inchbald deals with the same theme, also unsatisfactorily, in the Pri-
   ory marriage in *Wives as They Were, and Maids as They Are* (1797).
6. In *The Prostituted Muse: Images of Women and Women Dramatists,
   1642–1737* (New York: St. Martin's, 1988), Jacqueline Pearson notes
   that women playwrights were more likely than men to open their
   plays with female characters; women were also likely to include more
   female characters than men did and to let them speak more of the
   lines. *Sir Patient Fancy* opens with a scene between two young un-
   married women, and, as Pearson points out, this gives them an op-

portunity to articulate what they want, rather than passively accepting a role defined by the male characters.

7. According to Fidelis Morgan, "In all London's theaters during the sixty years from 1920 to 1980 . . . fewer plays by women writers have been performed than were played by the two London companies which held the dramatic monopoly from 1660 to 1720" *(The Female Wits,* xi).

# Aphra Behn
## (1640–89)

NOTHING is certainly known of Aphra Behn's early life, not even her maiden name; but it does seem that she lived in Surinam for some months, as she claimed in her novella *Oroonoko*. After a marriage, apparently brief, to Mr. Behn, she went to Antwerp as a spy during the second Dutch War (1666), returning to London penniless. Possibly influenced by her acquaintance with Thomas Killigrew, manager of one of the two licensed theaters in London, and doubtless encouraged by the voracious demand for new plays after the theaters reopened in 1660, Behn turned to playwriting to support herself. She wrote two conventional tragicomedies that were moderately successful, but found her style with *The Dutch Lover* (1673), a comedy. Nevertheless, it was not well received, partly because of poor acting and costuming, mostly because of prejudice against a woman author. The female playwright had become a serious competitor instead of an entertaining novelty. Provoked, Behn added a vigorously feminist preface to the published play.

She went on to write fifteen (or possibly nineteen) more plays, most of which were successful, and many of which were published under her name. They feature ingenious intrigue, amusing characters, and witty courtship scenes. The best are *Sir Patient Fancy* (1678) and *The Rover* (1677); the latter, together with her farce *The Emperor in the Moon* (1687), held the stage well into the eighteenth century. Behn used her plays to promote her political sympathies, vigorously supporting the Court party and satirizing Protestant Dissenters, the successors of the Puritans who had rebelled against King Charles I. She also wrote poems (including some lovely songs), translations, and novellas, of which the best is *Oroonoko* (1688).

Behn seems to have been an attractive woman, a witty conversationalist, and a warm friend. She knew the brilliant courtier the Earl of Rochester, the leading actress Elizabeth Barry, and the writers John Dryden and Thomas Otway. She attracted her full share of the ferocious lampoons characteristic of her period, infused with particular venom because of her sex; she was attacked for "the ruin of her face" (at forty-five), for sexual promiscuity, and for getting her lovers to write her plays. Actually, her only proven love affair was a long, unhappy one with a cold bisexual lawyer named John Hoyle. Despite the attacks, Behn, considered the first professional woman author in England, demonstrated that a woman could openly succeed as a writer if she was sufficiently tough.

*Sir Patient Fancy* was produced at the Duke's Theatre, Dorset Garden, in January 1678. Anthony Leigh, a big, fat man, starred as Sir Patient. The play was not as successful as some of her other works, but it was revived occasionally until 1692.

# Sir Patient Fancy

# To the Reader

I printed this play with all the impatient haste one ought to do, who would be vindicated from the most unjust and silly aspersion woman could invent to cast on woman, and which only my being a woman has procured me: *That is was bawdy,* the least and most excusable fault in the men writers, to whose plays they all crowd, as if they came to no other end than to hear what they condemn in this. *But from a woman it was unnatural;* but how so cruel an unkindness came into their imaginations I can by no means guess; unless by those whose lovers by long absence, or those whom age or ugliness have rendered a little distant from those things they would fain imagine here.—But if such as these durst profane their chaste ears with hearing it over again, or taking it into their serious consideration in their cabinets, they would find nothing that the most innocent virgins can have cause to blush at, but confess with me that no play either ancient or modern has less of that bugbear bawdry in it. Others to show their breeding (as Bayes[1] says) cried it was made out of at least four French plays, when I had but a very bare hint from one, the *Malade imaginaire,*[2] which was given me translated by a gentleman infinitely to advantage; but how much of the French is in this, I leave to those who do indeed understand it and have seen it at the Court. The play had no other misfortune but that of coming out for a woman's: had it been owned by a man, though the most dull, unthinking, rascally scribbler in town, it had been a most admirable play. Nor does its loss of fame with the ladies do it much hurt, though they ought to have had good nature and justice enough to have attributed all its faults to the author's unhappiness, who is forced to write for bread and not ashamed to own it, and consequently ought to write to please (if she can) an age which has given several proofs it was by this way of writing to be obliged, though it is a way too cheap for men of wit to pursue who write for glory, and a way which even I despise as much below me.

# Dramatis Personæ.

SIR PATIENT FANCY, an old rich alderman, and one that fancies himself always sick—Mr. Anthony Leigh

LEANDER FANCY, his nephew, in love with *Lucretia*—Mr. Crosby

WITTMORE, gallant to the *Lady Fancy*, a wild young fellow of a small fortune—Mr. Betterton

LODWICK KNOWELL, son to the *Lady Knowell*, in love with *Isabella*—Mr. Smith

SIR CREDULOUS EASY, a foolish Devonshire knight, designed to marry *Lucretia*—Mr. Nokes

CURRY, his groom—Mr. Richards

ROGER, footman to the *Lady Fancy*

ABEL (BARTHOLOMEW), clerk to *Sir Patient Fancy*

BRUNSWICK, a friend to *Lodwick Knowell*

MONSIEUR TURBOON, a French doctor

A FAT DOCTOR

AN AMSTERDAM DOCTOR

A LEYDEN DOCTOR

PAGE to the *Lady Knowell*

Guests, six servants to *Sir Patient,* ballad-singers and serenaders

THE LADY FANCY, young wife to *Sir Patient*—Mrs. Currer

THE LADY KNOWELL, an affected learned woman, mother to *Lodwick* and *Lucretia*—Mrs. Gwin

LUCRETIA, daughter to the *Lady Knowell*—Mrs. Price

ISABELLA, daughter to *Sir Patient Fancy*—Mrs. Betterton

FANNY, a child of seven years old, daughter to *Sir Patient Fancy*

MAUNDY, the *Lady Fancy*'s woman—Mrs. Gibbs

BETTY, waiting-woman to *Isabella*

ANTIC, waiting-woman to *Lucretia*

NURSE

# PROLOGUE.

## Spoken by Mr. Betterton.

We write not now, as th' ancient poets writ,
For your applause of Nature, Sense, and Wit;
But, like good tradesmen, what's in fashion vent,
And cozen you, to give ye all content.
True comedy, writ even in Dryden's[3] style,
Will hardly raise your humors to a smile.
Long did his sovereign muse the sceptre sway,
And long with joy you did true homage pay:
But now, like happy states, luxurious grown,
The Monarch Wit unjustly you dethrone,
And a tyrannic commonwealth prefer,[4]
Where each small wit starts up and claims his share;
And all those laurels are in pieces torn,
Which did e'er while one sacred head adorn.
Nay, even the women now pretend to reign;
Defend us from a Poet Joan[5] again!
That congregation's in a hopeful way
To Heaven, where the lay-sisters teach and pray.
Oh, the great blessing of a little wit!
I've seen an elevated poet sit,
And hear the audience laugh and clap, yet say,
Gad, after all, 'tis a damned silly play:
He, unconcerned, cries only—Is it so?
No matter, these unwitty things will do,
When your fine, fustian, useless eloquence
Serves but to chime asleep a drowsy audience.
Who at the vast expence of wit would treat,
That might so cheaply please the appetite?

Such homely fare you're like to find tonight:
Our author
Knows better how to juggle than to write:
Alas! a poet's good for nothing now,
Unless he have the knack of conjuring too;
For 'tis beyond all natural sense to guess
How their strange miracles are brought to pass.
Your Presto Jack be gone, and come again,
With all the hocus art of legerdemain;
Your dancing tester, nutmeg, and your cups,
Outdoes your heroes and your amorous fops.[6]
And if this chance to please you, by that rule,
He that writes wit is much the greater fool.

scene: London, in two houses.

# ACT I.

## Scene i. A room in Lady Knowell's house.

*(Enter Lucretia with Isabella.)*

ISABELLA. 'Tis much I owe to Fortune, my dear Lucretia, for being so kind to make us neighbors, where with ease we may continually exchange our souls and thoughts without the attendance of a coach, and those other little formalities that make a business of a visit; it looks so like a journey, I hate it.

LUCRETIA. Attendance[7] is that curse to greatness that confines the soul, and spoils good humor; we are free whilst thus alone, and can laugh at the abominable fopperies of this town.

ISABELLA. And lament the numberless impertinences wherewith they continually plague all young women of quality.

LUCRETIA. Yet these are the precious things our grave parents still choose out to make us happy with, and all for a filthy jointure,[8] the undeniable argument for our slavery to fools.

ISABELLA. Custom is unkind to our sex, not to allow us free choice; but we above all creatures must be forced to endure the formal recommendations of a parent, and the more insupportable addresses of an odious fop; whilst the obedient daughter stands—thus—with her hands pinned before her, a set look, few words, and a mien that cries—Come marry me. Out upon't.

LUCRETIA. I perceive then, whatever your father designs, you are resolved to love your own way.

ISABELLA. Thou mayst lay thy maidenhead upon't, and be sure of the misfortune to win.

LUCRETIA. My brother Lodwick's like to be a happy man then.

ISABELLA. Faith, my dear Lodwick or nobody in my heart, and I hope thou art as well resolved for my cousin Leander.

LUCRETIA. Here's my hand upon't, I am; yet there's something sticks upon my stomach, which you must know.

ISABELLA. Spare the relation, for I have observed of late your mother to have ordered her eyes with some softness, her mouth endeavoring to sweeten itself into smiles and dimples, as if she meant to recall fifteen again, and gave it all to Leander, for at him she throws her darts.

LUCRETIA. Is't possible thou shouldst have perceived it already?

ISABELLA. Long since.

LUCRETIA. And now I begin to love him, 'twould vex me to see my mother marry him—well, I shall never call him Father.

ISABELLA. He'll take care to give himself a better title.

LUCRETIA. This Devonshire knight too, who is recommended to my mother as a fit husband for me, I shall be so tormented with—My brother swears he's the pertest, most unsufferable fool he ever saw; when he was at my uncle's last summer, he made all his diversion.

ISABELLA. Prithee let him make ours now, for of all fops your country fop is the most tolerable animal; those of the town are the most unmanageable beasts in nature.

LUCRETIA. And are the most noisy, keeping fops.

ISABELLA. Keeping[9] begins to be as ridiculous as matrimony, and is a greater imposition upon the liberty of man; the insolence and expense of their mistresses has almost tired out all but the old and doting part of mankind. The rest begin to know their value, and set a price upon a good shape, a tolerable face and mien:—and some there are who have made excellent bargains for themselves that way, and will flatter ye and jilt ye an antiquated lady as the most experienced miss[10] of 'em all.

LUCRETIA. Lord, Lord! what will this world come to?—but this mother of mine—Isabella. *(Sighs.)*

ISABELLA. Is discreet and virtuous enough, a little too affected, as being the most learned of her sex.

LUCRETIA. Methinks to be read in the arts, as they call 'em, is the peculiar province of the other sex.

ISABELLA. Indeed the men would have us think so, and boast their learning and languages; but if they can find any of our sex fuller of words, and to so little purpose as some of their gownmen, I'll be content to change my petticoats for pantaloons, and go to a grammar-school.

LUCRETIA. Oh, they're the greatest babelards[11] in Nature.

ISABELLA. They call us easy and fond, and charge us with all weakness; but look into their actions of love, state, or war, their roughest business, and you shall find 'em swayed by some who have the luck to find their foibles; witness my father, a man reasonable enough, till drawn away by doting love and religion: what a monster my young mother[12] makes of him! flattered him first into matrimony, and now into what sort of fool or beast she pleases to make him.

LUCRETIA. I wonder she does not turn him to Christianity; methinks a conventicle[13] should ill agree with her humor.

ISABELLA. Oh, she finds it the only way to secure her from his suspicion, which if she do not e'er long give him cause for, I am mistaken in her humor.—

*(Enter Lady Knowell and Leander.)*

But see your mother and my cousin Leander, who seems, poor man, under some great consternation, for he looks as gravely as a lay-elder conducting his spouse from a sermon.

LADY KNOWELL. Oh, fy upon't. See, Mr. Fancy, where your cousin and my Lucretia are idling. *Dii boni,*[14] what an insupportable loss of time's this?

LEANDER. Which might be better employed, if I might instruct 'em, Madam.

LADY KNOWELL. Ay, Mr. Fancy, in consultation with the ancients.—Oh, the delight of books! when I was of their age, I always employed my looser hours in reading—if serious, 'twas Tacitus, Seneca, Plutarch's *Morals,* or some such useful author; if in an humor gay, I was for poetry, Virgil, Homer, or Tasso. Oh, that love between Rinaldo and Armida, Mr. Fancy! Ah, the caresses that fair Corcereis gave, and received from the young warrior;[15] ah, how soft, delicate, and tender! Upon my honor, I cannot read them in the excellence of their original language, without I know not what emotions.

LEANDER. Methinks 'tis very well in our mother tongue, Madam.

LADY KNOWELL. Oh, faugh, Mr. Fancy, what have you said, mother tongue! Can any thing that's great or moving be expressed in filthy English?—I'll give you an energetical proof, Mr. Fancy; observe but divine Homer in the Grecian language— *Ton d'apamibominous prosiphe podas ochus Achilleus!*[16] Ah, how it sounds! which English'd dwindles into the most grating stuff:—Then the swift-foot Achilles made reply. Oh, faugh.

LUCRETIA. So now my mother's in her right sphere.

LADY KNOWELL. Come, Mr. Fancy, we'll pursue our first design of retiring into my cabinet, and reading a leaf or two in Martial;[17] I am a little dull, and would fain laugh.

LEANDER. Methinks, Madam, discourse were much better with these young ladies. Dear Lucretia, find some way to release me. *(Aside.)*

LADY KNOWELL. Oh, how I hate the impertinence of women, who for the generality have no other knowledge than that of dressing; I am uneasy with the unthinking creatures.

LUCRETIA. Indeed, 'tis much better to be entertaining a young lover alone; but I'll prevent her, if possible. *(Aside.)*

LADY KNOWELL. No, I am for the substantial pleasure of an author. *Philosophemur!*[18] is my motto,—I'm strangely fond of you, Mr. Fancy, for being a scholar.

LEANDER. Who, Madam, I a scholar? the greatest dunce in Nature—Malicious creatures, will you leave me to her mercy? *(To them, aside.)*

LUCRETIA. Prithee assist him in his misery, for I am Mudd,[19] and can do nothing towards it. *(Aside.)*

ISABELLA. Who, my cousin Leander a scholar, Madam?

LUCRETIA. Sure he's too much a gentleman to be a scholar.

ISABELLA. I vow, Madam, he spells worse than a country farrier when he prescribes a drench.

LEANDER. Then, Madam, I write the lewdest hand.[20]

ISABELLA. Worse than a politician or a statesman.

LUCRETIA. He cannot read it himself when he has done.

LEANDER. Not a word on't, Madam.

LADY KNOWELL. This agreement to abuse him, I understand— *(Aside.)*—Well, then, Mr. Fancy, let's to my cabinet—your hand.

LEANDER. Now shall I be teased unmercifully,—I'll wait on you, Madam.

*(Exit Lady Knowell.)*

—Find some means to redeem me, or I shall be mad.

*(Exit Leander. Enter Lodwick.)*

LODWICK. Hah, my dear Isabella here, and without a spy! what a blessed opportunity must I be forced to lose, for there is just now arrived my sister's lover,[21] whom I am obliged to receive: but if you have a mind to laugh a little—

ISABELLA. Laugh! why, are you turned buffoon, tumbler, or Presbyterian preacher?

LODWICK. No, but there's a creature below more ridiculous than either of these.

LUCRETIA. For love's sake, what sort of beast is that?

LODWICK. Sir Credulous Easy, your new lover just come to town bag and baggage, and I was going to acquaint my mother with it.

ISABELLA. You'll find her well employed with my cousin Leander.

LUCRETIA. A happy opportunity to free him: but what shall I do now, Brother?

LODWICK. Oh, let me alone to ruin him with my mother; get you gone, I think I hear him coming, and this apartment is appointed for him.

LUCRETIA. Prithee haste then, and free Leander; we'll into the garden. (*Exeunt Lucretia and Isabella.*)

(*A chair and a table. Enter Sir Credulous in a riding habit. Curry, his groom, carrying a portmantle.[22]*)

LODWICK. Yes—'tis the Right Worshipful. I'll to my mother with the news. (*Exit Lodwick.*)

SIR CREDULOUS. Come undo my portmantle, and equip me, that I may look like somebody before I see the ladies—Curry, thou shalt e'en remove now, Curry, from groom to footman; for I'll ne'er keep horse more, no, nor mare neither, since my poor Gillian's departed this life.

CURRY. 'Ds diggers, Sir, you have grieved enough for your mare in all conscience; think of your mistress now, Sir, and think of her no more.

SIR CREDULOUS. Not think of her! I shall think of her whilst I live, poor fool, that I shall, though I had forty mistresses.

CURRY. Nay, to say truth, Sir, 'twas a good-natured civil beast, and so she remained to her last gasp, for she could never have left this world in a better time, as the saying is, so near her journey's end.

SIR CREDULOUS. A civil beast! Why, was it civilly done of her, thinkest thou, to die at Branford, when had she lived till tomorrow, she had been converted into money and have been in my pocket? for now I am to marry and live in town, I'll sell off all my pads; poor fool, I think she e'en died for grief I would have sold her.

CURRY. 'Twas unlucky to refuse Parson Cuffet's wife's money for her, Sir.

SIR CREDULOUS. Ay, and to refuse her another kindness too, that shall be nameless, which she offered me, and which would have given me good luck in horse-flesh too. Zoz, I was a modest fool, that's truth on't.

CURRY. Well, well, Sir, her time was come you must think, and we are all mortal, as the saying is.

SIR CREDULOUS. Well, 'twas the lovingest tit:—but grass and hay, she's gone—where be her shoes, Curry?

CURRY. Here, Sir, her skin went for good ale at Branford. *(Gives him the shoes.)*

SIR CREDULOUS. Ah, how often has she carried me upon these shoes to Mother Jumble's; thou rememberest her handsome daughter, and what pure ale she brewed; between one and t'other my rent came short home there. But let that pass too, and hang sorrow; as thou sayst, I have something else to think on. *(Takes his things out, lays them upon the table.)* And, Curry, as soon as I am dressed, go you away to St. Clement's Churchyard, to Jackson, the cobbler there.

CURRY. What, your dog-tutor, Sir?

SIR CREDULOUS. Yes, and see how my whelp proves, I put to him last Parliament.

CURRY. Yes, Sir.

*(Enter Leander, and starts back, seeing Sir Credulous.)*

SIR CREDULOUS. And ask him what gamesters come to the ponds[23] nowadays, and what good dogs.

CURRY. Yes, Sir.

LEANDER. This is the beast Lodwick spoke of; how could I laugh were he designed for any but Lucretia! *(Aside.)*

SIR CREDULOUS. And dost hear, ask him if he have not sold his own dog Diver with the white ear; if I can purchase him, and my own dog prove right, I'll be Duke of Ducking-Pond, ads

zoz. *(Sir Credulous dresses himself.)* Well, I think I shall be fine
anon, he.

CURRY. But zo, zo, Sir, as the saying is, this suit's a little out of
fashion; 'twas made that very year I came to your worship,
which is five winters, and as many summers.

SIR CREDULOUS. What then, Mun; I never wear it, but when I go
to be drunk, and give my voice for a knight o'th'shire, and here
at London in term time, and that but eight times in eight visits
to eight several ladies to whom I was recommended.[24]

CURRY. I wonder that amongst eight you got not one, Sir.

SIR CREDULOUS. Eight! Zoz, I had eight score, Mun; but the Devil
was in 'em, they were all so forward, that before I could seal
and deliver, whip, quoth Jethro, they were either all married to
somebody else, or run quite away; so that I am resolved if this
same Lucretia proves not right, I'll e'en forswear this town and
all their false wares, amongst which, zoz, I believe they vent as
many false wives as any metropolitan[25] in Christendom, I'll say
that for't, and a fiddle for't, i'faith:—come, give me my watch
out,—so, my diamond rings too: so, I think I shall appear pretty
well all together, Curry, hah?

LEANDER. Like something monstrously ridiculous, I'll be sworn.
*(Aside.)*

CURRY. Here's your purse of broad gold, Sir, that your grandmother gave you to go a wooing withal; I mean to show, Sir.

SIR CREDULOUS. Ay, for she charged me never to part with it;—so,
now for the ladies. *(Shakes his ribbons.)*


*(Enter Lodwick.)*


LODWICK. Leander, what mak'st thou here, like a holiday fool gazing at a monster?

LEANDER. Yes. And one I hope I have no great reason to fear.

LODWICK. I am of thy opinion. Away, my mother's coming. Take
this opportunity with my sister; she's i'th'garden; and let me
alone with this fool, for an entertainment that shall show him
all at once. Away—*(Exit Leander.)*


*(Lodwick goes in to Sir Credulous.)*

Sir Credulous. Lodwick, my dear friend! and little spark of ingenuity—Zoz, man, I'm but just come to town. *(Embrace.)*

Lodwick. 'Tis a joyful hearing, Sir.

Sir Credulous. Not so joyful neither, Sir, when you shall know poor Gillian's dead, my little grey mare; thou knew'st her, Mun. Zoz, 'thas made me as melancholy as the drone of a Lancashire bagpipe. But let that pass; and now we talk of my mare, Zoz, I long to see this sister of thine.

Lodwick. She'll be with you presently, Sir Credulous.

Sir Credulous. But hark ye, Zoz, I have been so often fobbed off in these matters, that between you and I, Lodwick, if I thought I should not have her, Zoz, I'd never lose precious time about her.

Lodwick. Right, Sir; and to say truth, these women have so much contradiction in 'em, that 'tis ten to one but a man fails in the art of pleasing.

Sir Credulous. Why, there's it:—therefore prithee, dear Lodwick, tell me a few of thy sister's humors, and if I fail,—then hang me, ladies, at your door, as the song says.

Lodwick. Why, faith, she has many odd humors hard enough to hit.

Sir Credulous. Zoz, let 'em be as hard as Hercules his labors in the Vale of Basse, I'll not be frighted from attempting her.

Lodwick. Why, she's one of those fantastic creatures that must be courted her own way.

Sir Credulous. Why, let's hear her way.

Lodwick. She must be surprised with strange extravagancies wholly out of the road and method of common courtship.

Sir Credulous. Pshaw, is that all? Zoz, I'm the best in Christendom at your out-of-the-way businesses.—Now do I find the reason of all my ill success; for I used one and the same method to all I courted, whatever their humors were. Hark ye, prithee give me a hint or two, and let me alone to manage matters.

Lodwick. I have just now thought of a way that cannot but take—

Sir Credulous. Zoz, out with it, man.

Lodwick. Why, what if you should represent a dumb ambassador from the blind God of Love.

Sir Credulous. How, a dumb ambassador? Zoz, man, how shall I deliver my embassy then, and tell her how much I love her?—

besides, I had a pure[26] speech or two ready by heart, and that will be quite lost. *(Aside.)*

LODWICK. Fie, fie! how dull you are! why, you shall do it by signs, and I'll be your interpreter.

SIR CREDULOUS. Why, faith, this will be pure. I understand you now, Zoz; I am old excellent at signs;—I vow this will be rare.

LODWICK. It will not fail to do your business, if well managed—but stay, here's my sister; on your life, not a syllable.

*(Enter Leander, Lucretia, and Isabella.)*

SIR CREDULOUS. I'll be racked first, Mum budget,—prithee present me; I long to be at it, sure. *(He falls back, making faces and grimaces.)*

LODWICK. Sister, I here present you with a worthy knight, struck dumb with admiration of your beauty; but that's all one, he is employed Envoy Extraordinary from the blind God of Love: and since, like his young master, he must be defective in one of his senses, he chose rather to be dumb than blind.

LUCRETIA. I hope the small deity is in good health, Sir?

ISABELLA. And his mistress, Psyche, Sir?

*(He smiles and bows, and makes signs.)*

LODWICK. He says that Psyche has been sick of late, but somewhat recovered, and has sent you for a token a pair of jet bracelets, and a cambric handkerchief of her own spinning, with a sentence wrought in't, *Heart in hand, at thy command. (Looking every word upon Sir Credulous as he makes signs.)*

SIR CREDULOUS. Zoz, Lodwick, what do you mean? I'm the son of an Egyptian if I understand thee. *(Pulls him, he signs to him to hold his peace.)*

LODWICK. Come, Sir, the tokens; produce, produce— *(He falls back, making damnable signs.)* How! Faith, I'm sorry for that with all my heart,—he says, being somewhat put to't on his journey, he was forced to pawn the bracelets for half a crown, and the handkerchief he gave his landlady on the road for a kindness received,—this 'tis when people will be fooling—

SIR CREDULOUS. Why, the Devil's in this Lodwick, for mistaking my signs thus. Hang me if ever I thought of bracelets or a handkerchief, or ever received a civility from any woman breathing,—is he bewitched trow? *(Aside.)*

Leander. Lodwick, you are mistaken in the knight's meaning all this while. Look on him, Sir,—do not you guess from that look, and wrying of his mouth, that you mistook the bracelets for diamond rings, which he humbly begs, Madam, you would grace with your fair hand?

Lodwick. Ah, now I perceive it plain.

Sir Credulous. A pox of his compliment. Why, this is worse than t'other.—What shall I do in this case?—should I speak and undeceive them, they would swear 'twere to save my gems: and to part with 'em—Zoz, how simply should I look!—but hang't, when I have married her, they are my own again.[27] *(Gives the rings, and falls back into grimaces. Leander whispers to Lodwick.)*

Lodwick. Enough—Then, Sister, she has sent you a purse of her own knitting full of broad gold.

Sir Credulous. Broad gold! why, what a pox, does the man conjure?

Lodwick. Which, Sister, faith, you must accept of; you see by that grimace how much 'twill grieve him else.

Sir Credulous. A pretty civil way this to rob a man.—Why, Lodwick,—why, what a pox, will they have no mercy?—Zoz, I'll see how far they'll drive the jest. *(Gives the gold and bows, and scrapes and screws.)*

Lodwick. Say you so, Sir? Well, I'll see what may be done.— Sister, behold him, and take pity on him; he has but one more humble request to make you, 'tis to receive a gold watch which he designs you from himself.

Sir Credulous. Why, how long has this fellow been a conjurer? For he does deal with the Devil, that's certain,—Lodwick— *(Pulls him.)*

Lodwick. Ay, do, speak and spoil all, do.

Sir Credulous. Speak and spoil all, quoth he! and the Deuce take me if I am not provoked to't. Why, how the Devil should he light slap-dash, as they say, upon everything thus? Well, Zoz, I'm resolved to give it her, and shame her if she have any conscience in her. *(Gives his watch with pitiful grimaces.)*

Lodwick. Now, Sister, you must know there's a mystery in this watch, 'tis a kind of hieroglyphic that will instruct you how a married woman of your quality ought to live.

SIR CREDULOUS. How, my watch mysteries and hieroglyphics! The Devil take me, if I knew of any such virtues it had.

*(They are all looking on the watch.)*

LODWICK. Beginning at eight, from which down to twelve you ought to employ in dressing, till two at dinner, till five in visits, till seven at the play, till nine i'th'park, ten at supper with your lover, if your husband be not at home, or keep his distance, which he's too well bred not to do; then from ten to twelve are the happy hours the bergere,[28] those of entire enjoyment.—

SIR CREDULOUS. Say you so? Hang me if I shall not go near to think I may chance to be a cuckold by the shift.

ISABELLA. Well, Sir, what must she do from twelve till eight again?

LODWICK. Oh! those are the dull conjugal hours for sleeping with her own husband, and dreaming of joys her absent lover alone can give her.

SIR CREDULOUS. Nay, an she be for sleeping, Zoz, I am as good at that as she can be for her heart; or snoring either.

LODWICK. But I have done; Sir Credulous has a dumb oration to make you by way of farther explanation.

SIR CREDULOUS. A dumb oration! Now do I know no more how to speak a dumb speech than a dog.

LUCRETIA. Oh, I love that sort of eloquence extremely.

LODWICK. I told you this would take her.

SIR CREDULOUS. Nay, I know your silent speeches are incomparable, and I have such a speech in my head.

LODWICK. Your postures, your postures, begin, Sir. *(He puts himself into a ready posture as if he would speak, but only makes faces. Enter Page.)*

PAGE. Sir, my Lady desires to speak with you. *(To Leander.)*

LEANDER. I'll wait on her,—a Devil on't.—

PAGE. I have command to bring you, Sir, instantly.

LEANDER. This is ill luck, Madam, I cannot see the farce out; I'll wait on you as soon as my good fortune will permit me. *(Exit with Page.)*

LUCRETIA. He's going to my mother; dear Isabella, let's go and hinder their discourse. Farewell, Sir Ambassador, pray remember us to Psyche, not forgetting the little blind archer, ha, ha, ha.—

*(Exit Lucretia and Isabella, laughing.)*

Sir Credulous. So, I have undone all; they are both gone, flown I protest. Why, what a Devil ailed 'em? Now have I been dumb all this while to no purpose; you too never told her my meaning right. As I hope to breathe, had any but yourself done this, I should have sworn by Helicon and all the rest of the devils, you had had a design to have abused me, and cheated me of all my movables too.

Lodwick. What a hopeful project was here defeated by my mistake! But courage, Sir Credulous, I'll put you in a way shall fetch all about again.

Sir Credulous. Say you so? Ah, dear Lodwick, let me hear it.

Lodwick. Why, you shall this night give your mistress a serenade.

Sir Credulous. How! a serenade!

Lodwick. Yes, but it must be performed after an extravagant manner, none of your dull amorous night-walking noises so familiar in this town; Lucretia loves nothing but what's great and extravagant, and passes the reach of vulgar practice.

Sir Credulous. What think you of a silent serenade? Zoz, say but the word and it shall be done, Man; let me alone for frolics, i'faith.

Lodwick. A silent one! No, that's to wear a good humor to the stumps; I would have this want for no noise; the extremes of these two addresses will set off one another.

Sir Credulous. Say you so? What think you then of the bagpipe, tongs, and gridiron, cat-calls, and loud-sounding cymbals?

Lodwick. Naught, naught, and of known use; you might as well treat her with viols and flute-doux, which were enough to disoblige her forever.

Sir Credulous. Why, what think you then of the King of Bantam's own music.[29]

Lodwick. How! the King of Bantam's music?

Sir Credulous. Ay, Sir, the King of Bantam's: a friend of mine had a present sent him from thence, a most unheard of curiosity I'll assure you.

Lodwick. That, that by all means, Sir.

SIR CREDULOUS. Well, I'll go borrow 'em presently.

LODWICK. You must provide yourself of a song.

SIR CREDULOUS. A song! hang't, 'tis but rummaging the play-books,[30] stealing thence is lawful prize—Well, Sir, your servant. *(Exit. Enter Leander.)*

LODWICK. I hope 'twill be ridiculous enough, and then the Devil's in't if it do not do his business with my mother, for she hates all impertinent noises but what she makes herself. She's now going to make a visit to your uncle, purposely to give me an opportunity to Isabella.

LEANDER. And I'm engaged to wait on her thither; she designs to carry the fiddles too.[31] He's mad enough already, but such a visit will fit him for Bedlam.

LODWICK. No matter, for you have all a lewd hand with him;[32] between his continual imaginary sickness, and perpetual physic, a man might take more pleasure in an hospital. What the Devil did he marry a young wife for? and they say a handsome creature too.

LEANDER. To keep up his title of cuckold, I think; for she has beauty enough for temptation, and no doubt makes the right use on't. Would I could know it, that I might prevent her cheating my uncle longer to my undoing.

LODWICK. She'll be cunning enough for that, if she have wit: but now thou talkst of intrigues, when didst see Wittmore? That rogue has some lucky haunt which we must find out.—But my mother expects your attendance; I'll go seek my sister, and make all the interest there I can for you, whilst you pay me in the same coin to Isabella. Adieu.

LEANDER. Trust my friendship.—

*(Exeunt severally.)*

# ACT II.

## Scene i. A garden to Sir Patient Fancy's house.

*(Enter Lady Fancy, Wittmore, and Maundy.)*

WITTMORE. Enough, my charming mistress, you've set my soul at peace, and chased away those fears and doubts my jealousy created there.

MAUNDY. Mr. Wittmore's satisfied of your constancy, Madam; though had I been your Ladyship, I should have given him a more substantial proof, which you might yet do, if you would make handsome use of your time.

WITTMORE. Maundy advises well; my dearest, let's withdraw to yonder covert arbor, whose kind shades will secure us a happiness that gods might envy. *(Offers to lead her out.)*

LADY FANCY. I dare not for the world; Sir Patient is now asleep, and 'tis to those few minutes we are obliged for this enjoyment, which should love make us transgress, and he should wake and surprise us, we are undone forever. No, let us employ this little time we have in consulting how we may be often happy, and securely so: Oh, how I languish for the dear opportunity!

WITTMORE. And could you guess what torments I have suffered in these few fatal months that have divided us, thou wouldst pity me.

LADY FANCY. —But to our business; for though I am yet unsuspected by my husband, I am eternally plagued with his company; he's so fond of me, he scarce gives me time to write to thee, he waits on me from room to room, hands me in the garden, shoulders me in the balcony, nay, does the office of my women, dresses and undresses me, and does so smirk at his handywork. In fine, dear Wittmore, I am impatient till I can have less of his company, and more of thine.

WITTMORE. Does he never go out of town?

LADY FANCY. Never without me.

Wittmore. Nor to church?

Lady Fancy. To a meeting-house you mean, and then too carries me, and is as vainly proud of me as of his rebellious opinion, for his religion means nothing but that, and contradiction;[33] which I seem to like too, since 'tis the best cloak I can put on to cheat him with.

Wittmore. Right, my fair hypocrite.

Lady Fancy. But, dear Wittmore, there's nothing so comical as to hear me cant, and even cheat those knaves, the preachers themselves, that delude the ignorant rabble.

Wittmore. What miracles cannot your eyes and tongue perform!

Lady Fancy. Judge what a fine life I lead the while, to be set up with an old, formal, doting, sick husband, and a herd of snivelling, grinning hypocrites, that call themselves the teaching saints; who, under pretence of securing me to the number of their flock, do so sneer[34] upon me, pat my breasts, and cry fie, fie upon this fashion of tempting nakedness. *(Through the nose.)*

Wittmore. Dear creature, how could we laugh at thy new way of living, had we but some minutes allowed us to enjoy that pleasure alone.

Lady Fancy. Think, dear Wittmore, think, Maundy, and I have thought over all our devices to no purpose.

Wittmore. Pox on't, I'm the dullest dog at plotting, thinking, in the world; I should have made a damnable ill town poet. Has he quite left off going to the Change?[35]

Lady Fancy. Oh, he's grown cautiously rich, and will venture none of his substantial stock in transitory traffic.

Wittmore. Has he no mutinous cabal, nor coffee-houses, where he goes religiously to consult the welfare of the nation?

Lady Fancy. His imagined sickness has made this their rendezvous.

Wittmore. When he goes to his blind devotion, cannot you pretend to be sick? That may give us at least two or three opportunities to begin with.

Lady Fancy. Oh! Then I should be plagued with continual physic and extempore prayer till I were sick indeed.

Wittmore. Damn the humorous coxcomb and all his family; what shall we do?

Lady Fancy. Not all, for he has a daughter that has good humor, wit, and beauty enough to save her,—stay—that has jogged a thought, as the learned say, which must jog on, till the motion have produced something worth my thinking—

*(Enter Roger, running.)*

MAUNDY. Ad's me, here's danger near, our scout comes in such haste.

LADY FANCY. Roger, what's the matter?

ROGER. My master, Madam, is risen from sleep, and is come into the garden.—See, Madam, he's here.

LADY FANCY. What an unlucky accident was this!

WITTMORE. What shall I do? 'Tis too late to obscure myself.

LADY FANCY. He sees you already, through the trees,—here—keep your distance, your hat under your arm; so, be very ceremonious, whilst I settle a demure coutenance.—

MAUNDY. Well, there never came good of lovers that were given to too much talking; had you been silently kind all this while, you had been willing to have parted by this time.

*(Enter Sir Patient in a night-gown, reading a bill.)*

SIR PATIENT. Hum,—Twelve purges for this present January—as I take it, good Mr. Doctor, I took but ten in all December.—By this rule I am sicker this month, than I was the last.—And, good Master Apothecary, methinks your prices are somewhat too high: at this rate nobody would be sick.—Here, Roger, see it paid, however,—Ha, hum. *(Sees 'em, and starts back.)* What's here, my lady wife entertaining a lewd fellow of the town? a flaunting cap and feather blade.

LADY FANCY. Sir Patient cannot now be spoken with. But, Sir, that which I was going just now to say to you, was, that it would be very convenient in my opinion to make your addresses to Isabella,—'twill give us opportunities. *(Aside.)* We ladies love no imposition; this is counsel my husband perhaps will not like, but I would have all women choose their man, as I have done,—my dear Wittmore. *(Aside.)*

SIR PATIENT. I profess ingenuously an excellent good lady this of mine, though I do not like her counsel to the young man, who I perceive would be a suitor to my daughter, Isabella.

WITTMORE. Madam, should I follow my inclinations, I should pay my vows nowhere but there,—but I am informed Sir Patient is a man so positively resolved—

LADY FANCY. That you should love his wife. *(Aside.)*

WITTMORE. And I'll comply with that resolve of his, and neither love nor marry Isabella, without his permission; and I doubt not but I shall by my respects to him gain his consent,—to cuckold him. *(Aside.)*

SIR PATIENT. I profess ingenuously, a very discreet young man.

WITTMORE. But, Madam, when may I promise myself the satisfaction of coming again? For I'm impatient for the sight and enjoyment of the fair person I love.

LADY FANCY. Sir, you may come at night, and something I will do by that time shall certainly give you that access you wish for.

WITTMORE. May I depend upon that happiness?

LADY FANCY. Oh, doubt not my power over Sir Patient.

SIR PATIENT. My Lady Fancy, you promise largely.

LADY FANCY. Sir Patient here!

WITTMORE. A devil on him, would I were well off: now must I dissemble, profess, and lie most confoundedly.

SIR PATIENT. Your servant, Sir, your servant.—My Lady Fancy, your Ladyship is well entertained, I see. Have a care you make me not jealous, my Lady Fancy.

LADY FANCY. Indeed I have given you cause, Sir Patient; for I have been entertaining a lover, and one you must admit of too.

SIR PATIENT. Say you so, my Lady Fancy?—Well, Sir, I am a man of reason, and if you show me good causes why, can bid you welcome, for I do nothing without reason and precaution.

WITTMORE. Sir, I have—

SIR PATIENT. I know what you would say, Sir; few words denoteth a wise head,—you would say that you have an ambition to be my son-in-law.

WITTMORE. You guess most right, Sir.

SIR PATIENT. Nay, Sir, I'll warrant I'll read a man as well as the best, I have studied it.

WITTMORE. Now, Invention, help me, or never.

SIR PATIENT. Your name, I pray? *(Putting off his hat gravely at every word.)*

WITTMORE. Fainlove, Sir.

SIR PATIENT. Good Mr. Fainlove, your country?

WITTMORE. Yorkshire, Sir.

SIR PATIENT. What, not Mr. Fainlove's son of Yorkshire, who was knighted in the good days of the late Lord Protector?[36] *(Off his hat.)*

WITTMORE. The same, Sir.—I am in, but how to come off again, the Devil take me if I know. *(Aside.)*

SIR PATIENT. He was a man of admirable parts, believe me, a notable headpiece, a public-spirited person, and a good Commonwealths-man, that he was, on my word.—Your estate, Sir, I pray? *(Hat off.)*

WITTMORE. I have not impaired it, Sir, and I presume you know its value.—For I am a dog if I do. *(Aside.)*

SIR PATIENT. O' my word, 'tis then considerable, Sir; for he left but one son, and fourteen hundred pounds per annum, as I take it: which son, I hear, is lately come from Geneva, whither he was sent for virtuous education. I am glad of your arrival, Sir.—Your religion, I pray?

WITTMORE. You cannot doubt my principles, Sir, since educated at Geneva.

SIR PATIENT. Your father was a discreet man. Ah, Mr. Fainlove, he and I have seen better days, and wish we could have foreseen these that are arrived.

WITTMORE. That he might have turned honest in time, he means, before he had purchased bishops' lands.

SIR PATIENT. Sir, you have no place, office, dependence or attendance at Court, I hope?

WITTMORE. None, Sir,—Would I had—so you were hanged. *(Aside.)*

LADY FANCY. Nay, Sir, you may believe, I knew his capacities and abilities before I would encourage his addresses.

SIR PATIENT. My Lady Fancy, you are a discreet lady;—Well, I'll marry her out of hand, to prevent Mr. Lodwick's hopes: for though the young man may deserve well, that mother of his I'll have nothing to do with, since she refused to marry my nephew. *(Aside.)*

*(Enter Fanny.)*

FANNY. Sir Father, here's my Lady Knowell and her family come to see you.

SIR PATIENT. How! her whole family! I am come to keep open house; very fine, her whole family! she's plague enough to mortify any good Christian,—Tell her, my Lady and I am gone forth; tell her anything to keep her away.

FANNY. Should I tell a lie, Sir Father, and to a lady of her quality?

SIR PATIENT. Her quality and she are a couple of impertinent things, which are very troublesome, and not to be endured, I take it.

FANNY. Sir, we should bear with things we do not love sometimes, 'tis a sort of trial, Sir, a kind of mortification fit for a good Christian.

SIR PATIENT. Why, what a notable talking baggage is this! How came you by this doctrine?

FANNY. I remember, Sir, you preached it once to my sister, when the old alderman was the text, whom you exhorted her to marry, but the wicked creature made ill use on't.

SIR PATIENT. Go your way for a prating huswife,[37] go, and call your sister hither.


(Exit Fanny.)


—Well, I'm resolved to leave this town, nay, and the world too, rather than be tormented thus.

LADY FANCY. What's the matter, Dear, thou dost so fret thyself?

SIR PATIENT. The matter! my house, my house is besieged with impertinence; the intolerable lady Madam Romance, that walking library of profane books is come to visit me.

LADY FANCY. My Lady Knowell?

SIR PATIENT. Yes, that lady of eternal noise and hard words.

LADY FANCY. Indeed 'tis with pain I am obliged to be civil to her, but I consider her quality; her husband was too an alderman, your friend, and a great Ay and No man i'th' City, and a painful promoter of the good cause.[38]

SIR PATIENT. But she's a fop, my Lady Fancy, and ever was so, an idle, conceited she fop; and has vanity and tongue enough to debauch any nation under civil government. But, Patience, thou art a virtue, and affliction will come.—Ah, I'm very sick, alas, I have not long to dwell amongst the wicked, oh, oh.— Roger, is the doctor come? (Enter Roger.)

Roger. No, Sir, but he has sent you a small draught of a pint, which you are to take, and move upon't.

Sir Patient. Ah,—Well, I'll in and take it;—Ah—Sir, I crave your patience for a moment, for I design you shall see my daughter; I'll not make long work on't, Sir. Alas, I would dispose of her before I die. Ah,—I'll bring her to you, Sir, ah, ah.— *(Goes out with Roger.)*

Lady Fancy. He's always thus when visited, to save charges,—But how, dear Wittmore, cam'st thou to think of a name and country so readily?

Wittmore. Egad, I was at the height of my invention, and the alderman civilly and kindly assisted me with the rest; but how to undeceive him—

Lady Fancy. Take no care for that; in the meantime you'll be shrewdly hurt to have the way laid open to our enjoyment, and that by my husband's procurement too. But take heed, dear Wittmore, whilst you only design to feign a courtship, you do it not in good earnest.

Wittmore. Unkind creature!

Lady Fancy. I would not have you endanger her heart neither: for thou has charms will do't.—Prithee do not put on thy best looks, nor speak thy softest language; for if thou dost, thou canst not fail to undo her.

Wittmore. Well, my pretty flatterer, to free her heart and thy suspicions, I'll make such awkward love as shall persuade her, however she chance to like my person, to think most lewdly of my parts.[39]—But 'tis fit I take my leave, for if Lodwick or Leander see me here, all will be ruined; death, I had forgot that.

Lady Fancy. Leander's seldom at home, and you must time your visits: but see, Sir Patient's returned, and with him your new mistress.

*(Enter Sir Patient and Isabella.)*

Sir Patient. Here's my daughter, Isabella, Mr. Fainlove: she'll serve for a wife, Sir, as times go; but I hope you are none of those.—Sweetheart, this gentleman I have designed you; he's rich and young, and I am old and sickly, and just going out of the world, and would gladly see thee in safe hands.

Maundy. He has been just going this twenty years. *(Aside.)*

SIR PATIENT. Therefore I command you to receive the tenders of his affection.

*(Enter Fanny.)*

FANNY. Sir Father, my Lady Knowell's in the garden.

LADY FANCY. My dear, we must go meet her in decency.

SIR PATIENT. A hard case, a man cannot be sick in quiet. *(Exit with Lady Fancy.)*

ISABELLA. A husband, and that not Lodwick! Heaven forbid. *(Aside.)*

WITTMORE. Now Foppery assist to make me very ridiculous.—Death, she's very pretty and inviting; what an insensible dog shall I be counted to refuse the enjoyment of so fair, so new a creature, and who is like to be thrown into my arms too, whether I will or not?—But Conscience and my vows to the fair mother. No, I will be honest.—Madam,—as Gad shall save me, I'm the son of a whore, if you are not the most belle person I ever saw, and if I be not damnably in love with you; but a pox take all tedious courtship, I have a free-born and generous spirit; and as I hate being confined to dull cringing, whining, flattering, and the Devil and all of foppery, so when I give an heart, I'm an infidel, Madam, if I do not love to do't frankly and quickly, that thereby I may oblige the beautiful receiver of my vows, protestations, passions, and inclination.

ISABELLA. You're wonderful engaging, Sir, and I were an ingrate not to facilitate a return for the honor you are pleased to do me.

WITTMORE. Upon my reputation, Madam, you're a civil, well-bred person, you have all the agreemony of your sex, *la belle taille, la bonne mine, and repartee bien,* and are *tout oure torre,* as I'm a gentleman, *fort agréable.*[40]—If this do not please your lady, and nauseate her, the Devil's in 'em both for unreasonable women.—*(To Maundy.)*

FANNY. Gemini, Sister, does the gentleman conjure?

ISABELLA. I know not, but I'm sure I never saw a more affected fop.

MAUNDY. Oh, a damnable, impertinent fop! 'Tis pity, for he's a proper gentleman.

WITTMORE. Well, if I do hold out, egad, I shall be the bravest young fellow in Christendom. But, Madam, I must kiss your hand at present; I have some visits to make, devoirs to pay, necessities of gallantry only, no love engagements, by Jove, Madam; it is sufficient I have given my parole to your father, to do him the honor of my alliance; and an unnecessary jealousy will but disoblige, Madam, your slave.—Death, these rogues see me, and I'm undone.—*(Exit.)*

*(Enter Lady Fancy, Lady Knowell, Sir Credulous, and Lucretia, with other women and men, Roger attending.)*

LADY KNOWELL. Isabella, your servant. Madam, being sensible of the insociable and solitary life you lead, I have brought my whole family to wait on your Ladyship, and this my son *in futuro,* to kiss your hands. I beseech your Ladyship to know him for your humble servant: my son and your nephew, Madam, are coming with the music too; we mean to pass the whole day with your Ladyship:—and see, they are here.

*(Enter Lodwick pulling in Wittmore, Leander with them.)*

LODWICK. Nay, since we have met thee so luckily, you must back with us.

WITTMORE. You must excuse me, Gentlemen.

LODWICK. We'll show you two or three fine women.

WITTMORE. Death, these rogues will ruin me—but I have business, Gentlemen, that—

LEANDER. That must not hinder you from doing deeds of charity: we are all come to tease my uncle, and you must assist at so good a work;—come, gad, thou shalt make love to my aunt.—I would he would effectually. *(Aside.)*

LODWICK. Now I think on't, what the Devil dost thou make here?

WITTMORE. Here!—oh, Sir—a—I have a design upon the alderman.

LODWICK. Upon his handsome wife, thou meanest; ah, rogue!

WITTMORE. Faith, no,—a—'tis to—borrow money of him; and as I take it, Gentlemen, you are not fit persons for a man of credit to be seen with, I pass for a graver man.

LODWICK. Well, Sir, take your course—but, egad, he'll sooner lend thee his wife than his money.

*(Exit Wittmore, they come in.)*

LEANDER. Aunt, I have taken the boldness to bring a gentleman of
my acquaintance to kiss your Ladyship's hands.

LODWICK. Thy aunt!—death, she's very handsome.—Madam, your
most humble servant. *(Kisses the Lady Fancy.)*

LEANDER. Prithee employ this fool, that I may have an opportunity to entertain thy sister.

LODWICK. Sir Credulous, what, not a word? not a compliment?
Hah,—be brisk, man, be gay and witty, talk to the ladies.

SIR CREDULOUS. Talk to 'em! Why, what shall I say to 'em?

LODWICK. Anything, so it be to little purpose.

SIR CREDULOUS. Nay, Sir, let me alone for that matter—but who
are they, prithee?

LODWICK. Why, that's my Lady Fancy, and that's her daughter-in-
law;[41] salute 'em, Man.—

SIR CREDULOUS. Fair lady,—I do protest and vow, you are the most
beautiful of all mothers-in-law, and the world cannot produce
your equal.

LODWICK. The rogue has but one method for all addresses.

*(They laugh.)*

LADY KNOWELL. Oh, absurd! this, Sir, is the beautiful mother-in-
law. *(To Lady Fancy.)*

*(Enter Sir Patient.)*

SIR CREDULOUS. Most noble lady, I cry your mercy. Then, Madam,
as the sun amongst the stars, or rather as the moon not in con-
junction with the sun, but in her opposition, when one rises the
other sets, or as the vulgar call it, full moon—I say, as the moon
is the most beautiful of all the sparkling lights, even so are you
the most accomplished lady under the moon—and, Madam, I
am extremely sensible of your charms and celestial graces. *(To
Isabella.)*

SIR PATIENT. Why, this is abominable and insupportable.

LUCRETIA. I find, Sir, you can talk to purpose when you begin
once.

SIR CREDULOUS. You are pleased to say so, noble lady: but I must

needs say, I am not the worst bred gentleman for a country gentleman that ever you saw; for you must know, incomparable
lady, that I was at the university three years, and there I learned
my logic and rhetoric, whereby I became excellent at repartee,
sweet lady. As for my estate, my father died since I came of age,
and left me a small younger brother's portion, dear lady.

LUCRETIA. A younger brother's, Sir?

SIR CREDULOUS. Ha, ha, I know what you would infer from that
now: but you must know, delicious lady, that I am all the children my father had.

LUCRETIA. Witty, I protest.

SIR CREDULOUS. Nay, Madam, when I set on't I can be witty.

LEANDER. Cruel Lucretia, leave 'em, and let us snatch this opportunity to talk of our own affairs.

SIR CREDULOUS. For you must know, bright lady, though I was
pleased to rally myself, I have a pretty competent estate of
about 3,000 pounds a year, and am to marry Madam Lucretia.

LADY FANCY. You are a happy man, Sir.

SIR CREDULOUS. Not so happy neither, inestimable lady, for I lost
the finest mare yesterday,—but let that pass: were you never in
Devonshire, Madam?

LADY FANCY. Never, Sir.

SIR CREDULOUS. In troth, and that's pity, sweet lady; for if you
loved hawking, drinking, and whoring,—oh, Lord, I mean
hunting; i'faith, there be good fellows would keep you company, Madam.

SIR PATIENT. This is a plot upon me, a mere plot.—My Lady Fancy,
be tender of my reputation; foppery's catching, and I had as
lieve be a cuckold as husband to a vain woman.

SIR CREDULOUS. Zoz, and that may be as you say, noble Sir. Lady,
pray what gentleman's this?—Noble Sir, I am your most humble
servant.

SIR PATIENT. Oh, cry your mercy, Sir. *(Walks away.)*

SIR CREDULOUS. No offense, dear Sir, I protest: 'slife, I believe 'tis
the master of the house, he looked with such authority;—why,
who cares, let him look as big as the four winds, east, west,
north, and south, I care not this,—therefore I beg your pardon, noble Sir.

SIR PATIENT. Pray spare your hat and legs, Sir, till you come to
Court; they are thrown away i'th' City.[42]

SIR CREDULOUS. Oh Lord! Dear Sir, 'tis all one for that, I value not a leg nor an arm amongst friends; I am a Devonshire knight, Sir, all the world knows, a kind of country gentleman, as they say, and am come to town to marry my Lady Knowell's daughter.

SIR PATIENT. I'm glad on't, Sir. *(Walks away, he follows.)*

SIR CREDULOUS. She's a deserving lady, Sir, if I have any judgment; and I think I understand a lady, Sir, in the right honorable way of matrimony.

SIR PATIENT. Well, Sir, that is to say, you have been married before, Sir; and what's all this to me, good Sir?

SIR CREDULOUS. Married before! incomparable, Sir! not so, neither, for there's difference in men, Sir.

SIR PATIENT. Right, Sir, for some are wits, and some are fools.

SIR CREDULOUS. As I hope to breathe, 'twas a saying of my grandmother's, who used to tell me, Sir, that bought wit was best. I have brought money to town for a small purchase of that kind; for, Sir, I would fain set up for a country wit.—Pray, Sir, where live the poets, for I would fain be acquainted with some of them.

SIR PATIENT. Sir, I do not know, nor do I care for wits and poets. Oh, this will kill me quite; I'll out of town immediately.

SIR CREDULOUS. But, Sir, I mean your fine railing bully wits, that have vinegar, gall, and arsenic in 'em, as well as salt, and flame, and fire, and the Devil and all.

SIR PATIENT. Oh, defend me! and what is all this to me, Sir?

SIR CREDULOUS. Oh, Sir, they are the very soul of entertainment; and, Sir, it is the prettiest sport to hear 'em rail and bawl at one another—Zoz, would I were a poet.

SIR PATIENT. I wish you were, since you are so fond of being railed at.—If I were able to beat him, I would be much angry,—but patience is a virtue, and I will into the country. *(Aside.)*

SIR CREDULOUS. 'Tis all one case to me, dear Sir,—but I should have the pleasure of railing again, *cum privilegio;*[43] I love fighting with those pointless weapons.—Zoz, Sir, you know if we men of quality fall out—(for you are a knight, I take it) why, there comes a challenge upon it, and ten to one somebody or other is run through the gills; why, a pox on't, I say, this is very damnable, give me poet's licence.—

LADY FANCY. Take him off in pity. *(To Leander.)*

LODWICK. Indeed, railing is a coin only current among the poets, Sir Credulous.

SIR PATIENT. Oh blessed deliverance!—what a profane wretch is here, and what a lewd world we live in—Oh London, London, how thou aboundest in iniquity! thy young men are debauched, thy virgins deflowered, and thy matrons all turned bawds! My Lady Fancy, this is not company for you, I take it; let us fly from this vexation of spirit, on the never-failing wings of discretion.—*(Going to lead Lady Fancy off,—the Lady Knowell speaking to Isabella all this while.)*

LADY KNOWELL. How! marry thee to such a fop, say'st thou? Oh, egregious!—as thou lovest Lodwick, let him not know his name, it will be dangerous; let me alone to evade it.

ISABELLA. I know his fiery temper too well to trust him with the secret.

LADY KNOWELL. Hark ye, Sir, and do you intend to do this horrible thing?—

SIR PATIENT. What thing, my Lady Knowell?

LADY KNOWELL. Why, to marry your daughter, Sir.

SIR PATIENT. Yes, Madam.

LADY KNOWELL. To a beastly town fool? *Monstrum horrendum!*[44]

SIR PATIENT. To any fool, except a fool of your race, of your generation.—

LADY KNOWELL. How! a fool of my race, my generation! I know thou meanest my son, thou contumelious knight, who, let me tell thee, shall marry thy daughter *invito te,* that is (to inform thy obtuse understanding), in spite of thee; yes, shall marry her, though she inherits nothing but thy dull enthusiasms, which had she been legitimate she had been possessed with.

SIR PATIENT. Oh, abominable! you had best say she is none of my daughter, and that I was a cuckold.—

LADY KNOWELL. If I should, Sir, it would not amount to *scandalum magnatum:*[45] I'll tell thee more, thy whole pedigree,—and yet for all this, Lodwick shall marry your daughter, and yet I'll have none of your nephew.

SIR PATIENT. Shall he so, my Lady Knowell? I shall go near to out-trick your Ladyship, for all your politic learning. 'Tis past the canonical hour, as they call it, or I would marry my daughter instantly; I profess we ne'er had good days since these canonical fopperies came up again, mere Popish tricks to give our children time for disobedience,—the next justice would ha' served turn, and have done the business at any hour:[46] but patience is a virtue—Roger, go after Mr. Fainlove, and tell him I would speak with him instantly.

*(Exit Roger.)*

LADY KNOWELL. Come, come, Ladies, we lose fleeting time, upon my honor, we do; for, Madam, as I said, I have brought the fiddles, and design to sacrifice the entire evening to your Ladyship's diversion.

SIR CREDULOUS. Incomparable lady, that was well thought on; Zoz, I long to be jigging.

SIR PATIENT. Fiddles, Good Lord! why, what am I come to?— Madam, I take it, Sir Patient Fancy's lady is not a proper person to make one at immodest revelings and profane masqueradings.

LADY FANCY. Why, ah, 'tis very true, Sir; but we ought not to offend a brother that is weak, and, consequently, a sister.

SIR PATIENT. An excellent lady, this; but she may be corrupted, ah, she may fall. I will therefore, without delay, carry her from this wicked town.

LADY KNOWELL. Come, come, Gentlemen, let's in. Mr. Fancy, you must be my man;—Sir Credulous, come, and you, sweet Sir, come, Ladies,—*Nunc est saltandum, &c.*[47] *(Exeunt.)*

Scene ii. Changes to a chamber.

*(Enter Sir Patient, as before, Lady Fancy, Wittmore, Maundy, and Roger with things.)*

SIR PATIENT. Maundy, fetch my clothes, I'll dress me and out of town instantly,—persuade me not. *(To Wittmore.)* Roger, is the coach ready, Roger?

ROGER. Yes, Sir, with four horses.

LADY FANCY. Out of town! Oh, I'm undone then, there will be no hopes of ever seeing Wittmore. *(Aside.)*—Maundy, oh, help me to contrive my stay, or I'm a dead woman.—Sir, sure you cannot go and leave your affairs in town.

SIR PATIENT. Affairs! what affairs?

LADY FANCY. Why, your daughter's marriage, Sir:—and—Sir,—not,

Sir, but that I desire of all things in the world the blessing of being alone with you, far from the noise and lewd disorders of
this filthy town.

SIR PATIENT. Most excellent woman! ah, thou art too good for sin-
ful man, and I will therefore remove thee from the temptations
of it.—Maundy, my clothes—Mr. Fainlove, I will leave Isabella
with my Lady Fidget, my sister, who shall tomorrow see you
married, to prevent farther inconveniences.

LADY FANCY. What shall I do?

MAUNDY. Madam, I have a design which, considering his spleen,[48]
must this time do our business,—'tis—*(Whispers.)*

LADY FANCY. I like it well, about it instantly, hah—

*(Exit Maundy.)*

Alas, Sir, what ails your face? Good Heaven,—look, Roger.

SIR PATIENT. My face! why, what ails my face? hah!

LADY FANCY. See, Mr. Fainlove, oh, look on my dear; is he not
strangely altered?

WITTMORE. Most wonderfully.

SIR PATIENT. Altered, hah—why, where, why, how altered?—hah,
altered, say you?

WITTMORE. Lord, how wildly he stares!

SIR PATIENT. Hah, stare wildly!

ROGER. Are you not very sick, Sir?

LADY FANCY. Sick! oh, Heavens forbid!—How does my dearest
love?

SIR PATIENT. Methinks I feel myself not well o'th' sudden—ah—a
kind of shivering seizes all my limbs,—and am I so much
changed?

WITTMORE. All over, Sir, as big again as you were.

LADY FANCY. Your face is frightfully blown up, and your dear eyes
just starting from your head; oh, I shall sound[49] with the apprehension on't. *(Falls into Wittmore's arms.)*

SIR PATIENT. My head and eyes so big, say you? Oh, I'm wondrous
sick o'th' sudden,—all over say you—oh, oh—Ay, I perceive it
now; my senses fail me too.

LADY FANCY. How, Sir, your senses fail you?

WITTMORE. That's a very bad sign, believe me.

SIR PATIENT. Oh, ay, for I can neither feel nor see this mighty growth you speak of. *(Falls into a chair, with great signs of disorder.)*

WITTMORE. Alas, I'm sorry for that, Sir.

ROGER. Sure, 'tis impossible, I'll run and fetch a glass,[50] Sir. *(Offers to go.)*

LADY FANCY. Oh, stay, I would not for the world he should see what a monster he is,—and is like to be before tomorrow. *(Aside.)*

ROGER. I'll fit him with a glass,—I'll warrant ye, it shall advance our design. *(Exit Roger.)*

*(Enter Maundy with the clothes, she starts.)*

MAUNDY. Good Heaven, what ails you, Sir?

SIR PATIENT. Oh—oh—'tis so.

MAUNDY. Lord, how he's swollen! see how his stomach struts.[51]

SIR PATIENT. Ah, 'tis true, though I perceive it not.

MAUNDY. Not perceive it, Sir! Put on your clothes and be convinced,—try 'em, Sir. *(She pulls off his gown, and puts on his doublet and coat, which come not near by a handful or more.)*

SIR PATIENT. Ah, it needs not,—mercy upon me!—*(Falls back.)* I'm lost, I'm gone! Oh, Man, what art thou but a flower? I am poisoned, this talking lady's breath's infectious; methought I felt the contagion steal into my heart; send for my physicians, and if I die I'll swear she's my murderer. Oh, see, see, how my trembling increases; oh, hold my limbs, I die.—

*(Enter Roger with a magnifying glass, shows him the glass; he looks in it.)*

ROGER. I'll warrant I'll show his face as big as a bushel. *(Aside.)*

SIR PATIENT. Oh, oh,—I'm a dead man, have me to bed, I die away, undress me instantly, send for my physicians, I'm poisoned, my bowels burn, I have within an Etna, my brains run round, Nature within me reels. *(They carry him out in a chair.)*

WITTMORE. And all the drunken universe does run on wheels, ha, ha, ha. Ah, my dear creature, how finely thou hast brought him to his journey's end!

LADY FANCY. There was no other way but this to have secured my happiness with thee; there needs no more than that you come anon to the garden back-gate, where you shall find admittance.—Sir Patient is like to lie alone tonight.

WITTMORE. Till then 'twill be a thousand ages.

LADY FANCY. At games of love husbands to cheat is fair,
'Tis the gallant we play with on the square.[52]

*(Exeunt severally.)*

# ACT III.

## Scene i

*(Scene draws off[53] to a room in Sir Patient Fancy's house, and discovers Lady Knowell, Isabella, Lucretia, Lodwick, Leander, Wittmore, Sir Credulous, other men and women, as going to dance.)*

LADY KNOWELL. Come, one dance more, and then I think we shall have sufficiently teased the alderman, and 'twill be time to part.—Sir Credulous, where's your mistress?

SIR CREDULOUS. Within a mile of an oak, dear Madam, I'll warrant you.—Well, I protest and vow, sweet lady, you dance most nobly,—Why, you dance—like—like a—like a hasty pudding, before Jove.

*(They dance some antic,[54] or rustic antic. Lodwick speaking to Isabella.)*

### SONG, made by a gentleman

Sitting by yonder river side,
Parthenia thus to Cloe cried,
Whilst from the fair nymph's eyes apace
Another stream o'erflowed her beauteous face;
Ah, happy nymph, said she, that can
So little value that false creature, man.

Oft the perfidious things will cry,
Alas they burn, they bleed, they die;
But if they're absent half a day,
Nay, let 'em be but one poor hour away,

No more they die, no more complain,
But like unconstant wretches live again.

LODWICK. Well, have you considered of that business yet, Isabella?
ISABELLA. What business?
LODWICK. Of giving me admittance tonight.
ISABELLA. And may I trust your honesty?
LODWICK. Oh, doubt me not; my mother's resolved it shall be a match between you and I, and that very consideration will secure thee: besides, who would first sully the linen they meant to put on?
ISABELLA. Away, here's my mother.

*(Enter Lady Fancy and Maundy.)*

LADY FANCY. Madam, I beg your pardon for my absence, the effects of my obedience, not will; but Sir Patient is taken very ill o'th' sudden, and I must humbly entreat your Ladyship to retire, for rest is only essential to his recovery.
LADY KNOWELL. Congruously spoken, upon my honor. Oh, the impudence of this fellow, your Ladyship's husband, to espouse so fair a person only to make a nurse of!
LADY FANCY. Alas, Madam!—
LADY KNOWELL. A slave, a very household drudge.—Oh, faugh, come, never grieve—for, Madam, his disease is nothing but imagination, a melancholy which arises from the liver, spleen, and membrane called *mesenterium;* the Arabians name the distemper *myrathial,* and we here in England, *hypochondriacal melancholy;* I could prescribe a most potent remedy, but that I am loth to stir the envy of the College.[55]
LADY FANCY. Really, Madam, I believe—
LADY KNOWELL. But as you say, Madam, we'll leave him to his repose; pray do not grieve too much.
LODWICK. Death! would I had the consoling her, 'tis a charming woman!
LADY KNOWELL. Mr. Fancy, your hand; Madam, your most faithful servant.—Lucretia, come; Lucretia.—Your servant, Ladies and Gentlemen.
LADY FANCY. A Devil on her, would the nimbleness of her Lady-

ship's tongue were in her heels; she would make more haste away. Oh, I long for the blest minute.

LODWICK. Isabella, shall I find admittance anon?

ISABELLA. On fair conditions.

LODWICK. Trust my generosity.—Madam, your slave. *(To Lady Fancy, gazing on her, goes out.)*

SIR CREDULOUS. Madam, I would say something of your charms and celestial graces, but that all praises are as far below you, as the moon in her opposition is below the sun;—and so, luscious lady, I am yours. Now for my serenade—

*(Exeunt all but Lady Fancy and Maundy.)*

LADY FANCY. Maundy, have you commanded all the servants to bed?

MAUNDY. Yes, Madam, not a mouse shall stir, and I have made ready the chamber next the garden for your Ladyship.

LADY FANCY. Then there needs no more but that you wait for Wittmore's coming to the garden gate, and take care no lights be in the house for fear of eyes.

MAUNDY. Madam, I understand lovers are best by dark, and shall be diligent: the doctor has secured Sir Patient by a sleeping pill, and you are only to expect your approaching happiness.

*(Exeunt.)*

Scene ii. Lady Knowell's chamber.

*(Enter Lady Knowell and Leander.)*

LADY KNOWELL. Leander, raise your soul above that little trifle Lucretia;—cannot you guess what better fate attends you? Fie, how dull you are! must I instruct you in plain right down terms? and tell you, that I propose you master of my fortune.— Now possibly you understand me.

*(Enter Lucretia, and peeps.)*

LEANDER. I wish I did not, Madam,

Unless I'd virtue to deserve the bounty;
I have a thousand faults dissimulation hides,
Inconstant, wild, debauched as youth can make me.
Lucretia. All that will not do your business. *(Aside.)*
Lady Knowell. Yet you would have my daughter take you with
all these faults; they're virtues there, but to the name of mother,
they all turn retrograde: I can endure a man
As wild and as inconstant as she can;
I have a fortune too that can support that humor,
That of Lucretia does depend on me,
And when I please is nothing;
I'm far from age or wrinkles, can be courted
By men, as gay and youthful as a new summer's morn,
Beauteous as the first blossoms of the spring,
Before the common sun has kissed their sweets away,
If with salacious appetites I loved.
Leander. Faith, Madam, I could wish—
Lady Knowell. That I were but fifteen: but
If there be inequality in years,
There is so too in fortunes, that might add
A lustre to my eyes, charms to my person,
And make me fair as Venus, young as Hebe.
Leander. Madam, you have enough to engage any unconquered
heart; but 'twas, I thought, with your allowance I disposed of
mine, and 'tis a heart that knows not how to change.
Lady Knowell. Then 'tis a foolish, unambitious heart, unworthy
of the elevation it has not glorious pride enough to aim at.—
Farewell, Sir,—when you are wiser, you may find admittance.
*(Goes out.)*
Leander. Stay, Madam—

*(Enter Lucretia.)*

Lucretia. For what? To hear your penitence! Forgive me,
Madam, I will be a villain, forget my vows of love, made to
Lucretia.
And sacrifice both her and those to interest.
Oh, how I hate this whining and dissembling!
Leander. Do, triumph o'er a wretched man, Lucretia.
Lucretia. How! wretched in loving me so entirely, or that you

cannot marry my mother, and be master of her mighty fortune?
'Tis a temptation indeed so between love and interest; hang me
if ever I saw so simple a look as you put on when my mother
made love to you.

Leander. You may easily guess the confusion of a man in my circumstances, to be languishing for the loved daughter, and pursued by the hated mother, whom if I refuse will ruin all my
hopes of thee.

Lucretia. Refuse her! I hope you have more wit.

Leander. Lucretia, could she make a monarch of me, I could not
marry her.

Lucretia. And you would be so wise to tell her so?

Leander. I would no more abuse her, than I could love her.

Lucretia. Yet that last must be done.

Leander. How!

Lucretia. Dost believe me so wicked to think I mean in earnest?
No, tell her a fine story of love and liking, gaze on her, kiss her
hands, and sigh, commend her face and shape, swear she's the
miracle of the age for wit, cry up her learning, vow you were
an ass not to be sensible of her perfections all this while; what
a coxcomb, to dote upon the daughter when such charms were
so visible in the mother! Faith, she'll believe all this.

Leander. It may be so, but what will all this serve for?

Lucretia. To give us time and opportunity to deceive her, or I'm
mistaken.

Leander. I cannot teach my tongue so much deceit.

Lucretia. You may be a fool, and cry, Indeed, forsooth, I cannot
love, for alas I have lost my heart, and am unworthy of your
proffered blessings—do, and see her marry me in spite to this
fop Easy, this knight of nonsense: no, no, dissemble me handsomely and like a gentleman, and then expect your good fortune.

*(Enter Antic.)*

Antic. Madam, your mother's coming.

Lucretia. Away, then, she must not see us together; she thinks
you gone.

Leander. But must I carry off no comfort with me?

LUCRETIA. Will you expose me to the incensed jealousy of a parent? Go, or I shall hate ye. *(Thrusts him out.)*

## Scene iii. A garden.

*(Enter Maundy by dark, opens the garden door.)*

MAUNDY. Now am I returned to my old trade again, fetch and carry my lady's lovers; I was afraid when she had been married, these night-works would have ended; but to say truth, there's a conscience to be used in all things, and there's no reason she should languish with an old man when a young man may be had.—The door opens, he's come.—

*(Enter Lodwick.)*

I see you're a punctual lover, Sir; pray follow me as softly as you can.

LODWICK. This is someone whom I perceive Isabella has made the confidant to our amours. *(Exeunt.)*

## Scene iv.

*(Draws off, and discovers Lady Fancy in her night-gown, in a chamber as by the dark.)*

LADY FANCY. Oh, the agreeable confusion of a lover high with expectation of the approaching bliss! What tremblings between joy and fear possess me? All my whole soul is taken up with Wittmore; I've no ideas, no thoughts but of Wittmore, and sure my tongue can speak no other language, but his name.—Who's there?

*(Enter Maundy, leading Lodwick.)*

MAUNDY. Madam, 'tis I, and your expected lover here—I put him into your hands, and will wait your commands in the next chamber. *(Exit Maundy.)*

LODWICK. Where are you, my dearest creature?

LADY FANCY. Here—give me your hand, I'll lead you to those joys we both so long have sighed for.

LODWICK. Hah! To joys; sure, she doth but dally with me. *(Aside.)*

LADY FANCY. Why come you not on, my dear?

LODWICK. And yet, why this admission, and i'th' dark too, if she designed me none but virtuous favors?—What damned temptation's this?

LADY FANCY. Are you bewitched? What is't that frights you?

LODWICK. I'm fixed. Death, was ever such a lover?
Just ready for the highest joys of love,
And like a bashful girl restrained by fear
Of an ensuing infamy—I hate to cuckold my own expectations.

LADY FANCY. Heavens! what can you mean?

LODWICK. Death, what's this?—Sure 'tis not virtue in me,—Pray Heaven it be not impotence!—Where got I this damned honesty,[56] which I never found myself master of till now!—why should it seize me when I had least need on't?

LADY FANCY. What ails you? are you mad?—we are safe, and free as winds let loose to ruffle all the groves; what is't delays you then? Soft.

LODWICK. Pox o' this thought of wife, the very name
destroys my appetite.
Oh, with what vigor I could deal my love
To some fair lewd unknown,
To whom I'd never made a serious vow!

LADY FANCY. Tell me the mystery of this sudden coldness: have I kept my husband in town for this? Nay, persuaded him to be very sick to serve our purpose, and am I thus rewarded—ungrateful man!

LODWICK. Hah,—'tis not Isabella's voice,—your husband, say you? *(Takes hold greedily of her hand.)*

LADY FANCY. Is safe, from any fear of interrupting us.
Come—these delays do ill consist with love.
And our desires; at least if they are equal.

LODWICK. Death, 'tis the charming mother!
What lucky star directed me tonight?
Oh, my fair dissembler, let us haste
To pay the mighty tributes due to love.

LADY FANCY. Follow me then with careful silence,—for Isabella's chamber joins to this, and she may hear us.

Lodwick. Not flowers grow, nor smooth streams glide away,
  Not absent lovers sigh, nor breaks the day,
  More silently than I'll those joys receive,
  Which Love and Darkness do conspire to give. *(Exeunt.)*

Scene v. Changes again to a garden.

*(Enter Isabella and Fanny in their night-gowns.)*

Isabella. Well, I have no mind to let this dear mad devil Lodwick in tonight.

Fanny. Why, Sister, this is not the first venture you have made of this kind, at this hour, and in this place; these arbors, were they tell-tales, could discover many pretty stories of your loves, and do you think they'll be less faithful now? pray trust them once again. Oh, I do so love to hear Mr. Lodwick protest, and vow, and swear, and dissemble, and when you don't believe him, rail at you,—avads, 'tis the prettiest man—

Isabella. I have a strange apprehension of being surprised tonight.

Fanny. I'll warrant you, I'll sit on yon bank of pinks, and when I hear a noise I'll come and tell you; so Lodwick may slip out at the back gate, and we may be walking up and down as if we meant no harm.

Isabella. You'll grow very expert in the arts of love, Fanny.

Fanny. When I am big enough I shall do my endeavor, for I have heard you say, Women were born to no other end than to love; and 'tis fit I should learn to live and die in my calling.—Come, open the gate, or you'll repent it; we shall have my father marry you within a day or two to that ugly man that speaks hard words,—avads, I can't abide him.

Isabella. What noise is that?

Fanny. Why, 'tis Mr. Lodwick at the garden-door;—let him in whilst I'll to my flowery bank, and stand sentinel.—

*(Runs off. Isabella opens the gate. Enter Wittmore.)*

Wittmore. Who's there?

Isabella. Speak low; who should it be but the kind fool herself, who can deny you nothing but what you dare not take?

Wittmore. Not take! what's that? hast thou reserves in store?

—Oh, come and let me lead thee to thy bed,
Or seat thee on some bank of softer flowers,
Where I may rifle all thy unknown store.

ISABELLA. How! Surely you're not in earnest?—Do you love me?

WITTMORE. Love thee! by thy dear self, all that my soul adores,
I'm all impatient flame! all over love!
—You do not use to doubt, but since you do,
Come, and I'll satisfy thy obliging fears,
And give thee proofs how much my soul is thine,
I'll breathe it all anew into thy bosom.—
Oh, thou art fit for the transporting play,
All loose and wanton, like the Queen of Love
When she descends to meet the youth in shades.

ISABELLA. And are you, Sir, in earnest? can it be?

WITTMORE. That question was severe, what means my love?
What pretty art is this to blow my flames?
Are you not mine? did we not meet t'enjoy?
I came not with more vigorous, eager haste,
When our first sacrifice to Love we paid,
Than to perform that ceremony now.
Come, do not let the sacred fire burn out,
Which only was prepared for Love's rich altar,
And this is the divine, dark, silent minute—(*Goes to lead her off.*)

ISABELLA. Hold, Ravisher, and know this saucy passion
Has rendered back your interest.[57] Now I hate ye,
And my obedience to my father's will
Shall marry me to Fainlove, and I'll despise ye. (*Flings from him.*)

WITTMORE. Hah! Isabella! Death, I have made sweet work,—stay, gentle maid,—she'll ruin all if she go:—stay—she knew me, and cunningly drew me to this discovery; I'll after her and undeceive her. (*Runs after her.*)

(*A confused noise of the serenade.*)

Scene vi. Draws off to Lady Fancy's antechamber.

(*Enter Isabella, groping as in the dark.*)

ISABELLA. Pray Heaven I get undiscovered to my chamber, where I'll make vows against this perjured man; hah, sure he follows still; no wood-nymph ever fled before a satyr with half that trembling haste I flew from Lodwick.—Oh, he has lost his virtue, and undone me. *(Goes out groping, and the noise of serenade again.)*

## Scene vii.

*(Changes to Lady Fancy's bedchamber, discovers her as before; Lodwick has just risen in disorder from the bed, buttoning himself and setting himself in order; and noise at the door of unlatching it.)*
*(Enter Isabella, groping, Sir Patient without.)*

LADY FANCY. It is this door that opened, and which I thought I had secured.

SIR PATIENT *(within)*. Oh, insupportable, abominable, and not to be endured!

ISABELLA. Hah, my father! I'm discovered and pursued,—grant me to find the bed.

LADY FANCY. Heavens! 'twas my husband's voice, sure we're betrayed. It must be so, for what devil but that of jealousy could raise him at this late hour?

ISABELLA. Hah, where am I, and who is't that speaks—*(To herself.)*

LODWICK. So, he must know that I have made a cuckold of him. *(Aside.)*

SIR PATIENT. *(within)*. Call up my men, the coachman, groom and butler, the footmen, cook, and gardener; bid 'em all rise and arm, with long staff, spade, and pitchfork, and sally out upon the wicked.

LODWICK. S'heart! what a death shall I die:—is there no place of safety hereabouts—for there is no resisting these unmerciful weapons.

ISABELLA. A man's voice!

LADY FANCY. I know of none, nor how to prevent your discovery.

SIR PATIENT *(within)*. Oh, oh, lead me forward; I'll lie here on the garden side, out of the hearing of this hellish noise.

LADY FANCY. Hah, noise!—what means he?

LODWICK. Nay, I know not. Is there no escaping?—

Isabella. Who can they be that talk thus? Sure I have mistook my chamber.

Lady Fancy. Oh, he's coming in—I'm ruined; what shall we do? Here—get into the bed—and cover yourself with the clothes—quickly—oh, my confusion will betray me.

*(Lodwick gets into the bed, Isabella hides behind the curtain very near to him.)*
*(Enter Sir Patient, led by Nurse and Maundy, with lights.)*

Maundy. Pray go back, Sir, my poor lady will be frighted out of her wits at this danger you put yourself into; the noise shall be stilled.

Lady Fancy. Oh, what's the matter with my love? What, do you mean to murder him? Oh, lead him instantly back to his bed.

Sir Patient. Oh, oh, no, I'll lie here,—put me to bed, oh, I faint,—my chamber's possessed with twenty thousand evil spirits.

Lady Fancy. Possessed! what sickly fancy's this?

Sir Patient. Ah, the house is beset, surrounded, and confounded with profane tinkling, with popish hornpipes and Jesuitical cymbals, more antichristian and abominable than organs or anthems.

Nurse. Yea, verily, and surely it is the spawn of cathedral instruments played on by Babylonish minstrels, only to disturb the brethren.

Sir Patient. Ay, 'tis so; call up my servants, and let them be first chastised and then hanged; accuse 'em for French papishes, that had a design to fire the city, or anything;[58]—oh, I shall die—lead me gently to this bed.

Lady Fancy. To hinder him will discover all:—stay, Sir.—

Sir Patient. Hah, my Lady turned rebellious!—put me to bed, I say;—*(Throws himself forward to the bed.)*—hah—what's here?—what are thou,—a man,—hah, a man. Treason! betrayed! my bed's defiled, my Lady polluted, and I am cornuted; oh, thou vile serpent of my bosom!

*(She stands with her face toward the stage in signs of fear.)*

ISABELLA. A man, and in my virtuous lady mother's chamber! How fortunate was I to light on this discovery!

LADY FANCY. Well, Sir, since you have seen him, I beseech you for my sake, Dear, pardon him this one time. *(Coaxing him.)*

SIR PATIENT. Thou beg his pardon! Oh, was ever heard such impudence!

LADY FANCY. Indeed, my love, he is to blame; but we that are judicious should bear with the frailties of youth.

SIR PATIENT. Oh insupportable audacity!—what canst thou say, false woman?

LADY FANCY. Truly, not much in his defence, my dear.

ISABELLA. Oh, cunning devil!—

LADY FANCY. But, Sir, to hide the weakness of your daughter, I have a little strained my modesty,—

ISABELLA. Heavens! what says she?—

LADY FANCY. 'Tis Isabella's lover, Sir, whom I've concealed.

LODWICK. A good hint to save both our credits.

SIR PATIENT. How, Mr. Fainlove, mean you?

*(Lodwick rises and comes a little more forward, Isabella does the like, till both meet at the foot of the bed, and start, Lodwick looking simply.)*

LADY FANCY. Ay, my dear, Mr. Fainlove.

LODWICK. Isabella here! must she know too what a fine inconstant dog I am?—

ISABELLA. Lodwick! and in my mother's chamber! may I believe my eyes!

SIR PATIENT. But how got he hither?—tell me that. Oh, youth, youth, to what degree of wickedness art thou arrived?

LADY FANCY. She appointed him to come this night, Sir, and he going to her chamber, by mistake came into mine, it being the next to hers.

MAUNDY. But, Lord, Sir, had you heard how my Lady schooled him, whilst I ran down to fetch a light!

LODWICK. Now does my conscience tell me, I am a damned villain.—*(Aside, looking pitifully on Isabella.)*

LADY FANCY. But the poor man presently perceived his mistake, and begged my pardon in such feeling terms—that I vow I had not the heart to deny it him.

ISABELLA. Oh traitor! would thou hadst been that ravisher I took thee for, rather than such a villain—false! and with my mother too!

LADY FANCY. And just then, Sir, you came to the door, and lest you should see him, [he] entreated me to hide him from your anger,—the offence is not so heinous, Sir, considering he is so soon to marry her.

SIR PATIENT. Well, Sir, and what have you to say in your defence?—hah, how, Mr. Knowell,—worse and worse,—why, how came you hither, Sir? hah.—

LADY FANCY. Not Wittmore! oh, I am ruined and betrayed. *(Falls almost in a swoon.)*

SIR PATIENT. Hah, Isabella here too!

ISABELLA. Yes, Sir, to justify her innocence.

SIR PATIENT. Hah! Innocence! and justify! Take her away; go out of my sight, thou limb of Satan,—take her away, I say; I'll talk with you tomorrow, Lady Finetricks—I will.—

ISABELLA.—And I'll know before I sleep, the mystery of all this, and who 'twas this faithless man sent in his room to deceive me in the garden. *(Goes out.)*

LODWICK. A plague of all ill luck—how the Devil came she hither? I must follow and reconcile her. *(Going out, Sir Patient stays him.)*

SIR PATIENT. Nay, Sir, we must not part so till I have known the truth of this business, I take it.

LODWICK. Truth, Sir! oh, all that your fair Lady has said, Sir; I must confess her eyes have wounded me enough with anger, you need not add more to my shame.—

LADY FANCY. Some little comfort yet, that he proved indeed to be Isabella's lover. Oh, that I should mistake so unluckily! *(Aside.)*

SIR PATIENT. Why, I thought it had been Mr. Fainlove.

LADY FANCY. By all that's good, and so did I.

LODWICK. I know you did, Madam, or you had not been so kind to me. Your servant, dear Madam.—*(Going, Sir Patient stays him.)*

LADY FANCY. Pray, Sir, let him go; oh, how I abominate the sight of a man that could be so wicked as he has been!

SIR PATIENT. Hah,—good Lady, excellent woman. Well, Sir, for my Lady's sake I'll let you pass with this; but if I catch you here again, I shall spoil your intrigues, Sir, marry, shall I, and so rest ye satisfied, Sir.—

LODWICK. At this time, I am, Sir—Madam, a thousand blessings on you for this goodness.

LADY FANCY. Ten thousand curses upon thee,—go, boast the ruin you have made. *(Aside to Lodwick.)*

SIR PATIENT. Come, no more anger now, my Lady; the gentleman's sorry, you see. I'll marry my pert huswife tomorrow for this.— Maundy, see the gentleman safe out:—ah, put me to bed; ah, this night's work will kill me, ah, ah.

*(Exeunt Lodwick and Maundy.)*
*(The scene draws over Sir Patient and Lady, draws again and discovers.)*

Scene viii. The garden, Wittmore, Fanny, and Isabella.

ISABELLA. How, Mr. Fainlove, it cannot be.

FANNY. Indeed, Sister, 'tis the same, for all he talks so; and he told me his coming was but to try your virtue only.

*(Enter Lodwick and Maundy as passing over, but stand.)*

ISABELLA. That Fainlove! whom I am so soon to marry! and but this day courted me in another dialect!

WITTMORE. That was my policy, Madam, to pass upon your father with. But I'm a man that knows the value of the fair, and saw charms of beauty and of wit in you, that taught me to know the way to your heart was to appear myself, which now I do. Why did you leave me so unkindly but now?

LODWICK. Hah, what's this? whilst I was grafting horns on another's head, some kind friend was doing that good office for me.

MAUNDY. Sure, 'tis Wittmore!—oh, that dissembler—this was his plot upon my Lady, to gain time with Isabella. *(Aside.)*

WITTMORE. And being so near my happiness, can you blame me, if I made a trial whether your virtue were agreeable to your beauty, great, and to be equally adored?

LODWICK. Death, I've heard enough to forfeit all my patience!—
Draw, Sir, and make a trial of your courage too.—

WITTMORE. Hah, what desperate fool art thou? *(Draws.)*

LODWICK. One that will see thee fairly damned, e'er yield his interest up in Isabella—oh, thou false woman! *(They fight out;
Isabella, Fanny, and Maundy run off.)*

Scene ix.

*(Changes to the long street, a pageant of an elephant coming from
the farther end with Sir Credulous on it, and several others playing on strange confused instruments.)*

SIR CREDULOUS. This sure is extraordinary, or the Devil's in't, and
I'll ne'er trust serenade more. *(Comes forward, and all play
again.)*—Hold, hold, now for the song, which because I would
have most deliciously and melodiously sung, I'll sing myself;
look ye,—hum—hum.—

*(Sir Credulous should have sung.)*

Thou grief of my heart, and thou pearl of my eyes,
Don thy flannel petticoat quickly, and rise;
And from thy resplendent window discover
A face that would mortify any young lover:
For I, like great Jove transformed, do woo,
And am amorous owl, tu-whit tu-whoo, tu-whit tu-whoo.


A lover, Ads Zoz, is a sort of a tool
That of all things you best may compare to an owl:
For in some dark shades he delights still to sit,
And all the night long he cries whoo tu-whit.
Then rise, my bright Cloris, and don on slip shoe:
And hear thy amorous owl chant, wit tu-whoo, wit tu-whoo.

—Well, this won't do, for I perceive no window open, nor lady
bright appear, to talk obligingly:—perhaps the song does not
please her: you ballad-singers, have you no good songs of another fashion?

I MAN. Yes, Sir, several, *Robin—Hark how the waters fall, all, fall!*

SIR CREDULOUS. How, Man! Zoz, remove us farther off, for fear of wetting.

I MAN. No, no, Sir, I only gave my fellow a hint of an excellent ballad that begins—*Ill-wedded joys, how quickly do you fade! (Sings.)*

SIR CREDULOUS. Ay, ay, that, we'll have that,—*Ill-wedded joys, how quickly do you fade,—(Sings.)* That's excellent! Oh, now the windows open, now, now show your capering tricks.

*(Vaulting. They all play again.)*
*(Enter Roger and a company of fellows as out of Sir Patient's house, led on by Abel, a precise clerk, all armed with odd weapons.)*

ABEL. Verily, verily, here be these babes of perdition, these children of iniquity.

ROGER. A pox of your babes and children; they are men, and sons of whores, whom we must bang confoundedly, for not letting honest godly people rest quietly in their beds at midnight.

SIR CREDULOUS. Who's there?

ROGER. There, with a pox to you; cannot a right-worshipful knight, that has been sick these twenty years with taking physic, sleep quietly in his own house for you; and must we be raised out of our beds to quiet your hell-pipes, in the Devil's name?

ABEL. Down with Gog and Magog, there; there's the rotten bellwether that leads the rest astray, and defiles the whole flock.

ROGER. Hang your preaching, and let's come to him, we'll maul him. *(Beats Sir Credulous.)*

SIR CREDULOUS. Oh, Quarter, Quarter, Murder, Help, Murder, Murder!

*(Enter Lodwick.)*

LODWICK. Damn these rascals, whoe'er they were, that so unluckily redeemed a rival from my fury,—Hah, they are here,—Egad, I'll have one touch more with 'em,—the dogs are spoiling my designed serenade too—have amongst ye.—*(Fights and beats 'em off.)*

Sir Credulous, how is't?

SIR CREDULOUS. Who's there? Lodwick? Oh dear lad, is't thou that hast redeemed me from the enchanted cudgels that demolished my triumphant pageant, and confounded my serenade? Zoz, I'm half killed, Man,—I have never a whole bone about me, sure.

LODWICK. Come in with me—a plague upon the rascal that escaped me.

*(Exeunt.)*

# ACT IV.

## Scene i. Lady Knowell's house.

*(Enter Lucretia, followed by Sir Credulous.)*

LUCRETIA. Married tomorrow! and leave my mother the possession of Leander! I'll die a thousand deaths first.—How the fool
haunts me! *(Aside.)*

SIR CREDULOUS. Nay, delicious lady, you may say your pleasure; but
I will justify the serenade to be as high a piece of gallantry as was
ever practised in our age, though not comparable to your charms
and celestial graces, which should I praise as I ought, 'twould require more time than the sun employs in his natural motion between the tropics; that is to say, a whole year (for by the way, I
am no Copernican), for, dear Madam, you must know, my rhetoric master,—I say, my rhetoric master, who was—

LUCRETIA. As great a coxcomb as yourself;—pray leave me, I am
serious—I must go seek out Lodwick.

SIR CREDULOUS. Leave ye! I thank you for that, i'faith, before I
have spoke out my speech; therefore I say, Divine Lady—
because my rhetoric master commanded the frequent use of hy-
pallages,[59] allegories, and the richest figures of that beauteous
art,—because my rhetoric—

LUCRETIA. I must leave the fool; follow if you dare, for I have no
leisure to attend your nonsense. *(Goes out.)*

*(Enter Lady Knowell.)*

LADY KNOWELL. What, alone, Sir Credulous? I left you with
Lucretia.

SIR CREDULOUS. Lucretia! I'm sure she makes a very Tarquinius
Sextus of me,[60] and all about this serenade,—I protest and vow,
incomparable lady, I had begun the sweetest speech to her—
though I say't, such flowers of rhetoric—'twould have been the

very nosegay of eloquence, so it would; and like an ungrateful illiterate woman as she is, she left me in the very middle on't, so snuffy[61] I'll warrant.

LADY KNOWELL. Be not discouraged, Sir, I'll adapt her to a reconciliation: lovers must sometimes expect these little *belli fugaces;* the Grecians therefore truly named love *Glucupicros Eros.*[62]

SIR CREDULOUS. Nay, bright lady, I am as little discouraged as another, but I'm sorry I gave so extraordinary a serenade to so little purpose.

LADY KNOWELL. Name it no more, 'twas only a gallantry mistaken; but I'll accelerate your felicity, and tomorrow shall conclude the great dispute, since there is such volubility and vicissitude in mundane affairs. *(Goes out.)*

*(Enter Lodwick, stays Sir Credulous as he is going out the other way.)*

LODWICK. Sir Credulous, whither away so fast?

SIR CREDULOUS. Zoz, what a question's there? dost not know I am to untie the virgin zone tomorrow, that is, barter maidenheads with thy sister, that is, to be married to her, Man; and I must to Lincoln's Inn to my counsel about it?[63]

LODWICK. My sister just now told me of it; but, Sir, you must not stir.

SIR CREDULOUS. Why, what's the matter?

LODWICK. Have you made your will?

SIR CREDULOUS. My will! No, why my will, Man?

LODWICK. Then, for the good of your friends and posterity, stir not from this place.

SIR CREDULOUS. Good Lord, Lodwick, thou art the strangest man,—what do you mean to fright a body thus?

LODWICK. You remember the serenade last night?

SIR CREDULOUS. Remember it? Zoz, I think I do; here be the marks on't, sure—*(Pulls off his peruke, and shows his head broke.)*

LODWICK. Ads me, your head's broke.

SIR CREDULOUS. My head broke! why, 'twas a hundred to one that my neck had been broke.

LODWICK. Faith, not unlikely,—you know the next house is Sir Patient Fancy's; Isabella, too, you know, is his daughter.

Sir Credulous. Yes, yes, she was by when I made my dumb oration.

Lodwick. The same,—this lady has a lover, a mad, furious, fighting, killing Hector (as you know there are enough about this town). This monsieur, supposing you to be a rival, and that your serenade was addressed to her—

Sir Credulous. Enough, I understand you—set those rogues on to murder me.

Lodwick. Would 'twere no worse.

Sir Credulous. Worse! Zoz, Man, what the Devil can be worse?

Lodwick. Why, he has vowed to kill you himself wherever he meets you, and now waits below to that purpose.

Sir Credulous. Pshaw, pshaw, if that be all, I'll to him immediately, and make affidavit I never had any such design. Madam Isabella! ha, ha, alas, poor man, I have somebody else to think on.

Lodwick. Affidavit! why, he'll not believe you, should you swear your heart out: somebody has possessed him that you are a damned fool, and a most egregious coward, a fellow that to save your life will swear anything.

Sir Credulous. What cursed luck's this!—why, how came he to know I lived here?

Lodwick. I believe he might have it from Leander, who is his friend.

Sir Credulous. Leander! I must confess I never liked that Leander since yesterday.

Lodwick. He has deceived us all, that's the truth on't; for I have lately found out too, that he's your rival, and has a kind of a—

Sir Credulous. Smattering to my mistress, hah, and therefore would not be wanting to give me a lift out of this world; but I shall give her such a go-by—my Lady Knowell understands the difference between three thousand a year and—prithee, what's his estate?

Lodwick. Pshaw—not sufficient to pay surgeons' bills.

Sir Credulous. Alas, poor rat, how does he live, then?

Lodwick. Hang him, the ladies keep him; 'tis a good handsome fellow, and has a pretty town wit.

Sir Credulous. He a wit! what, I'll warrant he writes lampoons, rails at plays, curses all poetry but his own, and mimics the players—hah.

Lodwick. Some such common notions he has that deceives the ignorant rabble, amongst whom he passes for a very smart fellow,—'life, he's here.

*(Enter Leander.)*

SIR CREDULOUS. Why, what shall I do; he will not affront me before company? hah!

LODWICK. Not in our house, Sir,—bear up and take no notice on't. *(Lodwick whispers to Leander.)*

SIR CREDULOUS. No notice, quoth he? why, my very fears will betray me.

LEANDER. Let me alone—Lodwick, I met just now with an Italian merchant, who has made me such a present!

LODWICK. What is't, prithee?

LEANDER. A sort of specific poison for all the senses, especially for that of smelling; so that had I a rival, and I should see him at any reasonable distance, I could direct a little of this scent up to his brain so subtly that it shall not fail of execution in a day or two.

SIR CREDULOUS. How—Poison! *(Showing great signs of fear, and holding his nose.)*

LEANDER. Nay, should I see him in the midst of a thousand people, I can so direct it that it shall assault my enemy's nostrils only, without any effects on the rest of the company.

SIR CREDULOUS. Oh,—I'm a dead man!

LODWICK. Is't possible?

LEANDER. Perhaps some little sneezing or so, no harm; but my enemy's a dead man, Sir, killed.

SIR CREDULOUS. Why, this is the most damned Italian trick I ever heard of; why, this outdoes the famous poisoner Madame Brinvilliers.[64] Well, here's no jesting; I perceive that, Lodwick.

LODWICK. Fear nothing, I'll secure you. *(Aside to him.)*

*(Enter Wittmore.)*

—Wittmore! how is't Friend! thou lookest cloudy.

WITTMORE. You'll hardly blame me, Gentlemen, when you shall know what a damned unfortunate rascal I am.

LODWICK. Prithee, what's the matter?

WITTMORE. Why, I am to be married, Gentlemen, married today.

LODWICK. How, married! nay, Gad, then thou'st reason; but to whom, prithee?

WITTMORE. There's the Devil on't again, to a fine, young, fair, brisk woman, that has all the temptations Heaven can give her.

LODWICK. What pity 'tis they should be bestowed to so wicked an end! Is this your intrigue, that has been so long concealed from your friends?

LEANDER. We thought it had been some kind amour, something of love and honor.

LODWICK. Is she rich? If she be wondrous rich, we'll excuse thee.

WITTMORE. Her fortune will be suitable to the jointure I shall make her.

LODWICK. Nay, then, 'tis like to prove a hopeful match; what a pox can provoke thee to this; dost love her?

WITTMORE. No, there's another plague; I am cursedly in love elsewhere, and this was but a false address, to hide that real one.

LODWICK. How, love another? in what quality and manner?

WITTMORE. As a man ought to love, with a good substantial passion, without any design but that of right-down honest enjoyment.

LODWICK. Ay, now we understand thee; this is something. Ah, Friend, I had such an adventure last night.—You may talk of your intrigues and substantial pleasures, but if any of you can match mine,—Egad, I'll forswear womankind.

LEANDER. An adventure! prithee, where?

SIR CREDULOUS. What, last night, when you rescued me from the bilbo-blades! Indeed, ye looked a little furiously.

LODWICK. I had reason; I was just then come out of a garden from fighting with a man whom I found with my mistress; and I had at least known who't had been, but for the coming of those rascals that set on you, who parted us, whilst he made his escape in the crowd.

WITTMORE. Death! that was I, who for fear of being known got away: was't he then that I fought with, and whom I learned loved Isabella? (Aside.)

LODWICK. You must know, Gentlemen, I have a sort of a matrimonial kindness for a very pretty woman, she whom I tell you I disturbed in the garden; and last night she made me an assignation in her chamber. When I came to the garden door by which I was to have admittance, I found a kind of necessary called a bawdy waiting-woman, whom I followed, and thought she would have conducted me to the right woman; but I was luckily and in the dark led into a lady's chamber, who took me for a lover she expected: I found my happy mistake, and would not undeceive her.

WITTMORE. This could be none but Lucia. *(Aside.)*—Well, Sir, and what did you do there?

LODWICK. Do! why, what dost think? All that a man inspired by love could do; I followed all the dictates of Nature, Youth, and Vigor.

WITTMORE. Oh, hold, my heart—or I shall kill the traitor. *(Aside.)*

SIR CREDULOUS. Followed all the dictates of Nature, Youth, and Vigor! prithee, what's that?

LODWICK. I kissed a thousand times her balmy lips, and greedily took in the nimble sighs she breathed into my soul.

WITTMORE. Oh, I can scarce contain myself. *(Aside.)*

SIR CREDULOUS. Pshaw, is that all, Man?

LODWICK. I clasped her lovely body in my arms,
And laid my bosom to her panting breast.
Trembling she seemed all love and soft desire,
And I all burnings in a youthful fire.

SIR CREDULOUS. Bless us, the man's in a rapture!

WITTMORE. Damnation on them both.

SIR CREDULOUS. Well, to the point, Man: what didst do all this while?

LEANDER. Faith, I Fancy he did not sleep, Sir Credulous.

LODWICK. No, Friend, she had too many charms [not?] to keep me waking.

SIR CREDULOUS. Had she so? I should have begged her charms pardon, I tell her that though.

WITTMORE. Curse on my sloth; Oh, how shall I dissemble? *(Aside.)*

LEANDER. Thy adventure was pretty lucky—but, Wittmore, thou dost not relish it.

WITTMORE. My mind's upon my marriage, Sir; if I thought he loved Isabella, I would marry her to be revenged on him; at least I'll vex his soul, as he has tortured mine.—Well, Gentlemen, you'll dine with me,—and give me your opinion of my wife.

LODWICK. Where dost thou keep the ceremony?

WITTMORE. At Sir Patient Fancy's, my father-in-law.

LODWICK. How! Sir Patient Fancy to be your father-in-law?

LEANDER. My uncle?

WITTMORE. He's fired,—'tis his daughter, Sir, I am to marry.—

LODWICK. Isabella! Leander, can it be? can she consent to this? and can she love you?

WITTMORE. Why, Sir, what do you see in me, should render me unfit to be beloved? *(Angry.)*

LODWICK. Married today! By Heaven, it must not be, Sir. *(Draws him aside.)*

WITTMORE. Why, Sir, I hope this is not the kind lady who was so soft, so sweet and charming last night.

LODWICK. Hold, Sir,—we yet are friends.—

WITTMORE. And might have still been so, hadst thou not basely robbed me of my interest.

LODWICK. Death, do you speak my language? *(Ready to draw.)*

WITTMORE. No, take a secret from my angry heart, which all its friendship to thee could not make me utter;—it was my mistress you surprised last night.

LODWICK. Hah, my Lady Fancy his mistress? Curse on my prating tongue. *(Aside.)*

SIR CREDULOUS. What a Devil's all this—hard words, heart-burnings, resentments, and all that?

LEANDER. You are not quarrelling, I hope, my friends?

LODWICK. All this, Sir, we suspected, and smoked[65] your borrowing money last night; and what I said was to gain the mighty secret that had been so long kept from your friends:—but thou hast done a baseness—*(Lays his hand on his sword.)*

LEANDER. Hold, what's the matter?

WITTMORE. Did you not rob me of the victory, then, I've been so long a toiling for?

LODWICK. If I had, 'twould not have made her guilty, nor me a criminal; she taking me for one she loved, and I her for one that had no interest in my friend; and who the Devil would have refused so fine a woman? Nor had I, but that I was prevented by her husband.—But Isabella, Sir, you must resign.

WITTMORE. I will, provided that our friendship's safe; I am this day to marry her, and if you can find a means to do't in my room, I shall resign my interest to my friend; for 'tis the lovely mother I adore.

LODWICK. And was it you I fought with in the garden?

WITTMORE. Yes, and thereby hangs a tale of a mistake almost equal to thine, which I'll at leisure tell you. *(Talks to Lodwick and Leander.)*

SIR CREDULOUS. I'm glad they're friends. Zoz, here was like to have been a pretty business; what damnable work this same womankind makes in a nation of fools that are lovers!

WITTMORE. Look ye, I am a damned dull fellow at invention; I'll therefore leave you to contrive matters by yourselves, whilst I'll go try how kind Fortune will be to me this morning, and see in what readiness my bride is. What you do must be thought on suddenly; I'll wait on you anon, and let you know how matters go.—I'm as impatient to know the truth of this, as for an opportunity to enjoy Lucia. *(Goes out.)*

LODWICK. Leander, what shall I do?

LEANDER. You were best consult your mother and sister; women are best at intrigues of this kind. But what becomes of me?

LODWICK. Let me alone to dispatch this fool; I long to have him out of the way, he begins to grow troublesome.—But now my mother expects you.

LEANDER. Prithee, be careful of me.—*(Exit Leander.)*

SIR CREDULOUS. What was this long whisper; something about me?

LODWICK. Why, yes, faith, I was persuading him to speak to his friend about this business; but he swears there's no hope of a reconciliation: you are a dead man, unless some cleanly conveyance of you be soon thought on.

SIR CREDULOUS. Why, I'll keep within doors, and defy malice and foul weather.

LODWICK. Oh, he means to get a warrant, and search for stolen goods, prohibited commodities, or conventicles; there's a thousand civil pretences in this town to commit outrages—let me see.—

*(They both pause a while.)*

SIR CREDULOUS. Well, I have thought,—and of such a business, that the Devil's in't if you don't say I am a man of intrigue.

LODWICK. What is't?

SIR CREDULOUS. Ha, ha, ha, I must have leave to laugh to think how neatly I shall defeat this son of a whore of a thunder thumping Hector.

LODWICK. Be serious, Sir, this is no laughing matter; if I might advise, you should steal into the country, for two or three days, till the business be blown over.

SIR CREDULOUS. Lord, thou art so hasty and conceited of thy own invention, thou wilt not give a man leave to think in thy company. Why, these were my very thoughts; nay more, I have found a way to get off clever, though he watch me as narrowly as an enraged sergeant upon an escape.

LODWICK. That indeed would be a masterpiece.

SIR CREDULOUS. Why, look ye, do you see that great basket there?

LODWICK. I do,—this, you mean—*(Pulls in a basket.)*

SIR CREDULOUS. Very well, put me into this basket, and cord me down, send for a couple of porters, hoist me away with a direction to an old uncle of mine, one Sir Anthony Bubbleton at Bubbleton-Hall in Essex; and then whip slap-dash, as Nokes says in the play;[66] I'm gone, and who's the wiser?

LODWICK. I like it well.

SIR CREDULOUS. Nay, lose no time in applauding; I'll in, the carrier goes this morning. Farewell, Lodwick.—*(Goes into the basket.)* I'll be here again on Thursday.

*(Lodwick writes a direction.)*
*(Enter Boy.)*

LODWICK. By all means, Sir,—Who's there,—call a couple of porters.

*(Exit Boy.)*

SIR CREDULOUS. One word more; the carrier lies at the Bell in Friday Street;[67] pray take care they set me not on my head.—*(Pops in again.)*

*(Enter Boy and two porters.)*

LODWICK. Come hither, cord up this basket, and carry it where he shall direct.—Leander will never think he's free from a rival, till he have him in his possession—To Mr. Leander Fancy's at the next door; say 'tis things for him out of the country.—Write a direction to him on the basket-lid. *(Aside to the Boy.)*

*(Porters going to carry off the basket on a long pole between 'em.)*
*(Enter Lady Knowell.)*

LADY KNOWELL. What's this? whither goes this basket?

SIR CREDULOUS. Ah Lord! they are come with the warrant. *(Peeps out of the basket.)*

LODWICK. Only books, Madam, offered me to buy, but they do not please me.

LADY KNOWELL. Books! nay, then, set down the basket, Fellows, and let me peruse 'em; who are their authors, and what their language?

SIR CREDULOUS. A pox of all learning, I say,—'tis my mother-in-law.

*(Porters going to set down the basket.)*

LODWICK. Hold, hold, Madam, they are only English and some law-French.[68]

LADY KNOWELL. Oh, faugh, how I hate that vile sort of reading! up with 'em again, Fellows, and away.

*(Porters take up and go out.)*

LODWICK. God-a-mercy, law-French. *(Aside.)*

LADY KNOWELL. Law-French! out upon't, I could find in my heart to have the porters bring it back, and have it burnt for a heresy to learning.

LODWICK. Or thrown into the Thames, that it may float back to Normandy, to have the language new modeled.

LADY KNOWELL. You say well; but what's all this *ad Iphicli bonis*,[69] where's Sir Credulous all this while? His affairs expect him.

LODWICK. So does Leander your Ladyship within.

LADY KNOWELL. Leander! *Hymen, Hymenae,*[70] I'll wait on him; Lodwick, I am resolved you shall marry Isabella too; I have a design in my head that cannot fail to give you the possession of her within this two or three hours.

LODWICK. Such an indulgence will make me the happiest of men, and I have something to say to your Ladyship that will oblige you to hasten the design.

LADY KNOWELL. Come in, and let me know it.

*(Exeunt.)*

Scene ii. A chamber in Sir Patient Fancy's house.
A table and chairs.

*(Enter Lady Fancy in a morning-dress, Maundy with pen, ink, and paper.)*

LADY FANCY. Wittmore in the garden, sayst thou, with Isabella! Oh perjured man! it was by his contrivance, then, I was betrayed last night.

MAUNDY. I thought so too at first, Madam, till going to conduct Mr. Knowell through the garden, he finding Mr. Wittmore there with Isabella drew on him, and they both fought out of the garden: what mischief's done, I know not.—But, Madam, I hope Mr. Knowell was not uncivil to your Ladyship. I had no time to ask what passed between you.

LADY FANCY. Oh, name it not: I gave him all I had reserved for Wittmore. I was so possessed with the thoughts of that dear false one, I had no sense free to perceive the cheat:—but I will be revenged.—Come let me end my letter; we are safe from interruption.

MAUNDY. Yes, Madam, Sir Patient is not yet up; the doctors have been with him, and tell him he is not so bad as we persuaded him.

LADY FANCY. And was he soft and kind?—By all that's good, she loves him, and they contrived this meeting.—My pen and ink—I am impatient to unload my soul of this great weight of jealousy.—*(Sits down and writes.)*

*(Enter Sir Patient, looking over her shoulder a tip-toe.)*

MAUNDY. Heaven! here's Sir Patient, Madam.

LADY FANCY. Hah,—and 'tis too late to hide the paper; I was just going to subscribe my name.

SIR PATIENT. Good morrow, my Lady Fancy, your Ladyship is well employed, I see.

LADY FANCY. Indeed, I was, and pleasantly too: I am writing a love-letter, Sir.—But, my dear, what makes you so soon up?

SIR PATIENT. A love-letter!—let me see't. *(Goes to take it.)*

LADY FANCY. I'll read it to you, Sir.

MAUNDY. What mean you, Madam? *(Aside.)*

LADY FANCY. *(Reads.).* It was but yesterday you swore you loved me, and I poor easy fool believed; but your last night's infidelity has undeceived my heart, and rendered you the falsest man that ever woman sighed for. Tell me, how durst you, when I had prepared all things for our enjoyment, be so great a devil to deceive my languishing expectations? and in your room send one that has undone

Your—

MAUNDY. Sure, she's mad to read this to him.

SIR PATIENT. Hum,—I profess ingenuously—I think it is indeed a love-letter. My Lady Fancy, what means all this? As I take it, here are riddles and mysteries in this business.

LADY FANCY. Which thus, Sir, I'll unfold.—*(Takes the pen and writes Isabella.)*

SIR PATIENT. How! undone—Your—Isabella, meaning my daughter?

LADY FANCY. Yes, my dear, going this morning into her chamber, she not being there, I took a letter that lay open on her table, and out of curiosity read it; as near as I can remember, 'twas to this purpose. I writ it out now, because I had a mind thou shouldst see't; for I can hide nothing from thee.

SIR PATIENT. A very good Lady, I profess! to whom is it directed?

LADY FANCY. Why,—Sir—What shall I say, I cannot lay it now on Lodwick—*(Aside.)* I believe she meant it to Mr. Fainlove; for whom else could it be designed? she being so soon to marry him.

SIR PATIENT. Hah,—Mr. Fainlove! so soon so fond and amorous!

LADY FANCY. Alas, 'tis the excusable fault of all young women; thou knowst I was just such another fool to thee, so fond—and so in love.—

SIR PATIENT. Hah,—thou wert indeed, my Lady Fancy, indeed thou wert.—But I will keep the letter, however, that this idle baggage may know I understand her tricks and intrigues. *(Puts up the letter.)*

LADY FANCY. Nay, then 'twill out. No, I beseech you, Sir, give me the letter; I would not for the world Isabella should know of my theft, 'twould appear malicious in me.—Besides, Sir, it does

not befit your gravity to be concerned in the little quarrels of
lovers.

Sir Patient. Lovers! Tell me not of lovers, my Lady Fancy; with
reverence to your good Ladyship, I value not whether there be
love between 'em or not. Pious wedlock is my business,—nay, I
will let him know his own too, that I will, with your Ladyship's
permission.

Lady Fancy. How unlucky I am!—Sir, as to his chastisement, use
your own discretion, in which you do abound most plentifully.
But pray let not Isabella hear of it; for as I would preserve my
duty to thee, by communicating all things to thee, so I would
conserve my good opinion with her.

Sir Patient. Ah, what a blessing I possess in so excellent a wife!
and in regard I am every day descending to my grave.—ah—I
will no longer hide from thee the provision I have made for
thee, in case I die.—

Lady Fancy. This is the music that I longed to hear.—
Die!—Oh,—that fatal word will kill me— (Weeps.)
Name it no more, if you'd preserve my life.

Sir Patient. Hah—now cannot I refrain joining with her in affec-
tionate tears.—No, but do not weep for me, my excellent Lady,
for I have made a pretty competent estate for thee. Eight thousand pounds, which I have concealed in my study behind the
wainscot on the left hand as you come in.

Lady Fancy. Oh, tell me not of transitory wealth, for I'm resolved
not to survive thee. Eight thousand pound, say you?—Oh, I
cannot endure the thoughts on't. (Weeps.)

Sir Patient. Eight thousand pounds just, my dearest Lady.

Lady Fancy. Oh, you'll make me desperate in naming it,—is it in
gold or silver?

Sir Patient. In gold, my dearest, the most part, the rest in silver.

Lady Fancy. Good Heavens! why should you take such pleasure
in afflicting me? (Weeps.) Behind the wainscot, say you?

Sir Patient. Behind the wainscot, prithee be pacified,—thou
makest me lose my greatest virtue, moderation, to see thee thus:
alas, we're all born to die.—

Lady Fancy. Again of dying! Uncharitable man, why do you delight in tormenting me?—On the left hand, say you, as you go
in?

Sir Patient. On the left hand, my Love: had ever man such a wife?

Lady Fancy. Oh, my spirits fail me—lead me, or I shall faint,—
lead me to the study, and show me where 'tis,—for I am able to
hear no more of it.

Sir Patient. I will, if you will promise, indeed and indeed, not to
grieve too much. *(Going to lead her out.)*


*(Enter Wittmore.)*


Wittmore. Heaven grant me some kind opportunity to speak
with Lucia! hah, she's here,—and with her the fond cuckold her
husband.—Death, he has spied me, there's no avoiding him.—

Sir Patient. Oh, are you there, Sir?—Maundy, look to my
Lady,—I take it, Sir, you have not dealt well with a person of
my authority and gravity. *(Gropes for the letter in his pocket.)*

Wittmore. So this can be nothing less than my being found out
to be no Yorkshire Esquire; a pox of my Geneva breeding. It
must be so; what the Devil shall I say now?

Sir Patient. And this disingenuous dealing does ill become the person you have represented, I take it.

Wittmore. Represented! ay, there 'tis; would I were handsomely
off o' this business. Neither Lucia nor Maundy have any intelligence in their demure looks that can instruct a man.—Why,
faith, Sir,—I must confess,—I am to blame—and that I
have—a—

Lady Fancy. Oh, Maundy, he'll discover all; what shall we do?

Sir Patient. Have what, Sir?

Wittmore. From my violent passion for your daughter—

Lady Fancy. Oh, I'm all confusion.—

Wittmore. Egad, I am i'th'wrong, I see by Lucia's looks.

Sir Patient. That you have, Sir, you would say, made a sport and
May-game[71] of the engagement of your word; I take it, Mr.
Fainlove, 'tis not like the stock you come from.

Wittmore. Yes, I was like to have spoiled all; 'sheart, what fine
work I had made—but most certainly he has discovered my
passion for his wife.—Well, Impudence assist me—I made, Sir,
a trifle of my word, Sir! from whom have you this intelligence?

Sir Patient. From whom should I, Sir, but from my daughter Isabella?

Wittmore. Isabella! The malicious baggage understood to whom my first courtship was addressed last night, and has betrayed me.

Sir Patient. And, Sir, to let you see I utter nothing without precaution, pray read that letter.

Wittmore. Hah—a letter! what can this mean,—'tis Lucia's hand, with Isabella's name to't.—Oh, the dear cunning creature, to make her husband the messenger too.—How, I send one in my room! *(He reads.)*

Lady Fancy. Yes, Sir, you think we do not know of the appointment you made last night; but having other affairs in hand than to keep your promise, you sent Mr. Knowell in your room,—false man.

Wittmore. I send him, Madam! I would have sooner died.

Sir Patient. Sir, as I take it, he could not have known of your designs and rendezvous without your informations.—Were not you to have met my daughter here tonight, Sir?

Wittmore. Yes, Sir, and I hope 'tis no such great crime, to desire a little conversation with the fair person one loves, and is so soon to marry, which I was hindered from doing by the greatest and most unlucky misfortune that ever arrived: but for my sending him, Madam, credit me, nothing so much amazes me and afflicts me, as to know he was here.

Sir Patient. He speaks well, ingenuously, he does.—Well, Sir, for your father's sake, whose memory I reverence, I will for once forgive you. But let's have no more night-works, no more gambols, I beseech you, good Mr. Fainlove.

Wittmore. I humbly thank ye, Sir, and do beseech you to tell the dear creature that writ this, that I love her more than life or fortune, and that I would sooner have killed the man that usurped my place last night than have assisted him.

Lady Fancy. Were you not false, then?—Now hang me if I do not credit him. *(Aside.)*

Sir Patient. Alas, good Lady! how she's concerned for my interest; she's even jealous for my daughter. *(Aside.)*

Wittmore. False! charge me not with unprofitable sins; would I refuse a blessing, or blaspheme a power that might undo me? would I die in my full vigorous health, or live in constant pain? All this I could, sooner than be untrue.

Sir Patient. Ingenuously, my Lady Fancy, he speaks discreetly, and to purpose.

LADY FANCY. Indeed, my dear, he does, and like an honest gentleman: and I should think myself very unreasonable not to believe him.—And, Sir, I'll undertake your peace shall be made with your mistress.

SIR PATIENT. Well, I am the most fortunate man in a wife that ever had the blessing of a good one.

WITTMORE. Madam, let me fall at your feet and thank you for this bounty.—Make it your own case, and then consider what returns ought to be made to the most passionate and faithful of lovers. *(Kneels.)*

SIR PATIENT. I profess a wonderful good natured youth, this; rise, Sir, my Lady Fancy shall do you all the kind offices she can, o' my word, she shall.

LADY FANCY. I'm all obedience, Sir, and doubtless shall obey you.

SIR PATIENT. You must, indeed you must; and, Sir, I'll defer your happiness no longer; this day you shall be married.

WITTMORE. This day, Sir!—why, the writings[72] are not made.

SIR PATIENT. No matter, Mr. Fainlove; her portion shall be equivalent to the jointure you shall make her; I take it, that's sufficient.

WITTMORE. A jointure, quoth he! it must be in new Utopian land, then.—And must I depart thus, without a kind word, a look, or a billet, to signify what I am to expect. *(Looking on her slily.)*

SIR PATIENT. Come, my Lady Fancy, shall I wait on you down to prayer! Sir, you will get yourself in order for your marriage, the great affair of human life; I must to my morning's devotion. Come, Madam.

*(She endeavors to make signs to Wittmore.)*

LADY FANCY. Alas, Sir, the sad discourse you lately made me has so disordered me, and given me such a pain in my head, I am not able to endure the psalm-signing.

SIR PATIENT. This comes of your weeping; but we'll omit that part of th' exercise, and have no psalm sung.

LADY FANCY. Oh, by no means, Sir, 'twill scandalize the brethren; for you know a psalm is not sung so much out of devotion as 'tis to give notice of our zeal and pious intentions: 'tis a kind of proclamation to the neighborhood, and cannot be omitted.— Oh, how my head aches!

Wittmore. He were a damned dull lover that could not guess what she meant by this. *(Aside.)*

Sir Patient. Well, my Lady Fancy, your Ladyship shall be obeyed,—come, Sir, we'll leave her to her women. *(Exit Sir Patient.)*

*(As Wittmore goes out, he bows and looks on her; she gives him a sign.)*

Wittmore. That kind look is a sufficient invitation. *(Exit.)*

Lady Fancy. Maundy, follow 'em down, and bring Wittmore back again.

*(Exit Maundy.)*

There's now a necessity of our contriving to avoid this marriage handsomely,—and we shall at least make two hours our own; I never wished well to long prayers till this minute.

*(Enter Wittmore.)*

Wittmore. Oh, my dear Lucia!

Lady Fancy. Oh Wittmore! I long to tell thee what a fatal mistake had like to have happened last night.

Wittmore. My friend has told me all, and how he was prevented by the coming of your husband from robbing me of those sacred delights I languish for. Oh, let us not lose inestimable time in dull talking, but haste to give each other the only confirmation we can give, how little we are our own.

Lady Fancy. I see Lodwick's a man of honor, and deserves a heart if I had one to give him. *(Exeunt.)*

Scene iii. A hall.

*(Enter Sir Patient and Roger.)*

Sir Patient. Roger, is prayer ready, Roger?

Roger. Truly nay, Sir, for Mr. Goggle has taken too much of the creature this morning, and is not in case, Sir.[73]

Sir Patient. How mean you, Sirrah—that Mr. Goggle is overtaken with drink?

ROGER. Nay, Sir, he hath overeaten himself at breakfast, only.

SIR PATIENT. Alas, and that's soon done, for he hath a sickly stomach as well as I, poor man. Where is Bartholomew the clerk? he must hold forth, then, today.

ROGER. Verily he is also disabled: for going forth last night by your commandment to smite the wicked, he received a blow over the pericranium.—

SIR PATIENT. Why, how now, Sirrah, Latin! the language of the beast![74] hah—and what then, Sir?

ROGER. Which blow, I doubt, Sir, hath spoiled both his praying and his eating.

SIR PATIENT. Hah! What a family's here? no prayer today! *(Enter Nurse and Fanny.)*

NURSE. Nay, verily it shall all out; I will be no more the dark lantern to the deeds of darkness.

SIR PATIENT. What's the matter here?

*(Exit Roger.)*

NURSE. Sir, this young sinner has long been privy to all the daily and nightly meetings between Mr. Lodwick and Isabella; and just now I took her tying a letter to a string in the garden, which he drew up to his window: and I have borne it till my conscience will bear it no longer.

SIR PATIENT. Hah, so young a bawd!—Tell me, Minion—private meeting! tell me truth, I charge ye, when? where? how? and how often? Oh, she's debauched!—her reputation ruined, and she'll need a double portion. Come, tell me truth, for this little finger here has told me all.

FANNY. Oh Gemini, Sir, then that little finger's the hugesest great liar as ever was.

SIR PATIENT. Hussy, hussy—I will have thee whipped most unmercifully. Nurse, fetch me the rod.

FANNY. Oh, pardon me, Sir, this one time, and I'll tell all. *(Kneels.)*— Sir—I have seen him in the garden, but not very often.

SIR PATIENT. Often! Oh, my family's dishonored. Tell me truly what he used to do there, or I will have thee whipped without cessation. Oh, I'm in a cold sweat; there's my fine maid, was he with her long?

FANNY. Long enough.

Sir Patient. Long enough!—oh, 'tis so, long enough,—for what, hah? my dainty miss, tell me, and didst thou leave 'em?

Fanny. They used to send me to gather flowers to make nosegays, Sir.

Sir Patient. Ah, demonstration; 'tis evident if they were left alone that they were naught, I know't.—And where were they the while? in the close arbor?—Ay, ay—I will have it cut down; it is the penthouse of iniquity, the very coverlid of sin.

Fanny. No, Sir, they sat on the primrose bank.

Sir Patient. What, did they sit all the while, or stand—or—lie—or—oh, how was't?

Fanny. They only sat indeed, Sir Father.

Sir Patient. And thou didst not hear a word they said all the while?

Fanny. Yes, I did, Sir, and the man talked a great deal of this, and of that, and of t'other, and all the while threw jessamine in her bosom.

Sir Patient. Well said, and did he nothing else?

Fanny. No, indeed, Sir Father, nothing.

Sir Patient. But what did she say to the man again?

Fanny. She said, let me see.—Ay, she said, Lord, you'll forget yourself, and stay till somebody catch us.

Sir Patient. Ah, very fine,—then what said he?

Fanny. Then he said, Well, if I must be gone, let me leave thee with this hearty curse—A pox take thee all over for making me love thee so confoundedly.

Sir Patient. Oh, horrible!

Fanny.—Oh, I could live here for ever,—that was when he kissed her—her hand only. Are you not a damned woman for making so fond a puppy of me?

Sir Patient. Oh unheard-of wickedness!

Fanny. Would the Devil had thee, and all thy family, e'er I had seen thy cursed face.

Sir Patient. Oh, I'll hear no more, I'll hear no more!—why, what a blasphemous wretch is this?

Fanny. Pray, Sir Father, do not tell my sister of this; she'll be horribly angry with me.

Sir Patient. No, no, get you gone.—Oh, I am heartsick—I'll up and consult with my Lady what's fit to be done in this affair. Oh, never was the like heard of.—(Goes out, Fanny and Nurse go the other way.)

Scene iv. The Lady Fancy's bedchamber.

*(She's discovered with Wittmore in disorder. A table, sword, and hat.)*

MAUNDY *(entering)*. Oh, Madam, Sir Patient's coming up.

LADY FANCY. Coming up, say you!

MAUNDY. He's almost on the top of the stairs, Madam.

WITTMORE. What shall I do?

LADY FANCY. Oh, damn him, I know not; if he sees thee here after my pretended illness, he must needs discover why I feigned.—I have no excuse ready,—this chamber's unlucky, there's no avoiding him here—step behind the bed; perhaps he has only forgot his psalm-book and will not stay long.

*(Wittmore runs behind the bed.)*
*(Enter Sir Patient.)*

SIR PATIENT. Oh, oh, pardon this interruption, my Lady Fancy,—Oh, I am half killed—my daughter, my honor—my daughter, my reputation.

LADY FANCY. Good Heavens, Sir, is she dead?

SIR PATIENT. I would she were; her portion and her honor would then be saved. But, oh, I'm sick at heart; Maundy, fetch me the bottle of *mirabilis*[75] in the closet,—she's wanton, unchaste.

*(Enter Maundy with the bottle.)*

Oh, I cannot speak it; oh, the bottle—*(Drinks.)* she has lost her fame, her shame, her name.—Oh, *(Drinks.)* that is not the right bottle, that with the red cork *(Drinks.)*,

*(Exit Maundy.)*

and is grown a very t'other-end-of-the-town creature, a very apple of Sodom, fair without and filthy within.[76] What shall we do with her? she's lost, undone; hah!

*(Enter Maundy.)*

Let me see, *(Drinks.)* this is *(Drinks.)* not as I take it—
*(Drinks.)*—no, 'tis not the right,—she's naught, she's lewd,
*(Drinks.)*—oh, how you vex me—*(Drinks.)* This is not the right
bottle yet,—*(Drinks.)* No, no, here. *(Gives her the bottle.)*

MAUNDY. You said that with the red cork, Sir. *(Goes out.)*

SIR PATIENT. I meant the blue;—I know not what I say.—In fine,
my Lady, let's marry her out of hand, for she is fallen, fallen to
Perdition; she understands more wickedness than had she been
bred in a profane nunnery, a court,

*(Enter Maundy.)*

or a playhouse, *(Drinks.)*—therefore let's marry her instantly,
out of hand *(Drinks.)*. Misfortune on misfortune. *(Drinks.)*—
But patience is a wonderful virtue, *(Drinks.)*—Hah—this is very
comfortable,—very consoling—I profess if it were not for these
creatures, ravishing comforts, sometimes a man were a very odd
sort of an animal *(Drinks.)*. But ah—see how all things were or-
dained for the use and comfort of man. *(Drinks.)*

LADY FANCY. I like this well. Ah, Sir, 'tis very true; therefore receive it plentifully and thankfully.

SIR PATIENT *(drinks)*. Ingenuously—it hath made me marvellous
lightsome; I profess it hath a very notable faculty,—very
knavish—and, as it were, waggish,—but hah, what have we
there on the table? a sword and hat? *(Sees Wittmore's sword
and hat on the table, which he had forgot.)*

LADY FANCY. Curse on my dullness.—Oh, these, Sir, they are Mr.
Fainlove's—he being so soon to be married and being straitened
for time, sent these to Maundy to be new trimmed with ribbon,
Sir—that's all. Take 'em away, you naughty baggage; must I
have men's things seen in my chamber?

SIR PATIENT. Nay, nay, be not angry, my little rogue; I like the
young man's frugality well. Go, go your ways, get you gone,
and finefy your knacks and tranghams,[77] and do your
business—go. *(Smiling on Maundy, gently beating her with his
hand: she goes out, he bolts the door after her, and sits down
on the bed's feet.)*

LADY FANCY. Heavens, what means he!

SIR PATIENT. Come hither to me, my little ape's face,—Come, come

I say—what, must I come fetch you?—Catch her, catch her—
catch her, catch her, catch her. *(Running after her.)*
LADY FANCY. Oh, Sir, I am so ill I can hardly stir.
SIR PATIENT. I'll make ye well, come hither, ye monkey-face, did it,
did it, did it? alas for it, a poor silly fool's face, dive it a blow,
and I'll beat it.
LADY FANCY. You neglect your devotion, Sir.
SIR PATIENT. No, no, no prayer today, my little rascal,—no prayer
today—poor Goggle's sick.—Come hither, why, you refractory
baggage you, come, or I shall touse you,[78] ingenuously I shall;
tom, tom, or I'll whip it.
LADY FANCY. Have you forgot your daughter, Sir, and your disgrace?
SIR PATIENT. A fiddle on my daughter, she's a chick of the old cock,
I profess; I was just such another wag when young.—But she
shall be married tomorrow, a good cloak for her knavery; therefore come your ways, ye wag, we'll take a nap together: good
faith, my little harlot, I mean thee no harm.
LADY FANCY. No, o' my conscience.
SIR PATIENT. Why then, why then, you little mongrel?
LADY FANCY. His precise Worship is as it were disguised,[79] the outward man is overtaken—pray, Sir, lie down, and I'll come to
you presently.
SIR PATIENT. Away, you wag, will you? will you?—Catch her there,
catch her.
LADY FANCY. I will indeed,—Death, there's no getting from him,—
pray lie down—and I'll cover thee close enough I'll warrant
thee.—*(Aside. He lies down, she covers him.)* Had ever lovers
such spiteful luck! hah—surely he sleeps, bless the mistaken
bottle.—Ay, he sleeps,—whilst, Wittmore—

*(He coming out falls; pulls the chair down; Sir Patient flings open
the curtain.)*

WITTMORE. Plague of my over-care, what shall I do?
SIR PATIENT. What's that, what noise is that? let me see, we are not
safe; lock up the doors, what's the matter? What thunder-clap
was that?

*(Wittmore runs under the bed; she runs to Sir Patient, and holds
him in his bed.)*

Lady Fancy. Pray, Sir, lie still, 'twas I was only going to sit down, and a sudden giddiness took me in my head, which made me fall, and with me the chair; there is no danger near ye, Sir—I was just coming to sleep by you.

Sir Patient. Go, you're a flattering huswife; go, catch her, catch her, catch her. *(Lies down, she covers him.)*

Lady Fancy. Oh, how I tremble at the dismal apprehension of being discovered! Had I secured myself of the eight thousand pound, I would not value Wittmore's being seen. But now to be found out would call my wit in question, for 'tis the fortunate alone are wise.—

*(Wittmore peeps from under the bed; she goes softly to the door to open it.)*

Wittmore. Was ever man so plagued?—hah—what's this?—confound my tell-tale watch, the 'larum goes, and there's no getting to't to silence it.—Damned misfortune!

*(Sir Patient rises, and flings open the curtains.)*

Sir Patient. Hah, what's that?

Lady Fancy. Heavens! what's the matter? we are destined to discovery. *(She runs to Sir Patient, and leaves the door still fast.)*

Sir Patient. What's that I say, what's that? let me see, let me see, what ringing's that; Oh, let me see what 'tis. *(Strives to get up, she holds him down.)*

Lady Fancy. Oh, now I see my fate's inevitable! Alas, that ever I was born to see't. *(Weeps.)*

Wittmore. Death, she'll tell him I am here. Nay, he must know't; a pox of all invention and mechanics, and he were damned that first contrived a watch.

Sir Patient. Hah, dost weep?—why dost weep? I say, what noise is that? what ringing? hah.—

Lady Fancy. 'Tis that, 'tis that, my dear, that makes me weep. Alas, I never hear this fatal noise, but some dear friend dies.

Sir Patient. Hah, dies! Oh, that must be I, ay, ay, oh.

Lady Fancy. I've heard it, Sir, this two days, but would not tell you of it.

SIR PATIENT. Hah! heard it these two days! Oh, what, is't a death-watch?—hah.—

LADY FANCY. Ay, Sir, a death-watch, a certain 'larum death-watch, a thing that has warned our family this hundred years, oh,—I'm the most undone woman!

WITTMORE. A blessing on her for a dear dissembling jilt—Death and the Devil, will it never cease?

SIR PATIENT. A death-watch! ah, 'tis so, I've often heard of these things—methinks it sounds as if 'twere under the bed.—*(Offers to look, she holds him.)*

LADY FANCY. You think so, Sir, but that 'tis about the bed is my grief; it therefore threatens you. Oh, wretched woman!

SIR PATIENT. Ay, ay, I'm too happy in a wife to live long. Well, I will settle my house at Hogsdowne, with the land about it, which is five hundred pounds a year, upon thee, live or die,—do not grieve.—*(Lays himself down.)*

LADY FANCY. Oh, I never had more cause; come try to sleep, your fate may be diverted—whilst I'll to prayers for your dear health.—*(Covers him, draws the curtains.)* I have almost run out all my stock of hypocrisy, and that hated art now fails me.—Oh all ye powers that favor distressed lovers, assist us now, and I'll provide against your future malice. *(She makes signs to Wittmore, he peeps.)*

WITTMORE. I'm impatient of freedom, yet so much happiness as I but now enjoyed, without this part of suffering had made me too blest.—Death and damnation! what curst luck have I? *(Makes signs to her to open the door, whilst he creeps softly from under the bed to the table, by which going to raise himself, he pulls down all the dressing-things: at the same instant Sir Patient leaps from the bed, and she returns from the door, and sits on Wittmore's back as he lies on his hands and knees, and makes as if she swooned.)*

SIR PATIENT. What's the matter? what's the matter? has Satan broke his everlasting chain and got loose abroad to plague poor mortals? hah—what's the matter? *(Runs to his Lady.)*

LADY FANCY. Oh, help, I die—I faint—run down, and call for help.

SIR PATIENT. My Lady dying? oh, she's gone, she faints,—what ho, who waits? *(Cries and bawls.)*

LADY FANCY. Oh, go down and bring me help; the door is locked,—they cannot hear ye,—oh—I go—I die.—

*(He opens the door, and calls help, help.)*

WITTMORE. Damn him! there's no escaping without I kill the dog.
  *(From under her, peeping.)*

LADY FANCY. Lie still, or we are undone.—

*(Sir Patient returns with Maundy.)*

MAUNDY. Hah, discovered!
SIR PATIENT. Help, help, my Lady dies.
MAUNDY. Oh, I perceive how 'tis.—Alas, she's dead, quite gone;
  oh, rub her temples, Sir.
SIR PATIENT. Oh, I'm undone then,—*(Weeps.)* Oh my dear, my vir-
  tuous Lady!
LADY FANCY. Oh, where's my husband, my dearest husband—Oh,
  bring him near me.
SIR PATIENT. I'm here, my excellent Lady.—

*(She takes him about the neck, and raises herself up, gives
Wittmore a little kick behind.)*

WITTMORE. Oh, the dear lovely hypocrite, was ever man so near
  discovery?—*(Goes out.)*
SIR PATIENT. Oh, how hard she presses my head to her bosom!
MAUNDY. Ah, that grasping hard, Sir, is a very bad sign.
SIR PATIENT. How goes my good, my dearest Lady Fancy?
LADY FANCY. Something better now, give me more air,—that dismal 'larum death-watch had almost killed me.
SIR PATIENT. Ah, precious creature, how she afflicts herself for
  me.—Come, let's walk into the dining room, 'tis more airy;
  from thence into my study, and make thyself mistress of that
  fortune I have designed thee, thou best of women.

*(Exeunt, leading her.)*

# ACT V.

Scene i. A room in Sir Patient Fancy's house.

*(A table and six chairs.)*
*(Enter Isabella reading a letter, Betty tricking[80] her.)*

ISABELLA. How came you by this letter?

BETTY. Miss Fanny received it by a string from his window, by which he took up that you writ to him this morning.

ISABELLA. What means this nicety? Forbear, I say—*(Puts Betty from her.)*

BETTY. You cannot be too fine upon your wedding day.

ISABELLA. Thou art mistaken, leave me,—whatever he says here to satisfy my jealousy, I am confirmed that he was false: yet this assurance to free me from this intended marriage makes me resolve to pardon him, however guilty.—

*(Enter Wittmore.)*

How now! what means this insolence? How dare you, having so lately made your guilty approaches, venture again into my presence?

WITTMORE. Why? Is there any danger, but what's so visible in those fair eyes?

ISABELLA. And there may lie enough, Sir, when they're angry. By what authority do you make this saucy visit?

WITTMORE. That of a husband, Madam; I come to congratulate the mighty joy this day will bring you.

ISABELLA. Thou dar'st not marry me; there will be danger in't.

WITTMORE. Why, sure, you do not carry death in your embraces; I find no terror in that lovely shape, no daggers in that pretty scornful look; that breath that utters so much anger now, last night was sweet as new-blown roses are,—and spoke such words, so tender and so kind.

ISABELLA. And canst thou think they were addressed to thee?

WITTMORE. No, nor could the shade of night hide the confusion which disordered you at the discovery that I was not he, the blessed he you looked for.

ISABELLA. Leave me, thou hated object of my soul.

WITTMORE. This will not serve your turn, for I must marry you.

ISABELLA. Then thou art a fool, and drawest thy ruin on; why, I will hate thee,—hate thee most extremely.

WITTMORE. That will not anger me.

ISABELLA. Why, I will never let thee touch me, nor kiss my hand, nor come into my sight.

WITTMORE. Are there no other women kind, fair, and to be purchased? he cannot starve for beauty in this age that has a stock to buy.

ISABELLA. Why, I will cuckold thee, look to't, I will most damnably.

WITTMORE. So would you, had you loved me, in a year or two; therefore, like a kind, civil husband, I've made provision for you—a friend, and one I dare trust my honor with,—'tis Mr. Knowell, Madam.

ISABELLA. Lodwick! What devil brought that name to his knowledge?—Canst thou know him, and yet dare hope to marry me?

WITTMORE. We have agreed it, and on these conditions.

ISABELLA. Thou basely injurest him, he cannot do a deed he ought to blush for. Lodwick do this! Oh, do not credit it,—prithee, be just and kind for thy own honor's sake; be quickly so, the hasty minutes fly and will anon make up the fatal hour that will undo me.

WITTMORE. 'Tis true; within an hour you must submit to Hymen, there's no avoiding it.

ISABELLA. Nay, then be gone, my poor submissive prayers and all that dull obedience custom has made us slaves to.—Do sacrifice me, lead me to the altar, and see if all the holy mystic words can conjure from me the consenting syllable. No, I will not add one word to make the charm complete, but stand as silent in the enchanting circle as if the priests were raising devils there.

(Enter Lodwick.)

LODWICK. Enough, enough, my charming Isabella; I am confirmed.

ISABELLA. Lodwick! what good angel conducted thee hither?

LODWICK. E'en honest Charles Wittmore here, thy friend and mine, no bugbear lover, he.

ISABELLA. Wittmore! that friend I've often heard thee name? Now some kind mischief on him: he has so frighted me, I scarce can bring my sense to so much order, to thank him that he loves me not.

LODWICK. Though shalt defer that payment to more leisure; we're men of business now. My mother, knowing of a consultation of physicians which your father has this day appointed to meet at his house, has bribed Monsieur Turboon, his French doctor in pension,[81] to admit of a doctor or two of her recommending, who shall amuse him with discourse till we get ourselves married; and to make it the more ridiculous, I will release Sir Credulous from the basket; I saw it in the hall as I came through. We shall have need of the fool.

*(Exit Wittmore.)*
*(Enter Wittmore, pulling in the basket.)*

WITTMORE. 'Twill do well.

LODWICK. Sir Credulous, how is't, Man? *(Opens the basket.)*

SIR CREDULOUS. What, am I not at the carrier's yet?—Oh Lodwick, thy hand, I'm almost poisoned—This basket wants airing extremely, it smells like an old lady's wedding gown of my acquaintance.—But what's [what, is?] the danger past, Man?

LODWICK. No, but there's a necessity of your being for some time disguised to act a physician.

SIR CREDULOUS. How! a physician! that I can easily do, for I understand simples.

LODWICK. That's not material, so you can but banter well, be very grave, and put on a starched countenance.

SIR CREDULOUS. Banter! what's that, Man?

LODWICK. Why, Sir, talking very much, and meaning just nothing; be full of words without any connection, sense, or conclusion. Come in with me, and I'll instruct you farther.

SIR CREDULOUS. Pshaw, is that all? say no more on't, I'll do't, let me alone for bantering—But this same damned rival—

Lodwick. He's now watching for you without and means to souse upon you; but trust to me for your security; come away, I have your habit ready. *(Goes out.)*—This day shall make thee mine, dear Isabella,—

*(Exit Lodwick and Wittmore.)*
*(Enter Sir Patient, Leander, and Roger.)*

Sir Patient. Marry Lucretia! is there no woman in the City fit for you but the daughter of the most notorious fantastical lady within the walls?

Leander. Yet that fantastical lady you thought fit for a wife for me, Sir.

Sir Patient. Yes, Sir, foppery with money had been something; but a poor fop, hang't, 'tis abominable.

Leander. Pray hear me, Sir.

Sir Patient. Sirrah, Sirrah, you're a jackanapes, ingenuously you are, Sir. Marry Lucretia, quoth he?

Leander. If it were so, Sir, where's her fault?

Sir Patient. Why, Mr. Coxcomb, all over. Did I with so much care endeavor to marry thee to the mother, only to give thee opportunity with Lucretia?

*(Enter Lady Knowell.)*

Leander. This anger shows your great concern for me.

Sir Patient. For my name I am, but 'twere no matter if thou wert hanged, and thou deservest it for thy lewd cavaliering opinion.—They say thou art a papist too, or at least a Church of England man, and I profess there's not a pin to choose.— Marry Lucretia!

Lady Knowell. Were I querimonious,[82] I should resent the affront this balatroon has offered me.

Isabella. Dear Madam, for my sake do not anger him now. *(Aside to her.)*

Lady Knowell. Upon my honor, you are very free with my daughter, Sir.

Sir Patient. How! she here! now for a peal from her eternal clapper; I had rather be confined to an iron-mill.

LADY KNOWELL. Sure, Lucretia merits a husband of as much worth as your nephew, Sir.

SIR PATIENT. A better, Madam, for he's the lewdest hector in the Town; he has all the vices of youth, whoring, swearing, drinking, damning, fighting,—and a thousand more, numberless and nameless.

LADY KNOWELL. Time, Sir, may make him more abstemious.

SIR PATIENT. Oh, never, Madam! 'tis in's nature, he was born with it, he's given over to reprobation, 'tis bred i'th' bone,—he's lost.

LEANDER. This is the first good office that ever he did me.

LADY KNOWELL. What think you, Sir, if in defiance of your inurbanity, I take him with all these faults myself?

SIR PATIENT. How, Madam!

LADY KNOWELL. Without more ambages, Sir, I have considered your former desires, and have consented to marry him, notwithstanding your exprobrations.[83]

SIR PATIENT. May I believe this, Madam? and has your Ladyship that goodness?—and hast thou, my boy, so much wit? Why, this is something now.—Well, he was ever the best and sweetest-natured youth.—Why, what a notable wag's this? and is it true, my boy, hah?

LEANDER. Yes, Sir, I had told you so before, had you permitted me to speak.

SIR PATIENT. Well, Madam, he is only fit for your excellent Ladyship, he is the prettiest, civilest lad.—Well, go thy ways; I shall never see the likes of thee; no—Ingenuously, the boy's made forever; two thousand pounds a year, besides money, plate, and jewels; made for ever.—Well, Madam, the satisfaction I take in this alliance has made me resolve to give him immediately my writings of all my land in Berkshire, five hundred pounds a year, Madam: and I would have you married this morning with my daughter, so one dinner and one rejoicing will serve both.

LADY KNOWELL. That, Sir, we have already agreed upon.

SIR PATIENT. Well, I'll fetch the writings. Come, Isabella, I'll not trust you out of my sight today.

*(Exeunt Sir Patient and Isabella.)*

LEANDER. Well, then, Madam, you are resolved upon this business of matrimony.

Lady Knowell. Was it not concluded between us, Sir, this morning? and at the near approach do you begin to fear?

Leander. Nothing, Madam, since I'm convinced of your goodness.

Lady Knowell. You flatter, Sir, this is mere adulation.

Leander. No, I am that wild extravagant my uncle rendered me, and cannot live confined.

Lady Knowell. To one woman, you mean? I shall not stand with you for a mistress or two; I hate a dull, morose, unfashionable blockhead to my husband; nor shall I be the first example of a suffering wife, Sir. Women were created poor obedient things.

Leander. And can you be content to spare me five or six nights in a week?

Lady Knowell. Oh, you're too reasonable.

Leander. And for the rest, if I get drunk, perhaps I'll give to you: yet in my drink I'm damned ill-natured too, and may neglect my duty; perhaps shall be so wicked, to call you cunning, deceitful, jilting, base, and swear you have undone me, swear you have ravished from my faithful heart all that could make it blessed or happy.

*(Enter Lucretia, weeping.)*

Lady Knowell. How now, Lucretia!

Lucretia. Oh, Madam, give me leave to kneel before, and tell you, if you pursue the cruelty I hear you're going to commit, I am the most lost, most wretched maid that breathes; we two have plighted faiths, and should you marry him, 'twere so to sin as Heaven would never pardon.

Lady Knowell. Rise, Fool.

Lucretia. Never, till you have given me back Leander, or leave to live no more.—Pray kill me, Madam; and the same flowers that deck your nuptial bed,
Shall serve to strow my hearse, when I shall lie
A dead, cold witness of your tyranny.

Lady Knowell. Rise; I still designed him yours.—I saw with pleasure, Sir, your reclination from[84] my addresses.—I have proved both your passions, and 'twere unkind not to crown 'em with the due premium of each other's merits. *(Gives her to Leander.)*

Leander. Can Heaven and you agree to be so bountiful?

LADY KNOWELL. Be not amazed at this turn, *Rotat omne fatum.*[85]—But no more,—keep still that mask of love we first put on, till you have gained the writings: for I have no joy beyond cheating that filthy uncle of thine.—Lucretia, wipe your eyes and prepare for Hymen; the hour draws near. *Thalessio, Thalessio,* as the Romans cried.

LUCRETIA. May you still be admired as you deserve!

*(Enter Sir Patient with writings, and Isabella.)*

SIR PATIENT. How, Madam Lucretia, and in tears?

LADY KNOWELL. A little disgusted, Sir, with her father-in-law, Sir.

SIR PATIENT. Oh, is that all? hold up thy head, Sweetheart, thy turn's next.—Here, Madam, I surrender my title, with these writings, and with 'em my joy, my life, my darling, my Leander.—Now let's away; where's Mr. Fainlove?

ISABELLA. He's but stepped into Cheapside, to fit the ring, Sir, and will be here immediately.

SIR PATIENT. I have business anon about eleven of the clock, a consultation of physicians to confer about this carcase of mine.

LEANDER. Physicians, Sir, what to do?

SIR PATIENT. To do! why, to take their advice, Sir, and to follow it.

LEANDER. For what, I beseech you, Sir?

SIR PATIENT. Why, Sir, for my health.

LEANDER. I believe you are not sick, Sir, unless they make you so.

SIR PATIENT. They make me so!—Do you hear him, Madam—Am not I sick, Sir? not I, Sir Patient Fancy, sick?

LADY KNOWELL. He'll destroy my design.—How, Mr. Fancy, not Sir Patient sick? or must he be incinerated before you'll credit it?

SIR PATIENT. Ah, Madam, I want but dying to undeceive him, and yet I am not sick!

LEANDER. Sir, I love your life, and would not have you die with fancy and conceit.—

SIR PATIENT. Fancy and conceit! do but observe him, Madam,—what do you mean, Sir, by fancy and conceit?

LADY KNOWELL. He'll ruin all;—why, Sir,—he means—

SIR PATIENT. Nay, let him alone, let him alone (with your Ladyship's pardon)—Come, Sir,—fancy and conceit, I take it, was the question in debate.—

LEANDER. I cannot prove this to you, Sir, by force of argument, but by demonstration I will, if you will banish all your cozening quacks and take my wholesome advice.

SIR PATIENT. Do but hear him, Madam: not prove it!

LADY KNOWELL. Sir, he means nothing.—Not sick! alas, Sir, you're very sick.

SIR PATIENT. Ay, ay, your Ladyship is a lady of profound knowledge.—Why, have I not had the advice of all the doctors in England, and have I not been in continual physic this twenty years:—and yet I am not sick! Ask my dear lady, Sir, how sick I am; she can inform you. *(Lady Knowell goes and talks to Isabella.)*

LEANDER. She does her endeavor, Sir, to keep up the humor.

SIR PATIENT. How, Sir?

LEANDER. She wishes you dead, Sir.

SIR PATIENT. What said the rascal? wishes me dead!

LEANDER. Sir, she hates you.

SIR PATIENT. How! hate me! what, my Lady hate me?

LEANDER. She abuses your love, plays tricks with ye, and cheats ye, Sir.

SIR PATIENT. Was ever so profane a wretch! What, you will not prove this neither?

LEANDER. Yes, by demonstration too.

SIR PATIENT. Why, thou saucy varlet. Sirrah, Sirrah, thank my Lady here I do not cudgel thee.—Well, I will settle the rest of my estate upon her tomorrow, I will, Sir; and thank God you have what you have, Sir; make much on't.

LEANDER. Pardon me, Sir, 'tis not my single opinion, but the whole City takes notice on't: that I tell it you, Sir, is the effect of my duty, not interest. Pray give me leave to prove this to you, Sir.

SIR PATIENT. What, you are at your demonstration again?—come—let's hear.

LEANDER. Why, Sir, give her frequent opportunities,—and then surprise her;—or, by pretending to settle all upon her,—give her your power, and see if she do not turn you out of doors;—or—by feigning you are sick to death—or indeed by dying.

SIR PATIENT. I thank you, Sir,—this indeed is demonstration, I take it. *(Pulls off his hat.)*

LEANDER. I mean but feigning, Sir; and be a witness yourself of her sorrow, or contempt.

Sir Patient *(pauses)*. Hah—hum,—why, ingenuously, this may be a very pretty project.—Well, Sir, suppose I follow your advice?—nay, I profess I will do so, not to try her faith, but to have the pleasure to hear her conjugal lamentations, feel her tears bedew my face, and her sweet mouth kissing my cheeks a thousand times; verily a wonderful comfort.—And then, Sir, what becomes of your demonstration?—

*(Enter Wittmore with the ring.)*

Oh—Mr. Fainlove, come, come, you're tardy, let's away to church.

*(Enter Roger.)*

Roger. Sir, here is Doctor Turboon and those other doctors your Worship expected.

*(Enter Lady Fancy and Bartholomew.)*

Sir Patient. The doctors already!—well, bring 'em up; come, Madam, we have waited for your Ladyship,—bring up the doctors, Roger.

*(Exit Roger.)*

Lady Fancy. Wittmore, I have now brought that design to a happy conclusion, for which I married this formal ass; I'll tell thee more anon,—we are observed.
Lady Knowell. Oh, Lodwick's come!

*(Enter Lodwick, Monsieur Turboon, Fat Doctor, Amsterdam, Leyden, Sir Credulous.)*

Sir Patient. Doctor Turboon, your servant; I expected you not this two hours.
Turboon. Nor had ee com, Sir, bot for dese wordy gentlemen, whose affairs wode not permit dem to come at your hoar.
Sir Patient. Are they English, pray?
Turboon. Dis is, Sir,—*(Pointing to Lodwick.)* an admirable phy-

sician and a rare astrologer.—Dis speaks good English, bot a Collender born. *(Points to Sir Credulous.)*

Sir Credulous. What a pox, does the fellow call me a colander?

Lodwick. He means a High Dutchman[86] of the town of Collen, Sir.

Sir Patient. Sir, I have heard of your fame.—Doctor, pray entertain these gentlemen till my return; I'll be with you presently.

Lodwick. Sir, I hope you go not forth today. *(Gazing on his face.)*

Sir Patient. Not far, Sir.

Lodwick. There is a certain star has ruled this two days, Sir, of a very malignant influence to persons of your complexion and constitution.—Let me see—within this two hours and six minutes, its malice will be spent; till then it will be fatal.

Sir Patient. Hum, reigned this two days?—I profess and things have gone very cross with me this two days,—a notable man this.

Lady Knowell. Oh, a very profound astrologer, Sir, upon my honor; I know him.

Sir Patient. But this is an affair of that importance, Sir,—

Lodwick. If it be more than health or life, I beg your pardon, Sir.

Sir Patient. Nay, no offence, Sir, I beseech you; I'll stay, Sir.

Lady Knowell. How! Sir Patient not see us married?

Sir Patient. You shall excuse me, Madam.

Lady Fancy. This was lucky. Oh, Madam, would you have my dear venture out when a malignant star reigns! not for the world.

Sir Patient. No, I'll not stir; had it been any star but a malignant star, I had waited on your Ladyship: but these malignant stars are very pernicious stars. Nephew, take my Lady Knowell, Mr. Fainlove my daughter; and Bartholomew, do you conduct my Lady; the parson stays for you, and the coaches are at the door.

*(Exeunt Lady Knowell, Leander, Wittmore, Isabella, Fancy, and Bartholomew.)*
*(Enter Boy.)*

Boy. Sir, my Lady has sent for you. *(Exit.)*

Lodwick. Sir, I'll be with you presently; Sir Credulous, be sure you lug him by the ears[87] with any sort of stuff till my return. I'll send you a friend to keep you in countenance.

SIR PATIENT. Please you to sit, Gentlemen.

*(Exit Lodwick.)*

AMSTERDAM. Please you, Sir. *(To Sir Credulous, who bows and runs back.)*
SIR CREDULOUS. Oh Lord, sweet Sir, I hope you do not take me—Nay, I beseech you, Noble Sir—Reverend Sir. *(Turning from one to t'other.)*
LEYDEN. By no means, Sir, a stranger.
SIR CREDULOUS. I beseech you—*Savantissimi Doctores,*—incomparable Sir,—and you—or you.
FAT DOCTOR. In troth, Sir, these compliments are needless; I am something corpulent and love my ease. *(Sits.)*
SIR CREDULOUS. Generous Sir, you say well; therefore *con licentia,*[88] as the Grecians have it. *(Sits.)*
AMSTERDAM. —Brother.—
LEYDEN. Nay, good Brother,—Sir Patient—
SIR PATIENT. Ingenuously, not before you, Mr. Doctor.
LEYDEN. Excuse me, Sir, an alderman and a knight.—
SIR PATIENT. Both below the least of the learned society.
LEYDEN. Since you will have it so.

*(All sit and cry hum,—and look gravely.)*

SIR CREDULOUS. Hum—hum, most worthy and most renowned—*Medicinae Professores, qui hic assemblati estis, & vos altri Messiores;*[89] I am now going to make a motion for the public good of us all, but will do nothing without your doctorships' approbation.
SIR PATIENT. Judiciously concluded.
SIR CREDULOUS. The question then is, *Reverentissimi Doctores,* whether—for mark me, I come to the matter in hand, hating long circumstances of words; there being no necessity, as our learned brother Rabelais observes in that most notorious treatise of his called *Garagantua;* there is, says he, no necessity of going over the hedge when the path lies fair before ye: therefore, as I said before, I now say again, coming to my question; for as that admirable Welsh divine says, in that so famous sermon of his, upon her Creat Cranfather Hadam and her Creat

Cranmother Heeve concerning the Happell,—and her will, warrant her, her will keep to her text still,—so I stick close to my question, which is, *Illustrissimi Doctores,* whether it be not necessary to the affair in hand—to take—a bottle; and if your doctorships are of my opinion—hold up your thumbs.

*(All hold up their thumbs.)*

—Look, Sir, you observe the votes of the learned cabalists.

SIR PATIENT. Which shall be put in act forthwith—I like this man well, he does nothing without mature deliberation.

*(Enter Brunswick.)*

BRUNSWICK. By your leaves, Gentlemen—Sir Credulous— *(Whispers.)*

SIR CREDULOUS. Oh—'tis Lodwick's friend; the rascal's dressed like Vanderbergen in the Strand:—Sir Patient, pray know this glorious doctor, Sir.

SIR PATIENT. A doctor, Sir?

SIR CREDULOUS. A doctor, Sir! yes, and as eloquent a doctor, Sir, as ever set bill to post:[90] why, 'tis—the incomparable—Brunswick, High-Dutch doctor.

SIR PATIENT. You're welcome, Sir,—Pray sit; ah.—Well, Sir, you are come to visit a very crazy, sickly person, Sir.

BRUNSWICK. Pray let me feel your pulse, Sir;—What think you, Gentlemen; is he not very far gone?—*(Feels his pulse, they all feel.)*

SIR CREDULOUS. Ah, far, far.—Pray, Sir, have you not a certain wambling pain in your stomach, Sir, as it were, Sir, a—a pain, Sir.

SIR PATIENT. Oh, very great, Sir, especially in a morning fasting.

SIR CREDULOUS. I knew it by your stinking breath, Sir—and are you not troubled with a pain in your head, Sir?

SIR PATIENT. In my head, Sir?

SIR CREDULOUS. I mean a—kind of a—pain,—a kind of a vertigo, as the Latins call it; and a *whirligigoustiphon,*[91] as the Greeks have it, which signifies in English, Sir, a dizzy-swimming kind—of a do ye see—a thing—that—a—you understand me.

SIR PATIENT. Oh, intolerable, intolerable!—why, this is a rare man!

FAT DOCTOR. Your reason, Sir, for that? *(To Sir Credulous.)*

SIR CREDULOUS. My reason, Sir? why, my reason, Sir, is this: Haly the Moor, and Rabbi Isaac, and some thousands more of learned Dutchmen observe your dull wall-eye and your *whir—whirligigoustiphon,* to be inseparable.

BRUNSWICK. A most learned reason!

FAT DOCTOR. Oh, Sir, inseparable.

SIR CREDULOUS. And have you not a kind of a—something—do ye mark me, when you make water, a kind of a stopping—and—a—do ye conceive me, I have forgot the English term, Sir, but in Latin 'tis a *stronggullionibus.*

SIR PATIENT. Oh, Sir, most extremely, 'tis that which makes me desperate, Sir.

SIR CREDULOUS. Your ugly face is an infallible sign; your *dysuria,* as the Arabics call it, and your ill-favored countenance are constant relatives.

ALL. Constant, constant.

SIR CREDULOUS. Pray, how do you eat, Sir?

SIR PATIENT. Ah, Sir, there's my distraction. Alas, Sir, I have the weakest stomach—I do not make above four meals a day, and then indeed I eat heartily—but alas, what's that to eating to live?—nothing, Sir, nothing.—

SIR CREDULOUS. Poor heart, I pity him.

SIR PATIENT. And between meals, good wine, sweetmeats, caudles,—cordials and mirabilises, to keep up my fainting spirits.

SIR CREDULOUS. A pox of his aldermanship: an the whole bench were such notable swingers,[92] 'twould famish the City sooner than a siege.

AMSTERDAM. Brothers, what do you think of this man?

LEYDEN. Think, Sir? I think his case is desperate.

SIR CREDULOUS. Pshaw, Sir, we shall soon rectify the quiblets and quillities of his blood,[93] if he observes our directions and diet, which is to eat but once in four or five days.

SIR PATIENT. How, Sir, eat but once in four or five days? Such a diet, Sir, would kill me; alas, Sir, kill me.

SIR CREDULOUS. Oh no, Sir, no; for look ye, Sir, the case is thus, do you mind me—so that the business lying so obvious, do ye see, there is a certain method, do ye mark me—in a—Now, Sir, when a man goes about to alter the course of Nature,—the case is very plain, you may as well arrest the chariot of the sun, or alter the eclipses of the moon; for, Sir, this being of another nature, the nature of it is to be unnatural, you conceive me, Sir?—therefore we must crave your absence, Sir, for a few minutes, till we have debated this great affair.

SIR PATIENT. With all my heart, Sir; since my case is so desperate, a few hours were not too much. *(Exit Sir Patient.)*

SIR CREDULOUS. Now, Sir, my service to you. *(Drinks.)*

*(Enter Fanny.)*

FANNY. Oh living heart! what do all these men do in our house? Sure they are a sort of new-fashioned Conventiclers:—I'll hear 'em preach.

*(They drink round the while.)*

AMSTERDAM. Sir, my service to you, and to your good lady, Sir.

LEYDEN. Again to you, Sir, not forgetting your daughters: they are fine women, Sir, let scandal do its worst. *(Drinks.)*

TURBOON. To our better trading, Sir.

BRUNSWICK. Faith, it goes but badly on. I had the weekly Bill, and 'twas a very thin Mortality;[94] some of the better sort die indeed, that have good round fees to give.

TURBOON. Verily, I have not killed above my five or six this week.

BRUNSWICK. How, Sir, killed?

TURBOON. Killed, Sir! ever whilst you live, especially those who have the *grande verole;*[95] for 'tis not for a man's credit to let the patient want an eye or a nose, or some other thing. I have killed ye my five or six dozen a week—but times are hard.

BRUNSWICK. I grant ye, Sir, your poor for experiment and improvement of knowledge: and to say truth, there ought to be such scavengers as we to sweep away the rubbish of the nation.

*(Sir Credulous and Fat Doctor seeming in discourse.)*

SIR CREDULOUS. Nay, an you talk of a beast, my service to you, Sir—*(Drinks.)* Ay, I lost the finest beast of a mare in all Devonshire.

FAT DOCTOR. And I the finest spaniel, Sir.

*(Here they all talk together till you come to—)*

—purpose, Sir.

TURBOON. Pray, what news is there stirring?

BRUNSWICK. Faith, Sir, I am one of those fools that never regard whether Louis or Philip have the better or the worst.[96]

TURBOON. Peace is a great blessing, Sir, a very great blessing.

BRUNSWICK. You are i'th' right, Sir, and so my service to you, Sir.

LEYDEN. Well, Sir, Stettin held out nobly, though the gazettes are various.

AMSTERDAM. There's a world of men killed, they say; why, what a shame 'tis so many thousands should die without the help of a physician.

LEYDEN. Hang 'em, they were poor rogues and not worth our killing; my service to you, Sir, they'll serve to fill up trenches.

SIR CREDULOUS. Spaniel, Sir! No man breathing understands dogs and horses better than myself.

FAT DOCTOR. Your pardon for that, Sir.

SIR CREDULOUS. For look ye, Sir, I'll tell you the nature of dogs and horses.

FAT DOCTOR. So can my groom and dog-keeper; but what's this to th'purpose, Sir?

*(Here they leave off.)*

SIR CREDULOUS. To th'purpose, Sir! good Mr. Hedleburgh, do you understand what's to th'purpose? you're a Dutch butter-firkin, a kilderkin, a double jug.

FAT DOCTOR. You're an ignorant blockhead, Sir.

SIR CREDULOUS. You lie, Sir, and there I was with you again.

AMSTERDAM. What, quarreling, men of your gravity and profession.

SIR CREDULOUS. That is to say, fools and knaves: pray, how long is't since you left toping and napping[97] for quacking, good Brother Cater-tray?—but let that pass, for I'll have my humor, and therefore will quarrel with no man, and so I drink.—*(Goes to fill again.)*

BRUNSWICK.—But what's all this to the patient, Gentlemen?

SIR CREDULOUS. Ay,—the wine's all out,—and, quarrels apart,

Gentlemen, as you say, what do you think of our patient? for something I conceive necessary to be said for our fees.

FAT DOCTOR. I think that unless he follows our prescriptions he's a dead man.

SIR CREDULOUS. Ay, Sir, a dead man.

FAT DOCTOR. Please you to write, Sir; you seem the youngest doctor. *(To Amsterdam.)*

AMSTERDAM. Your pardon, Sir, I conceive there may be younger doctors than I at the board.

SIR CREDULOUS. A fine punctilio this, when a man lies a dying *(Aside.)*—Sir, you shall excuse me; I have been a doctor this seven years.

*(They shove the pen and paper from one to the other.)*

AMSTERDAM. I commenced at Paris twenty years ago.

LEYDEN. And I at Leyden, almost as long since.

FAT DOCTOR. And I at Barcelona, thirty.

SIR CREDULOUS. And I at Padua, Sir.

FAT DOCTOR. You at Padua?

SIR CREDULOUS. Yes, Sir, I at Padua; why, what a pox, do ye think I never was beyond sea?

BRUNSWICK. However, Sir, you are the youngest doctor, and must write.

SIR CREDULOUS. I will not lose an inch of my dignity.

FAT DOCTOR. Nor I.

AMSTERDAM. Nor I.

LEYDEN. Nor I.

*(Put the paper from each other.)*

BRUNSWICK. Death, what rascals are these?

SIR CREDULOUS. Give me the pen—here's ado about your Paduas and punctilios. *(Sets himself to write.)*

AMSTERDAM. Every morning a dose of my pills *merda queorusticon*,[98] or the amicable pill.

SIR CREDULOUS. Fasting?

LEYDEN. Every hour sixscore drops of *adminicula vitae*.

SIR CREDULOUS. Fasting too? *(Sir Credulous writes still.)*

FAT DOCTOR. At night twelve cordial pills, *gallimofriticus*.

TURBOON. Let blood once a week, a glister once a day.

BRUNSWICK. Cry mercy, Sir, you're a Frenchman.—After his first sleep, threescore restorative pills, called *cheatus redivivus*.

SIR CREDULOUS. And lastly, fifteen spoonfuls of my *aqua tetrachymagogon*, as often as 'tis necessary; little or no breakfast, less dinner, and go supperless to bed.

FAT DOCTOR. Hum, your *aqua tetrachymagogon?*

SIR CREDULOUS. Yes, Sir, my *tetrachymagogon;* for look ye, do you see, Sir, I cured the Archduke of Strumbulo of a *gondileero*, of which he died, with this very *aqua tetrachymagogon*.

*(Enter Sir Patient.)*

SIR PATIENT. Well, Gentlemen, am I not an intruder?

FAT DOCTOR. Sir, we have duly considered the state of your body; and are now about the order and method you are to observe.

BRUNSWICK. Ay, this distemper will be the occasion of his death.

SIR CREDULOUS. Hold, Brothers, I do not say the occasion of his death; but the occasional cause of his death.

*(Sir Patient reads the bill.)*[99]

SIR PATIENT. Why, here's no time allowed for eating, Gentlemen.

AMSTERDAM. Sir, we'll justify this prescription to the whole College.

LEYDEN. If he will not follow it, let him die.

ALL. Ay, let him die.

*(Enter Lodwick and Leander.)*

LODWICK. What, have you consulted without me, Gentlemen? *(Lodwick reads the bill.)*

SIR PATIENT. Yes, Sir, and find it absolutely necessary for my health, Sir, I should be starved: and yet you say I am not sick, Sir. *(To Leander.)*

LODWICK. Very well, very well.

SIR PATIENT. No breakfast, no dinner, no supper?

SIR CREDULOUS. Little or none, but none's best.

SIR PATIENT. But, Gentlemen, consider; no small thing?

ALL. Nothing, nothing.

Sir Credulous. Sir, you must write for your fee. *(To Lodwick.)*

Lodwick. Now I think on't, Sir, you may eat *(Writes.)* a roasted pippin cold upon a vine-leaf, at night.

Leander. Do you see, Sir, what damned canting rascals these doctors are?

Sir Patient. Ay, ay, if all doctors were such, ingenuously, I should soon be weary of physic.

Leander. Give 'em their fees, Sir, and send 'em to the Devil for a company of cheats.

Sir Patient. Truth is, there is no faith in 'em,—well, I thank you for your care and pains. *(Gives 'em fees.)*

Sir Credulous. Sir, if you have any occasion for me, I live at the Red-colored Lantern, with eleven candles in't, in the Strand;[1] where you may come in privately and need not be ashamed, I having no creature in my house but myself, and my whole family. —*Ick kwam van Neder Landt te spreken*
*End helpen van pocken end ander gebreken.*
That's a top of my bill, sweet Sir.

*(Exeunt doctors.)*

Fanny. Lord, Sir Father, why do you give 'em money?

Leander. For talking nonsense this hour or two upon his distemper.

Fanny. Oh lemini, Sir, they did not talk one word of you, but of dogs and horses, and of killing folks, and of their wives and daughters; and when the wine was all out, they said they would say something for their fees.

Sir Patient. Say you so!—Knaves, rogues, cheats, murderers! I'll be revenged on 'em all,—I'll ne'er be sick again,—or if I be, I'll die honestly of myself without the assistance of such rascals,—go, get you gone.—*(To Fanny, who goes out.)*

Leander. A happy resolution! would you would be so kind to yourself as to make a trial of your lady too; and if she prove true, 'twill make some kind of amends for your so long being cozened this way.

Sir Patient. I'll about it, this very minute about it,—give me a chair.— *(He sits.)*

Leander. So, settle yourself well, disorder your hair,—throw away your cane, hat, and gloves,—stare, and roll your eyes,

SIR PATIENT FANCY • 117

squeeze your face into convulsions,—clutch your hands, make your stomach heave, so, very well,—now let me alone for the rest—Oh, help, help, my Lady, my Aunt, for Heaven's sake, help,—come all and see him die. *(Weeps.)*

*(Enter Wittmore, Lady Fancy, Isabella, Lucretia, Lady Knowell, Roger, and Nurse.)*

WITTMORE. Leander, what's the matter?

LEANDER. See, Madam, see my uncle in the agonies of death.

LADY FANCY. My dearest husband dying, Oh! —*(Weeps.)*

LEANDER. How hard he struggles with departing life!

ISABELLA. Father, dear Father, must I in one day receive a blessing with so great a curse? Oh,—he's just going, Madam.—*(Weeps.)*

LADY FANCY. Let me o'ertake him in the shades below; why do you hold me, can I live without him? Do I dissemble well?— *(Aside to Wittmore.)*

SIR PATIENT. Not live without me!—do you hear that, Sirrah? *(Aside to Leander.)*

LEANDER. Pray mark the end on't, Sir,—feign,—feign.—

LADY KNOWELL. We left him well; how came he thus o'th' sudden?

LEANDER. I fear 'tis an apoplexy, Madam.

LADY FANCY. Run, run for his physician. But do not stir a foot. *(Aside to Roger.)* Look up, and speak but one kind word to me.

SIR PATIENT. What cries are these that stop me on my way?

LADY FANCY. They're mine,—your Lady's—oh, surely he'll recover. *(Aside.)* Your most obedient wife's.

SIR PATIENT. My wife's, my heir, my sole executrix.

LADY FANCY. Hah, is he in's senses? *(Aside to Wittmore.)* Oh my dear Love, my Life, my Joy, my All, *(Cries.)* Oh, let me go; I will not live without him. *(Seems to faint in Wittmore's arms. All run about her.)*

SIR PATIENT. Do ye hear that, Sirrah?

LEANDER. Have yet a little patience; die away,—very well—Oh, he's gone,—quite gone.

*(Lady Fancy swoons.)*

LADY KNOWELL. Look to my Lady there,

*(Swoons again.)*

—Sure, she can but counterfeit. *(Aside.)*

*(They all go about her.)*

Sir Patient. Hah, my Lady dying!

Leander. Sir, I beseech you wait the event. Death! the cunning
devil will dissemble too long and spoil all,—here—carry the
dead corpse of my dearest uncle to his chamber. Nurse, to your
care I commit him now. *(Exeunt with Sir Patient in a chair.)*

*(All follow but Wittmore, who going the other way, meets Sir
Credulous and Lodwick, as before.)*

Wittmore. Lodwick! the strangest unexpected news, Sir Patient's
dead!

Sir Credulous. How, dead! we have played the physicians to
good purpose, i'faith, and killed the man before we adminis-
tered our physic.

Wittmore. Egad, I fear so indeed.

Lodwick. Dead!

Wittmore. As a herring, and 'twill be dangerous to keep these
habits longer.

Sir Credulous. Dangerous! Zoz, Man, we shall all be hanged;
why, our very bill dispatched him, and our hands are to't.—Oh,
I'll confess all.—*(Offers to go.)*

Lodwick. Death, Sir, I'll cut your throat if you stir.

Sir Credulous. Would you have me hanged for company, Gentlemen? Oh, where shall I hide myself, or how come at my
clothes?

Lodwick. We have no time for that; go get you into your basket
again, and lie snug till I have conveyed you safe away,—or I'll
abandon you.—*(Aside to him.)* 'Tis not necessary he should be
seen yet; he may spoil Leander's plot. *(Aside.)*

Sir Credulous. Oh, thank ye, dear Lodwick,—let me escape this
bout, and if ever the fool turn physician again, may he be
choked with his own *tetrachymagogon.*

Wittmore. Go, haste and undress you, whilst I'll to Lucia.

*(Exeunt Lodwick and Sir Credulous.)*
*(As Wittmore is going out at one door, enter Sir Patient and Leander at the other door.)*

LEANDER. Hah, Wittmore there! he must not see my uncle yet. *(Puts Sir Patient back. Exit Wittmore.)*

SIR PATIENT. Nay, sir, never detain me, I'll to my Lady; is this your demonstration?—Was ever so virtuous a lady—Well, I'll to her, and console her poor heart; ah, the joy 'twill bring her to see my resurrection!—I long to surprise her. *(Going off cross the stage.)*

LEANDER. Hold, Sir, I think she's coming,—blest sight, and with her Wittmore! *(Puts Sir Patient back to the door.)*

*(Enter Lady Fancy and Wittmore.)*

SIR PATIENT. Hah, what's this?

LADY FANCY. Now, my dear Wittmore, claim thy rites of love without control, without the contradiction of wretched poverty or jealousy. Now undisguised thou mayst approach my bed and reign o'er all my pleasures and my fortunes, of which this minute I create thee lord, and thus begin my homage.—*(Kisses him.)*

SIR PATIENT. Sure 'tis some fiend! This cannot be my Lady.

LEANDER. 'Tis something uncivil before your face, Sir, to do this.

WITTMORE. Thou wondrous kind, and wondrous beautiful; that power that made thee with so many charms gave me a soul fit only to adore 'em; nor wert thou destined to another's arms, but to be rendered still more fit for mine.

SIR PATIENT. Hah, is not that Fainlove, Isabella's husband? Oh Villain! Villain! I will renounce my sense and my religion. *(Aside.)*

LADY FANCY. Another's arms! Oh, call not those hated
   Thoughts to my remembrance,
   Lest it destroy that kindly heat within me,
   Which thou canst only raise and still maintain.

SIR PATIENT. Oh Woman! Woman! damned dissembling woman. *(Aside.)*

LADY FANCY. Come, let me lead thee to that mass of gold he gave me to be despised;
   And which I render thee, my lovely conqueror,

As the first tribute of my glorious servitude.
Draw in the basket which I told you of, and is amongst the rubbish in the hall.

*(Exit Wittmore.)*

That which the slave so many years was toiling for, I in one moment barter for a kiss, as earnest of our future joys.

Sir Patient. Was ever so prodigal a harlot? was this the saint? was this the most tender consort that ever man had?

Leander. No, in good faith, Sir.

*(Enter Wittmore, pulling in the basket.)*

Lady Fancy. This is it, with a direction on't to thee, whither I designed to send it.

Wittmore. Good morrow to the day, and next the gold;
Open the shrine, that I may see my saint—
Hail the world's soul,[2] *(Opens the basket, Sir Credulous starts up.)*

Lady Fancy. Oh Heavens! what thing art thou?

Sir Credulous. Oh, pardon, pardon, sweet Lady, I confess I had a hand in't.

Lady Fancy. In what, thou slave?—

Sir Credulous. Killing the good, believing alderman;—but 'twas against my will.

Lady Fancy. Then I'm not so much obliged to thee,—but where's the money, the eight thousand pounds, the plate and jewels, Sirrah?

Wittmore. Death, the dog has eat it.

Sir Credulous. Eat it! Oh Lord, eat eight thousand pounds. Would I might never come out of this basket alive, if ever I made such a meal in my life.

Wittmore. Ye dog, you have eat it; and I'll make ye swallow all the doses you writ in your bill, but I'll have it upward or downward. *(Aside.)*

Sir Patient. Hah, one of the rogues my doctors.

Sir Credulous. Oh, dear Sir, hang me out of the way rather.

*(Enter Maundy.)*

MAUNDY. Madam, I have sent away the basket to Mr. Wittmore's lodgings.

LADY FANCY. You might have saved yourself that labor, I now having no more to do but to bury the stinking corpse of my quondam cuckold, dismiss his daughters, and give thee quiet possession of all. *(To Wittmore.)*

SIR PATIENT. Fair Lady, you'll take me along with you? *(Snaps, pulls off his hat, and comes up to her.)*

LADY FANCY. My husband!—I'm betrayed—

SIR PATIENT. Husband! I do defy thee, Satan, thou greater whore than she of Babylon; thou shame, thou abomination to thy sex.

LADY FANCY. Rail on, whilst I dispose myself to laugh at thee.

SIR PATIENT. Leander, call all the house in to be a witness of our divorce.

*(Exit Leander.)*

LADY FANCY. Do, and all the world, and let 'em know the reason.

SIR PATIENT. Methinks I find an inclination to swear,—to curse myself and thee, that I could no better discern thee; nay, I'm so changed from what I was, that I think I could even approve of monarchy and church-discipline, I'm so truly convinced I have been a beast and an ass all my life.

*(Enter Lady Knowell, Isabella, Lucretia, Leander, Lodwick, Fanny, etc.)*

LADY KNOWELL. Hah, Sir Patient not dead?

SIR PATIENT. Ladies and Gentlemen, take notice that I am a cuckold, a crop-eared, sniveling cuckold.

SIR CREDULOUS. A cuckold! sweet Sir, pshaw, that's a small matter in a man of your quality.

SIR PATIENT. And I beg your pardon, Madam, for being angry that you called me so. *(To Lady Knowell.)* And yours, dear Isabella, for desiring you to marry my good friend there *(Points to Wittmore.)*, whose name I perceive I was mistaken in:—and yours, Leander, that I would not take your advice long since: and yours, fair Lady, for believing you honest,—'twas done like a credulous coxcomb:—and yours, Sir, for taking any of your tribe for wise, learned, or honest. *(To Sir Credulous.)*

WITTMORE. Faith, Sir, I deceived ye only to serve my friend; and, Sir, your daughter is married to Mr. Knowell: your wife had all my stock of love before, Sir.

*(Lodwick and Isabella kneel.)*

SIR PATIENT. Why, God-a-mercy—some comfort that,—God bless ye.—I shall love disobedience while I live for't.

LODWICK. I am glad on't, Sir, for then I hope you will forgive Leander, who has married my sister, and not my mother.

SIR PATIENT. How! has he served me so?—I'll make him my heir for't; thou hast made a man of me, my boy, and, faith, we will be merry,—Fair Lady, you may depart in peace, fair Lady, restoring my money, my plate, my jewels, and my writings, fair Lady.—

LADY FANCY. You gave me no money, Sir; prove it if you can; and for your land, 'twas not settled with this proviso, if she be honest.

SIR PATIENT. 'Tis well thou dost confess I am a cuckold, for I would have it known, fair Lady.

LADY FANCY. 'Twas to that end I married you, good Alderman.

SIR PATIENT. I'faith, I think thou didst, Sweetheart, i'faith, I think thou didst.

WITTMORE. Right, Sir, we have long been lovers, but want of fortune made us contrive how to marry her to your good Worship. Many a wealthy citizen, Sir, has contributed to the maintenance of a younger brother's mistress; and you are not the first man in office that has been a cuckold, Sir.

SIR PATIENT. Some comfort that too; the Brethren of the Chain[3] cannot laugh at me.

SIR CREDULOUS. A very pleasant old fellow this: faith, I could be very merry with him now, but that I am damnable sad.— Madam, I shall desire to lay the saddle on the right horse. *(To Lady Knowell.)*

LADY KNOWELL. What mean you, Sir?

SIR CREDULOUS. Only, Madam, if I were as some men are, I should not be as I am.

LADY KNOWELL. It may be so, Sir.

SIR CREDULOUS. I say no more, but matters are not carried so swimmingly, but I can dive into the meaning on't.

*(Sir Patient talks this while to Lodwick.)*

LADY KNOWELL. I hate this hypothetical way of arguing; answer me categorically.

SIR CREDULOUS. Hypothetical and categorical! what does she mean now? *(Aside.)*—Madam, in plain English, I am made a John-a-Nokes of, Jack-hold-my-staff, a Merry Andrew doctor,[4] to give Leander time to marry your daughter; and 'twas therefore I was hoisted up in the basket;—but as the play says, 'tis well 'tis no worse: I'd rather lose my mistress than my life.

SIR PATIENT. But how came this rascal Turboon to admit you?

LODWICK. For the lucre of our fees, Sir, which was his recompence.

SIR PATIENT. I forgive it you, and will turn spark; they live the merriest lives—keep some City mistress, go to Court, and hate all conventicles.

You see what a fine City-wife can do
Of the true breed; instruct her husband too:
I wish all civil cuckolds in the nation
Would take example by my reformation.

# EPILOGUE.

## Spoken by Mrs. Gwin.

I here and there o'erheard a coxcomb cry, *(Looking about.)*
Ah, rot it—'tis a woman's comedy.
One, who because she lately chanced to please us,
With her damned stuff, will never cease to tease us.
What has poor woman done, that she must be
Debarred from sense and sacred poetry?
Why in this age has Heaven allowed you more,
And women less of wit than heretofore?

We once were famed in story, and could write
Equal to men; could govern, nay, could fight.
We still have passive valor and can show,
Would Custom give us leave, the active too,
Since we no provocations want from you.
For who but we could your dull fopperies bear,
Your saucy love and your brisk nonsense hear;
Endure your worse than womanish affectation,
Which renders you the nuisance of the nation;
Scorned even by all the misses of the Town,
A jest to vizard mask, the pit-buffoon;
A glass by which the admiring country fool
May learn to dress himself *en ridicule:*
Both striving who shall most ingenious grow
In lewdness, foppery, nonsense, noise, and show.
And yet to these fine things we must submit
Our reason, arms, our laurels, and our wit.
Because we do not laugh at you, when lewd,
And scorn and cudgel ye when you are rude.
That we have nobler souls than you, we prove,
By how much more we're sensible of love;
Quickest in finding all the subtlest ways
To make your joys, why not to make you plays?
We best can find your foibles, know our own,
And jilts and cuckolds now best please the Town;
Your way of writing's out of fashion grown.
Method and rule—you only understand;
Pursue that way of fooling, and be damned.
Your learned cant of action, time, and place,[5]
Must all give way to the unlabored farce.
To all the men of wit we will subscribe:
But for your half wits, you unthinking tribe,
We'll let you see, whate'er besides we do,
How artfully we copy some of you:
And if you're drawn to th' life, pray tell me then,
Why women should not write as well as men.

# Notes to *Sir Patient Fancy*

1. Bayes, the foolish poet lampooned in the Duke of Buckingham's *The Rehearsal* (1671), makes two of his characters "speak French to show their breeding" (2:2).
2. Actually, Behn took more than a hint from Molière's *The Imaginary Invalid* (1673), which centers on a hypochondriac. Like Sir Patient, Argan dotes upon his young second wife and plans to give her his fortune; she pretends devotion to him but is actually interested only in his money. Behn does not seem to have borrowed significantly from any other plays.
3. John Dryden, the greatest poet of the age, wrote many plays.
4. Behn supported King Charles II, an enthusiastic patron of the theater, while Puritan Dissenters like Sir Patient Fancy looked back regretfully to the republican Commonwealth of 1649–60, which restricted personal liberty.
5. No contemporary woman writer seems prominent enough to be appropriately described as "Poet Joan," but there was an imaginary "Pope Joan" in the Middle Ages.
6. *Presto, hocus,* and the *dancing tester* (sixpence), nutmeg, and cups suggest conjuring tricks. Behn repeats the common charge that present-day audiences prefer flashy stage-effects and tricky plots to well-written drama.
7. Young ladies would not have been able to go any distance without servants in attendance.
8. Money settled by a husband on his wife before marriage, for use after his death.
9. Keeping of mistresses.
10. Kept mistress.
11. Babblers.
12. Stepmother.
13. Worship service of Protestant Dissenters from the Church of England. Lucretia, sharing Behn's anti-Puritan bias, implies that Dissenters are not properly Christians.
14. Great gods.
15. Ancients are ancient classical authors. Tacitus wrote histories; Seneca and Plutarch, moral essays; Virgil and Homer, epics. Torquato Tasso, an Italian, wrote the romantic epic *Jerusalem Delivered* (1576), featuring the lovers Rinaldo and Armida (Corcereis).
16. *Iliad,* Book I, line 84, close to accurately quoted and translated.
17. Martial (A.D. c. 40–c. 104) wrote witty Latin epigrams.
18. Let us apply ourselves to philosophy!

19. I count for nothing (here).
20. Worst, most poorly formed handwriting.
21. Suitor.
22. Portmanteau, traveling bag for clothes.
23. Probably ponds at taverns, where water-dogs would show their skill, while their owners bet on them. Below: Ducking-pond = a pond on which ducks may be hunted.
24. Mun, a dialect form of Man. Sir Credulous only dresses up when he goes to vote for a member of Parliament (a knight of the shire), an occasion when voters were bribed with drinks, or when he comes to London to attend court sessions.
25. Metropolis.
26. Fine, excellent.
27. Until the mid-nineteenth century, a wife's personal property belonged legally to her husband.
28. *L'heure du berger,* the favorable moment for a lover.
29. Music = orchestra or band. Bantam was a province in Java, but the King of Bantam is probably imaginary. Behn's short story "The Court of the King of Bantam" turns on a practical joke played on a fop who is made to believe he has acceded to the throne of Bantam.
30. Printed plays.
31. Bring along fiddlers.
32. He makes you all miserable.
33. Dissenters met in meeting-houses, rather than churches. According to the anti-Puritan Lady Fancy, their dissent in religion resulted from perverse hostility to the government and prevailing opinion.
34. Grin.
35. The Exchange, where merchants met to transact business. Evidently Sir Patient is living on his capital, without taking the risk of further investments (next speech).
36. Oliver Cromwell, whose death in 1658 made possible the restoration of the monarchy. Men like Sir Patient and his friends would not have been knighted by the King. Below: after the Restoration, Puritans might send their sons to Geneva for a good Presbyterian education, unavailable in England. Further: Sir Patient has profited by buying church lands confiscated under the Commonwealth; now that the Church of England has been restored with the monarchy, their ownership is in dispute. Finally: the Puritans hated the Court, as the center of monarchy and worldly values.
37. Pert, worthless girl.
38. The term "Ay and No" (or "Yea and Nay") man was derisively applied to Puritans, alluding to Matthew 5:37; the text directs Christians to affirm rather than swear, and Puritans sometimes objected to

taking oaths. The City, the part of London within the old city walls, was the business center, where business was done and businessmen lived; it was distinguished from the Court and the Town, the fashionable area. The good cause was that of Dissenting Protestantism and republican politics.

39. To have a very poor opinion of my intelligence.

40. The agreeableness of your sex, a beautiful shape, a lovely face, good repartee, and all the rest *(tout autour)* . . . extremely agreeable. (His French is intentionally incorrect.)

41. Stepdaughter.

42. Sir Credulous has bowed (made a leg) and removed his hat with a flourish; Sir Patient tells him that such ostentatious manners are not appreciated in the City.

43. With legal license to rail (Sir Credulous humorously misapplies the Latin phrase, which refers to privilege to print). Below: as a poet, he could insult others with impunity, and he would rather fight with insults than swords; gentlemen were obligated to settle a quarrel with a duel.

44. A frightful monster.

45. Defaming someone holding a position of dignity; a legal offense.

46. According to ecclesiastical law, marriages could be performed only between 8 a.m. and noon. Sir Patient detests this law because it inconveniences him and because he objects to any Church regulation as "Popish."

47. Now we must dance.

48. Mental disease causing depression, psychosomatic ailments, etc.; here, equivalent to hypochondria.

49. Faint.

50. Mirror. Roger will bring a magnifying mirror.

51. Sticks out rigidly.

52. Honestly.

53. Scenes were changed on the Restoration stage by drawing back a set of painted flats to discover (reveal) different flats (and sometimes actors) behind them. Cf. Scene iv, below, where the flats were drawn apart to reveal a bedroom behind a garden scene, and Scene viii, where they cover the bedroom to show the garden again.

54. Grotesque dance.

55. The spleen, or hypochondriacal melancholy, was supposed to be caused by vapors arising from the abdominal organs. The College is the organized body of physicians.

56. Chastity.

57. Returned to you the interest you had previously held in my heart.

58. Puritans objected to all instrumental music in church. The Roman

Catholics were unjustly accused of starting the Great Fire of London (1666).

59. A figure of speech in which attributes are transferred from their proper subject to another.

60. The ancient Roman king Tarquinius Sextus raped the virtuous Lucretia.

61. Sulky.

62. Passing quarrels. Glucupicros (Glycypicros) Eros = Sweetly bitter Eros (the god of love).

63. Go to his lawyer's office to get advice on the terms of his marriage contract.

64. Executed in Paris (1676).

65. Were suspicious of.

66. James Nokes was actually speaking this line, since he played Sir Credulous. "Whip slap-dash" was a favorite expression of Sir Samuel Harty in Thomas Shadwell's *The Virtuoso* (1676), another role created by Nokes.

67. The freight delivery man is to be found at the Bell (an actual inn in Cheapside).

68. Many Norman French expressions persisted in seventeenth-century legal language.

69. To the property of Iphiclus. Apparently a lost proverbial reference; probably means "What's all this to the point at issue?"

70. From Catullus's "Hymn to Hymen" (the god of marriage), to be sung at a wedding.

71. Laughing-stock.

72. Legal documents; here, the contract of marriage. Below: the woman brought a portion (money) into her husband's family, which was proportional to the jointure he settled on her.

73. "The creature" could refer to food or any other material comfort; most commonly, it referred jocularly to strong drink. In case = in good shape.

74. Sir Patient's detestation of Roman Catholics leads him to detest Latin, the language of their services. Anti-Catholics identified the Church with a seven-headed beast described in Revelation, ch. 17.

75. Aqua mirabilis, a cordial distilled from wine and spices.

76. Sir Patient considers women in the fashionable districts at "t'other end" of London less virtuous than those in the City. The proverbial apples of Sodom looked beautiful but crumbled to ashes when touched.

77. Knick-knacks and ornaments.

78. Tumble, rumple you.

79. Drunk.

80. Dressing, adorning.
81. The French doctor he keeps on regular salary.
82. Prone to complaining. Balatroon = buffoon, contemptible fellow.
83. Accusations.
84. Aversion to.
85. Destiny turns everything around. Below: Thalessio (Talassio) was customarily shouted at Roman weddings.
86. German.
87. Tease him.
88. With your permission. The phrase is Latin.
89. Professors of medicine, who are assembled here, and you other gentlemen. These words, preceded by *Savantissimi Doctores* (most wise Doctors), above, are directly quoted from the Third Interlude that concludes Molière's *Imaginary Invalid:* a chorus in Latin mixed with French and Italian. Below: Most reverend doctors . . . most illustrious doctors. Francois Rabelais, a medical doctor, made fun of pedantry in his burlesque *Gargantua* (1534). The sermon of the Welsh clergyman is in stage Welsh.
90. Bills (advertisements) were put up on posts in the street.
91. *Whirligigoustiphon* and *stronggullionibus,* below, are evidently invented words made of English roots, suggesting whirling thing and intense fool, with a Greek and a Latin ending. *Dysuria,* however, is a real word, though it is Greek, not Arabic.
92. Hearty eaters (?).
93. Evidently faked medical jargon: quiblets and quillities refer to verbal quibbles.
94. The Bills of Mortality were official lists of deaths, with their causes, published weekly for parishes in and around London.
95. Syphilis.
96. Presumably Kings Louis XIV of France and Philip IV of Spain, but they were not at war at this time.
97. Heavy drinking and cheating, especially with dice. Cater-tray = quatre-trois, a cast at dice.
98. This and the following drugs are imaginary; their names combine English, Latin, and Greek roots: *merda queorusticon,* any excrement from the country; *adminicula vitae,* support of life; *gallimofriticus,* gallimaufry, a hash of leftover food; *cheatus redivivus,* revived cheat; *aqua tetrachymagogon,* strong elixir of four partially digested foods. A glister (clyster) is an enema. *Gondileero* may be derived from gondola, since Strumbulo is presumably in Italy.
99. Prescription.
1. Houses on a street (such as the Strand) were identified by shop signs. The Dutch lines mean: I came from the Netherlands to talk / and

help with the pox and other illnesses. That's a top of my bill: That puts the finishing touch on my prescription.

2. Opening lines of Ben Jonson's *Volpone* (1606), with *my* gold changed to *the* gold.

3. Other public officials in the City, who wore large neck chains as insignia of office.

4. Fictitious names suggesting nonentity, tool, clown.

5. Male writers, who normally have a classical education, write plays according to the neoclassical rules of unity of action, time, and place.

# Mary Griffith Pix
## (1666–1709)

MARY GRIFFITH, daughter of an Oxfordshire vicar, married George Pix, a merchant tailor in London, when she was eighteen. Nothing more is known of George Pix, who may have died young; their only known child was a daughter who died in 1690.

In 1696, Mary Pix emerged into public view with a novel, a tragedy, and a comedy. *The Inhumane Cardinal, or, Innocence Betrayed* describes the sufferings of a young woman ruined by a secret marriage; and *Ibrahim, the Thirteenth Emperor of the Turks,* produced in late spring, is a bloody, sensational tragedy that proved to be her most popular work. *The Spanish Wives,* called a farce but differing from regular comedies only in its shorter length, appeared in August.

The appearance of these two plays, within a few months of two by Delarivier Manley and one by Catharine Trotter, prompted an anonymous contemporary to lampoon the three women in *The Female Wits* in the fall of 1696. (Mutually complimentary poems and prologues among these women suggest that they were acquaintances, if not friends.) The fact that Pix is much less roughly handled than her sister authors suggests that she was personally amiable and unassertive. She appears as Mrs. Wellfed, "a fat female author, a good, sociable, well-natured companion"; in contrast to Marsilia's (Manley's) raging ego and Calista's (Trotter's) intellectual pretentiousness, Mrs. Wellfed's manner is pleasant and unassuming. Her alleged fondness for drink is presented as a minor foible, and her natural pride in her works is moderated by good sense and good humor.

Pix went on to publish five more comedies and tragedies with her name on the title page or a signed dedication; five additional plays have been convincingly attributed to her. All of her plays were produced in London and were at least moderately successful. Her comedies offer lively plots and interesting heroines; her tragedies succeeded as effective vehicles for the acting of Thomas Betterton, Elizabeth Barry, and Anne Bracegirdle.

Some time before 1700, William Congreve befriended Pix. She was a close friend of Susanna Centlivre, and they both contributed complimentary verses to the feminist Sarah Fyge Egerton's *Collection of Poems on Several Occasions* (1706). In 1709, Centlivre's *The Busy Body* was performed for the benefit of Pix's estate.

Although the original cast of *The Spanish Wives* has been lost, its epilogue makes clear that Susanna Verbruggen, who excelled in "variety of humor," played the leading role of the Governor's Lady. It is likely that William Bullock played Friar Andrew and William Pinkethman, Hidewell. *The Spanish Wives* was successful enough to be revived in 1699, 1703, 1711, and possibly 1726.

# The Spanish Wives

To the Honorable,
Colonel TIPPING,
OF
WHITFIELD

*SIR,*

You may please to remember, when I had the honor to be in your company last, at *Soundess;* part of our discourse was upon *Dedications.* I believe you did not then apprehend the danger so near. But, this play being kindly received by the audience, I hope it will not meet with a worse fate, when it claims your protection. You have known me from my childhood, and my inclination to poetry; and 'tis from the happiness of that acquaintance, I presume to make so worthless an offering. This also, joined with your good humor, secures me from the severity of your judgment, which gives you power to be the greatest of critics. I need not tell England how much you have always served your country, since that would be like proclaiming it to be light at noonday. I know all witty men, especially yourself, hate anything that tends towards flattery; therefore I shall only in sincerity tell you: I am,

*SIR,*
*Your very humble, and*
*most obliged servant,*
MARY PIX.

# The Actors' Names.

GOVERNOR OF BARCELONA A merry old Lord, that has travelled,
and gives his wife more liberty than is usual in Spain.[1]
MARQUESS OF MONCADA A jealous Lord, guest to the Governor
CAMILLUS A Roman Count, following the Marquess's lady, as
contracted to her before
COLONEL PEREGRINE An English Colonel
FRIAR ANDREW One that attends the Count
HIDEWELL Retained by the Count
DIEGO Servant to the Governor


# The Women.

THE GOVERNOR'S LADY A brisk and airy lady
ELENORA Wife to the Marquess
SPYWELL Woman to the Governor's Lady
ORADA Woman to Elenora


Scene, *Barcelona*.

# PROLOGUE.

## Spoken by Mr. Pinkethman, in a press-master's habit.[2]

What cheer, my lads? Egad, I'm come to say,
I'll press to sea all those who damn this play:
Lord! how our ship might here be manned today!
Sea-fights, 'tis thought, won't much agree with those
Whom they call wits, and less with mealy[3] beaus.
Mayhaps 'twou'd make them sink; for, every tear,
We don't go to drink punch, and take French air.
But sure, the gentlewomen are at rest,
None of them are afraid of being pressed.
Well, how's the wind here? Still that's veering round,
Like your church-weathercocks, on English ground,
Then hiss it goes; Oh, that's a plaguy sound:
Egad, 'tis worse to every actor's ear,
Than frets of wind to your huge mops of hair.
For thus your cri—critics serve nine plays in ten,
Worse than Jack Frenchman does our merchantmen.
Like pirates too, while honest men they're breaking,
The damned fresh-water sharks aren't worth the taking:
Yet long to maul these same new plays as much
As we, when homeward bound, to take a touch;[4]
Or, as Dubart, to snap his brother Dutch.
Yet why should they hiss plays not worth regarding?
Do we bombard a town not worth bombarding?
Drolls shortly will amuse ye at the fair:[5]
To like this, think yourselves already there.
As for you spruce gallants, pray be n't too nice,

But show you can oblige a woman twice.
The first time she was grave, as well she might,[6]
For women will be damned sullen the first night;
But faith, they'll quickly mend, so be n't uneasy:
Tonight she's brisk, and tries new tricks to please ye.

# ACT I.

## Scene i. Hall in the Governor's Palace.

*(Enter the Governor of Barcelona and the Marquess of Moncada.)*

GOVERN. Prithee, my Lord Marquess, don't trouble me with thy jealous whims: You say, there was masqueraders last night under the windows,—why there let 'em be a God's name! I am sorry 'twas such a cold raw night for the honest lads. By the honor of Spain, if I had heard 'em, I would ha' sent the rogues a glass of malaga to warm 'em.

MARQUESS. O Lard! O Lard! I shall run mad! Sure, my Lord Governor, your horns will exceed the largest in the Palace-Hall.—Oh! that my wife were out of your house, and Barcelona! Methinks I am not secure, though she's under eleven locks.

GOV. By my Holy Dame, I am of your mind: I don't think you are secure.

MARQ. How! Do you know anything to the contrary?

GOV. Why, by th' mass, this I believe: her head's at work; And, I dare say, she has made ye a cuckold, in imagination, with every Don she has through any peep-hole seen, since your first marriage.

MARQ. Oh! damn her! damn her!

GOV. You'll never take my advice. *(Sings.)*

> —Give but a woman her freedom still,
> Then she'll never act what's ill:
> 'Tis crossing her, makes her have the will.

—Phough! I have been in England—There they are the happiest husbands—If a man does happen to be a cuckold, which, by the way, is almost as rare as in Spain: But, I say, if it does fall

out, all his wife's friends are his; and he's caressed,—nay, Gad-
zooks, many times rises to his preferment by it.

MARQ. Oh, insufferable! I am not able to bear your discourse.

*(Enter a Country Fellow.)*

—A man coming from my wife's apartments!—Oh, the Devil!
the Devil!

GOV. I see no cloven foot he has.

MARQ. No; but he is one of his imps; a letter-carrier. I read it in
his face.

GOV. Oh! I begin to perceive it now,—here's the superscription
writ in his forehead:—*To the beauteous Donna Elenora, Marchioness of, & C,* Ay, 'tis very plain.

MARQ. Well, Governor, these jeers won't be put up so.

COUNTRY FELLOW. What a wanion ails ye, trow? What do ye mean
by letters? Ich am no schollard; my calling is to zell fruit; and
zum o' the meads o' this hause (meads Ich think 'em) beckoned
me in;—I zould 'em zum; and that's all I knaw.

GOV. Ay, honest fellow, I dare swear 'tis:—why, if thou wert a
monkey, he'd be jealous on thee.

MARQ. You may think what you please, but I fear other things.
Therefore, if, as a guest, you will let me have the freedom of
your house, I'll take this fellow in, and search him.

GOV. Ay, with all my heart.—Oh these jealous fools! *(Aside.)*

MARQ. Come along, sirrah; I'll look as much in thy mouth.

GOV. Ay, for fear there should be a note in a hollow tooth.

COUNT. FELLOW. Why,—de ye zee, as for matter o' that,—ye ma'
look in my a—

GOV. Hold, Beast, 'tis a man of quality you speak to.

COUNT. FELL. Zooks, I think 'tis a madman.

MARQ. Come your ways, Impudence!

COUNT. FELL. But, Sir, Sir,—must the meads zerch me, or the men?

MARQ. I'll tell you presently, ye wanton rogue.

*(Exit. driving him before him.)*
*(Enter the Governor's Lady.)*

GOV. How now, Tittup?

LADY. Morrow, Deary.

GOV. Why, Tittup, here the Marquess has been fretting, fuming, swearing, raging: he is just horn-mad—Hark ye, Tittup, did you hear any serenading last night?

LADY. Yes, Deary; 'twas the English Colonel to me;—You are not angry, Deary.

GOV. Not I. *(Sings.)*

> He that has a handsome buxom wife,
> Must surely be always pleased,
> Blest with a pleasant quiet life,
> And never, never teased.

But hark ye, Tittup, that English Colonel has such a leer, such a tongue, such a nose, such a—have a care on him, Tittup.

LADY. I warrant ye, Deary, the honest freedom you allow is sufficient: I'll never go farther. You know, he dines here today, and brings his music to entertain us in the afternoon.

GOV. Yes, yes; I must dispatch some business, to be ready to receive him,—B'w'ye Tittup!

LADY. B'w'ye, Deary: Buss, before ye go.—

GOV *(kisses her)*. A pize! a pize![7] your kisses glow! Fie, fie! I don't love ye. *(Exit laughing.)*

LADY. 'Tis my Colonel, my Peregrine, sets my heart on fire, and gives that warmth my old husband found upon my lips—But then such a husband,—So good, so honest, preventing every wish.——Then such a Colonel, so handsome, so young, so charming,—Where's the harm to give a worthy begging stranger a little charity from a love's store, when the kind old Governor can never never miss it?

*(Exit.)*

Scene ii. A Palace. Camillus's Lodgings.

*(Enter Count Camillus and Friar Andrew.)*

FRIAR. Well, my Lord! now we are come to Barcelona, I fear this devil of a Marquess will be too hard for us.

CAMIL. How, Father Andrew, desponding!—'Twas but this morning, over your Malaga, you swore by the Eleven Thousand Virgins, and all your catalogue of saints, you'd bring my Elenora to my arms.

FRIAR. And by fifty thousand more, so I will, if it be possible: If not, my oath is void: You know the Marquess hates me heartily, as I do him, because once he caught me carrying your letter to his wife.

CAM. For the good office, I think, used ye most scurvily.

FRIAR. Scurvily! basely, barbarously; without respect to these sacred robes; tossed me in a blanket; covered me with filth and dust; and so sent me by force to our convent. For which, and my natural inclination to cuckoldom, I have joined in your attempts, and waited on you to Barcelona, to be revenged.

CAM. You know there's justice in my cause.—Elenora was, by contract, mine, at Rome,[8] before this old Marquess had her. And could I again Recover her, I don't question but to get leave of his Holiness For a divorce, and marry her myself.

FRIAR. Nay, that's as you please; when she's in your possession, marry or not, 'tis all one to Father Andrew; it never shall trouble my conscience. I must own, were I in your condition, I should not marry; because daily experience shows, a wife's a cloy, and a mistress a pleasure.

CAM. Well, we'll discourse that when we have the lady; and in the mean time, good Father, be diligent.

FRIAR. I think I am diligent; I am sure, I am worn to mere skin and bone in your service. This morning I found for ye a Mercury, a letter-carrier, that can slip through a key-hole to deliver a billet-doux to a fair lady.

CAM. I wish he were returned; I fear some misfortune has befallen him.

FRIAR. O! here he comes, sound wind and limb!

*(Enter Hidewell [the Country Fellow before].)*

—So, my dear tool of gallantry! how hast thou sped?

HIDEWELL. Gad, the hardest task I ever undertook.—Sir, you gave me five ducats,—as I hope for preferment, and to be made pimp-master general, it deserves double the sum.

CAM. Nor shalt thou fail of it, Boy, if thou hast succeeded.

HIDEW. First then, the damned old jealous Marquess caught me, and notwithstanding my counterfeit speech and simplicity, had me amongst his varlets, to be searched. They knew his custom, and no sooner entered, but they flew upon me like so many furies: I feared it had been to tear me limb from limb; but it proved only to tear my clothes off; which was done in a twinkling, and I left as naked as my mother bore me; whilst the old Marquess groveled all over my habiliments, and run pins in 'em, so thick that a poor louse would not have 'scaped spitting. The only thing which pleased me, was to observe a peep-hole the maids (knowing this to be their master's searching-room) had made; and sometimes one eye, sometimes another, viewing my proportions.

CAM. But had you any letter? was that safe? Satisfy me there.

HIDEW. Pray let me take my own method.—Nothing being found, they gave me again my clothes, and the Marquess a ducat for my trouble: Yet I had a letter—

CAM. Which thou ingeniously swallowedst.

HIDEW. No; which I more ingeniously brought.

CAM. What, in thy hat?

HIDEW. My hat had the same severe trial.

CAM. Thy shoes—

HIDEW. They passed the same scrutiny,—impossible in any of them to hide a scrip, the least shred of paper.

CAM. How then?

HIDEW. My Lord, do ye observe this stick?

CAM *(viewing it)*. Yes; 'tis an honest crabtree-stick—I see no more in it.

FRIAR *(taking the stick, and putting on his spectacles to view it)*. Come, come, let me see it; I can smell out a note that comes from a fair hand;—By St. Dominic, here's neither paper nor writing upon it.

HIDEW. Give it me. *(He unscrews the ferrule at the bottom, takes out the letter, and gives it to Camillus.)*

FRIAR. Thou dear abstract of invention, let me kiss thee.

CAM. Excellent Hidewell! if thou wilt stay with me, whilst I am in Barcelona, I'll satisfy thy utmost wishes.

HIDEW. Most willingly.

CAM. Here Father, here dear confidant! Orada writes that the tormented Marquess has removed her from those apartments that were next the streets to some that overlook the gardens,— thither, she says, my Elenora would have me come this night;

And if they can find a place to 'scape at, before the lodgings are better secured, they will: If not, we shall hear of them,—a gentle whistle is the sign.—Hidewell, you shan't appear in this, because if seen, you'd be known again.

FRIAR. Pray let me go: Gad, if the business should be done without my help, I should take it very ill.

CAM. Well, well, we'll in, and consider on't. *(Exeunt.)*

Scene iii. Scene draws, and discovers the Governor, his Lady, Colonel Peregrine, several Gentlemen and Ladies.

A Song.

I.

Alas! when charming Sylvia's gone,
I sigh, and think myself undone.
But when the lovely nymph is here,
I'm pleased, yet grieve and hope, yet fear
Thoughtless of all but her I rove;
Ah! tell me, is not this to love?

II.

Ah me! what power can move me so?
I die with grief when she must go;
But I revive at her return;
I smile, I freeze, I pant, I burn:
Transports so sweet, so strong, so new,
Say, can they be to Friendship due?

III.

Ah! no, 'tis Love, 'tis now too plain,
I feel, I feel the pleasing pain:
For, whoe'er saw bright Sylvia's eyes,
But wished, and longed, and was her prize?
Gods! if the truest must be blest,
Oh! let her be by me possest.

*(Colonel Peregrine and the Governor's Lady dance; all the time the Governor cries,—)*

> Ha boy, Tittup!
> Well done, Tittup!
> Ha boy, Tittup!

Gov *(the Dance done, he goes to her).*—You are hot, you are hot, Child.

LADY. A little warm.

Gov. Well, Tittup, do but carry thy body swimmingly, without tripping, and we'll begin a reformation in Barcelona, shall thou go through Spain,—The ladies shall live like cherubims,—But have a care, Tittup, have a care of a *faux pas.*

LADY. Fear not, Deary.

Gov. Come, now let's sit down, and see the rest perform—Let me have some lively songs—

*(Colonel Peregrine goes to sit next the Governor's Lady.)*

—Hold, Friend, hold! I have not learnt so much of your English fashion yet, to let another man sit by my wife, and I decently keep at a distance.

COL. I beg your pardon, Sir.

Gov. Nay,—no harm;—*(Sings.)*

> If an old man has a beauteous treasure,
> Let her sing, and dance, and laugh without measure,
> And then she'll think of no other pleasure.

COL. Your own, Sir?

Gov. Ay, ay, Boy; I have a thousand of 'em in a day, *extempore.*

COL. Is't possible?

Gov. Come, now I ha' done, do you strike up.—

*(Songs and dances. The music ended, enter a Servant.)*

SERV. My Lord, there is to wait on Your Honor,—His Excellency the Duke Gonsalvo de Medina, de Sidonia, de—

Gov. Hold, hold, enough, enough,—Where is he?

SERV. In the Hall of Ceremonies.

Gov. Gadso! I must go to him, sit you merry, I'll be with you presently.

*(Exeunt all but Colonel Peregrine, the Lady, and Spywell.)*

LADY. Spywell, stand at yonder door, and give me information, as soon as ever my Lord comes up the great stairs.

SPYWELL. I will, Madam.

COL. My Angel! by Heaven, I am raging mad; burnt up with violent love.—Thy shape—Thy every motion fires me,—but thy eyes—They set me in a blaze—Oh! I must die, unless the cordial of returning kindness save me!

LADY. Can you be so ungenerous to wrong this noble Governor, who is so fond of you, and even dotes on me?

COL. He wronged thee more, when he condemned thy lovely youth to withered sapless arms.—Can little foolish tricks of fondness make amends for extasies, paintings, the joys unutterable of vigorous love?

LADY. I must not hear ye.

COL. You must, you must—I'll, kneeling, fix ten thousand burning kisses on thy beauteous hand; And the little wanton god swims and revels in thy sprightly eyes.

LADY. Why am I fastened here!—too rigorous Heaven! Take from this wondrous stranger his conquering charms, or give me more insensibility!

*(Enter Spywell.)*

SPYW. Madam, my Lord's upon the stairs.

LADY. Away, away; mark what I say, and keep up the discourse.

COL. This is but living upon the rack; you might contrive a better opportunity.

LADY. Peace, and observe.—But are your ladies then so free and yet so innocent in England?—

GOV *(peeping)*.—Gadso,—they are together; though I am not jealous, 'tis convenient to hear a little what their conversation is.

COL.—Chaster in their thoughts than your nuns, yet merrier: more frolicsome than your carnivals.

LADY. Very pleasant! just so I would live,—yet if a bold encouraged wretch once offered at my honor, I would not stay to use my husband's sword,[9]—but with my own hands stab the vile presumer.

COL. You need not, Madam, talk of weapons; your eyes, though they roll in fire, yet shoot chaste beams, and show your heart as cold as ice.

GOV. So, so; very, very well, by th' mass! How is't my Ganymede o' the war, who look'st fitter to storm hearts than towns?—Yet, Egad, you English boys fear not their pretty faces, but fight like rugged Romans, or the old rough Gauls.

COL. You compliment us, My Lord.

GOV. No faith, I hate 'em.—Well, Tittup, are ye almost ready for your dinner?

LADY. When you please, Deary.

GOV. I warrant the Marquess would not let his wife dine with us for the King of Spain's next plate-fleet.[10]

LADY. He has let me see her but once;—when I offered it again, he plainly told me, my company was unfit for her:—rude brute!

COL. To us who have been bred otherwise it seems a miracle, That men can be so barbarous to the fair sex.

GOV. But I'll set 'em an example, if Tittup holds her ground.— Come along—*(Sings.)*

> Merrily, merrily let's pass our time,
> In freedom, joy and plenty:
> At sixty appear but in our prime,
> Whilst the thinking so is old at twenty.

*(Exeunt.)*

# ACT II.

## Scene i. A Chamber
## (in the Governor's Palace).

*(Enter Elenora, Marchioness of Moncada, and Orada.)*

ELEN. Dost think the messenger got off, Orada?

OR. Faith I know not, Madam,—I thought I heard the Marquess's voice as he went out.—The fellow seemed very cunning.—

ELEN. All his policy but little would avail him, if my husband met him,—by Heaven 'tis kindly done of Count Camillus to leave his wealth, his palaces, and all the pleasures of delightful Rome to follow wretched me to Barcelona. I am a thing accursed by cruel guardians, for my parents died when I was young; they would not else, sure, have forced me, condemned to an old jealous madman.—I saw his follies and his humors, and I begged, like a poor slave, who views the rack before him,—All in vain; they were inexorable.—so may just Heaven prove to them in their greatest need!

OR. This is a melancholy thought, complaints won't break locks; we must set our wits at work to free ourselves. I have searched the lodgings round, but there's no passage; an imprisoned mouse could scarce escape.

ELEN. But prithee, dear Orada, how got you in favor with My Lord? He used to hate ye abominably.

OR. True; and whilst he did so, it was impossible for me to serve Your Ladyship.—So I wheeled about,—Railed at you and all your ways most heartily, and immediately obtained his grace.

ELEN. Would that do?

OR. Yes, with a bantering letter I showed him, pretending I had got it from you; and a long harangue how wives ought to hear with their husbands' ears, see with their eyes, and make use of no sense without permission. In fine, I ravished him with my discourse, till he threw those withered sticks, his arms, about me, and swore I should remain his heart's joy.

ELEN. 'Tis a great point gained; you must wheedle him this night with some story, and keep him in the closet—whilst I watch for Camillus, or his agent.

OR. I warrant you, Madam.

ELEN. Orada, get me the song I love, the succeeding tedious; imprisoned wretches thus count the succeeding hours, and groan the melancholy time away.

### A Song

> Be gone, be gone, thou hag despair;
>   Be gone, back to thy native Hell:
> Leave the bosom of the fair,
>   Where only joy should dwell.
> Or else, with misers, willing revels keep;
> And stretch thy wretched lids from sleep.
>   But hence be gone, and in thy hated room
>   Let hope, with all its gentle blessings, come.

*(A noise of unlocking doors.)*

—So! now my jailor comes.

OR. Then I'll observe my cue.—Come, come, Madam, you must not complain.—Suppose your husband kept you in an oven, or a cellar, you ought to be content—I say,—Wives must submit.

EL. Hold thy tongue, Impertinence!—When you were good for anything, my husband would not let ye come at me: now he has brought you to his turn, I must be perpetually plagued with you.

*(Enter the Marquess.)*

MARQ. You are a perpetual plague to me, I'm sure—You hate everybody that tells you your duty.

EL. Inhuman Spaniard!—what wouldst thou have?—Am I not immured, buried alive?

MARQ. Yes, yes; I have your body, but your heart is with the young Count Camillus. D'ye blush, ye strumpet, in imagination?—Ye Eve! Dalilah! Devil! I'll let out that bounding blood.—Orada—get a surgeon to take away fifty ounces.

ORAD. My Lord, you are not mad! What! have a surgeon quiddling her white arm, and looking babies[11] in her eyes!

EL. Monster! be thyself the butcher, and let my heart's blood out: That gentleman you named has honor, truth, and virtue.

MARQ. Thou lyest, false woman! he's a rake, a hellhound, and wallowing now in Rome's brothels.

OR. I could contradict him if I durst. *(Aside.)*

ELEN *(laughing).* Perhaps so.

MARQ. D'ye fleer, poisonous witch? I am going to dispatch the last business that brought me to Barcelona. Then, Minion, thou shalt be immured in a remote castle, where thou shalt not see the face of humankind, except thy women, and when I design to visit thee.

ELEN. Know this, and let it gnaw thy jealous heart: Thy visits will be my severest punishment.

MARQ. Watch her, Orada; preach those maxims thy zeal for me suggests; let her not have liberty to think.

OR. Fear not; let me alone to tease her.

*(Exit Marquess, locking the doors after him.)*

ELEN. Ay,—make all fast—Insufferable tyrant!—Come Orada, let's go view the dear place, which at wished-for night brings my dear Camillus to me.

*(Exeunt.)*

Scene ii. A hall.

*(Enter the Marquess.)*

MARQ. Where's this plaguy Governor? I must have him with me, because 'tis about the King's business; though I hate him for breaking our Spanish customs, in letting his jilting wife have such liberty.—Ha! here she comes,—and a spark with her;—I'll abscond, and see how virtuously she carries herself.

*(Enter Colonel Peregrine and the Governor's Lady.)*

LADY. I dare not stay,—my husband thinks I am gone into my chamber; if by any chance he should come this way, all our hopes are ruined.

COL. Were he by, I'd seal my vows upon thy melting lips— Oh! receive my heart; it flutters near thee, and struggles for passage.

LADY. I am covered o'er with blushes!

MARQ *(aside, peeping)*. Confound your modesty! were you mine, you should be covered o'er with blood.

COL. My life! can't ye contrive some way to bless me? Your sex were ever most ingenious lucky at invention.

LADY. Suppose you pretended a quarrel in England,—for which you were pursued, and begged leave to hide here.—If you were in the house, I might get an opportunity to visit ye,—But sure you would not be such a naughty man to ruin me, if I did.

COL. Not for the world!

LADY. I would fain love ye, and preserve my honor.

COL. That is preserved whilst 'tis concealed: The roses in your cheeks will only wear a fresher dye,—and those dear eyes are no tell-tales, Love will make 'em shine and sparkle more.—I'll put your advice in execution.

LADY. I must not venture on another moment.—Farewell.

*(Exeunt severally.)*

COL. Farewell, my blessing.

*(Enter Marquess.)*

MARQ. Oh Women! Women! Women!—They are crocodiles, they are painted serpents, gilded toys, disguised fiends,—But why name I these? They are *women*—Just such another is my damsel of darkness; if Fortune would but throw a handsome fellow in her way.—Here comes the Governor, singing, I warrant ye,— poor credulous fool,—I cannot but laugh—ha, ha, he!

*(Enter the Governor singing.)*

Gov. Let her have her will, &c.—Hey da! I am glad to find you so merry. 'Tis as great a wonder to see you laugh, as 'twould be to see me cry—And that I han't done these fifty years, old Boy.

MARQ. My Lord, which is best, for a man's wife to cuckold him in imagination or reality?

Gov. Lord! Lord! your head is always upon cuckolding. All the cuckolds may be hanged, for what I care.

MARQ. Oh fie, no! Hanging would be a scurvy death for a man of your quality.

Gov. Why—what d'ye mean by that, now, ha?—Don't provoke me, I say—do not—I shall make old Toledo walk[12] if you do, for all 'tis in my own house.

MARQ. I must not tell him now,—It will put him so out of humor, he won't go with me,—'Twas only a jest, My Lord,—I would beg the honor of your company to the Duke of Sidonia's.

Gov. With all my heart—come, come: (Sings.)

> Tormented still's the jealous fool,
>     Himself, nor bosom wife can never rest:
> Yet he often proves the woman's tool,
>     Whilst the contented man is ever blest.

(Exeunt.)

Scene iii. A chamber (in Camillus's lodgings).

(Enter Camillus, Friar Andrew, and Hidewell, with a ladder of ropes.)

CAM. So, Hidewell! Hast thou got the ladder of ropes?

HIDEW. Yes, My Lord, here's all the tackling.

FRI. Is it strong?—for I am something weighty.

CAM. How, Father! just now you said you were worn to skin and bone.

FRI. Ay, My Lord; but you know bones ill covered will soonest be broken.

CAM. True; take care of yourself be sure.—Hidewell, I have altered my mind,—Thou shalt along with us; watch on the outside the wall, and give us notice when the coast is clear.

HIDEW. With all my heart.

FRI. Let me see, have I got my holy water about me?

CAM. Holy water! for what?

FRI. Oh! I always love to say my prayers, and have those trinkets, when I undertake a dangerous design.

CAM. Don't be so prophane, *Domine,*—you'll never thrive,—yet, if your devotion's strong, you've time enough—We shan't go this hour or two.

FRI. Nay. I won't hinder ye,—an ejaculation as I go along does the business.

*(Enter a servant.)*

SERV. My lord, the English Colonel, that lodges in the house, sends to know if you are at leisure.

CAM. Tell him, I am,—and long to kiss his hands.—I like that gentleman, he appears brave

*(Exit Servant.)*

And bold—should our designs grow desperate, I dare believe he would not scruple his assistance.

FRI. Faith and troth, I like him too,—he treats like an emperor; I dined with him to day,—and he so genteelly, so agreeably forced flesh upon me, that by St. Dominic, I could not refuse him; though 'tis a strict fast, a horrible strict fast, as I hope to be an abbot.—Then the obliging toad has such a waggish eye, I'll pawn my beads, a plaguy dog for the women, and they are ever good-natured:—By His Holiness's toe, I love the sex myself,—for all this dangling robe, and my foolish vow of chastity.

CAM. 'Tis pity you were not a Knight-Errant,—the Church has robbed the ladies of a famous adorer.

FRI. No, faith, my Lord, I do 'em more service in these weeds: I have saved many a desperate soul.

CAM. How!

FRI. Thus: in procuring them the full possession of their desires; and that surely brought 'em to repentance; and you know what repentance brings 'em to.

HIDEW. Truly, Father, I shall grow angry with you; for, if once the priests take up the office of procuring, there will be no business for a lay-pimp.

CAM. Peace,—the Colonel comes.

*(Enter Colonel Peregrine.)*

COL.—I am your Lordship's humble servant,—I have just had some music to compliment me,—I am a great lover of it,—if Your Lordship is so, we'll have the entertainment there.

CAM. Nothing can oblige me more.—Some chairs there!

*(A dialogue-song and dances: at the time of the dances Camillus and Peregrine seem in discourse.)*

HIDEW. If your Lordship pleases, being in this dress, I will aim at a jig, I danced thus once in a masquerade.

CAM. Prithee do.

*(A jig by Hidewell.)*


A Song

Betwixt Mr. Leveridge, a Spaniard,
and Mrs. Cross, an English Lady.

HE.　Fairest nymph that ever blessed our shore,
　　Let me those charming eyes adore,
　　And fly no more, and fly no more.

SHE.　Spaniard, thy suit is all in vain;
　　I was born where women reign,
　　And cannot brook the laws of Spain.

HE.　For thee my native customs I'll forgo,
　　Cut my black locks, and turn a beau.

SHE.　Ere I submit to be your wife,
　　Listen to an English husband's life;
　　With sparks abroad I'm every day,
　　Gracing the gardens, park, or play,
　　Hearing all the pretty things they say;
　　Give and take presents, and when that's done,
　　You thank the beaux when I come home.

HE.    Oh! I now my temper fear.
SHE.   Oh! sigh not yet, there's more to hear:
       At my levee crowding adorers stand,
       Fixed on my eyes, and grasping my white hand;
       All their courts and oglings bent on me,
       Not one regardful look towards thee:
       At this thou must be pleased, or else not see.
HE.    Then we must part, and I must die.
SHE.   If thou art such a fool, what care I?
HE.    I cannot share thee, so I am undone.
SHE.   A wiser will supply thy room.
CHORUS.   Then we must part, &c.
          If thou art such a fool, &c.
          I cannot share thee, &c.
          A wiser will supply, &c.


COL *(to the Singers and Dancers).*—So, well performed;—return to my apartments, I'll be with ye presently. *(Exeunt.)*
CAM. The oddness of our adventures surprise me:—Both our mistresses in the same house!—I hope 'twill further our designs.
COL. It must.—My Lord, I have a favor to beg: That you would lend me one of your implements tomorrow, to manage a plot I have in agitation.
CAM. Most willingly; take your choice.
FRI. I am at your service.
HIDEW. You are so forward,—Canonical fornication-broker,—I believe I am fittest for the gentleman's service.
FRI. Goodlack, Upstart! I helped ye to My Lord,—and now ye are for engrossing all business to yourself.
COL. Nay,—I must have the most expert, because the case is difficult.
FRI. Well! I'll not say much!—But here stands little Andrew, who has undertook to bring a smock-faced[13] cardinal to a madonna secured with a guard more numerous than Argus' eyes, and more dreadful than the dragon you wot of—yet spite of massy doors, impenetrable bolts, and Italian padlocks, effected it.
HIDEW. Phough! what's that! I have carried on an amour for the Queen of Spain,—conveyed her letters made up in wax-candles,

love-complaints writ in the inside of her glove, besides a thousand other contrivances you never dreamt of.—'Tis true, at last the fate of all court-pimps was mine: I fell into disgrace; as that had raised me, so it ruined me; I lost a coach and six by my profession,—And shall you pretend to rival me?

FRI. You lost! why, Sirrah, Sirrah! I tell thee, if I had employed my parts in church-politics, in tricks of priestcraft, by this time I had been Pope.—But the bringing kind loving things together, was dearer to me than the Triple Crown,—and shall a varlet contend with me?

COL. Gentlemen! dispute no more; I find either of you is qualified for my purpose.—My Noble Lord, Good Night,—if you want me, on the least notice, I am ready. *(Exit Col.)*

CAM. I thank you, dear neighbor, Good Night.—Hidewell, take up the ropes, and come away.

FRI. Along, Blunderbuss.

HIDEW. I hope, Father Peremptory, before tomorrow morning, you'll stand in need of my cunning, to deliver that loved carcass from some imminent danger.

FRI. I defy thee, and all thy shallow imaginations.

CAM. Leave jangling, and make haste.

*(Exeunt.)*

Scene iv. (The Governor's) palace.

*(Enter the Marquess, Orada following him.)*

ORA.—My Lord, I have a thousand things of greater consequence to say.—Pray return.

MARQ. Dear Orada, by and by; I must see where my devil of a wife is.

ORA. You know she cannot pass the lodgings, perhaps she's at her devotions.

MARQ. No, she's too foul to pray.

ORA *(taking him by the arm).*—But, my Lord,—as I was saying,—

MARQ *(flinging from her).* I'll return immediately.—

ORA. There's no keeping this mad fool out of his wife's sight;— They must e'en to bed, whilst I parle[14] with the lover.

*(Enter Marquess, pulling in Elenora.)*

MARQ.—So, Gentlewoman! I have caught ye!—How? With your head out at window, making your amorous complaints!

ELEN. I was almost stifled for want of air.—Sure you are not jealous of the trees and stars,—They were my only objects.

MARQ. Oh Impudence! did I not hear you say, When will he come; my Light, my Life, break through this veil of darkness, and shoot with rays of comfort on me?

ORA *(aside).* A deuce of these thinking minds! So brimful of cogitations, they must run over.

ELEN. I knew you behind me, and therefore did it to torment ye.

MARQ. It may be so; but I shan't trust ye—Come, into the bedchamber.—Orada, do you school her,—I'll watch for your Light and Life myself.

ORA. My Lord, you had better go to bed with her, and then you'll be secure.

MARQ. No, no; in, in. *(Shuts 'em in and locks the door.)*—Now for my pistols—that I may give this midnight-guest the welcome he deserves. *(Exit.)*

Scene v. Changes to an orchard (by the Governor's palace).

*(Count Camillus and Friar Andrew come down the wall by a ladder of ropes.)*

FRIAR.—So!—We are got well in; Heaven send us safe out again!

CAM. Father, Father! don't trouble Heaven in this affair, you'll never prosper.

FRIAR. Bless me, My Lord! Prayers are natural to me: if you are so wicked to neglect 'em, I can't help that.

CAM. Come, mind your business: where's the whistle?

FRIAR. Here, here,—now for a delicious vision of a peeping Angel! *(Whistles.)*

*(The Marquess above.)*

MARQ. The signal's given, and here's the answer. *(Shoots off a pistol. Friar Andrew falls flat.)*

CAM. We are discovered; and if I stay, all other opportunities are left for ever.—

*(A cry within of Thieves! Thieves!)*

—Why Friar! Friar! Father! You are not hurt, the bullets went over our heads.

FRIAR. Are ye sure I am not hurt?—I did conceive I was killed.

CAM. No, no; but I know not what you may be if you stay— Follow me, with speed. *(Cam. gets over the ladder.)*

FRIAR. Oh Pox! the devil of all ill luck! ruined, hanged, drawn, and quartered! No possibility of escaping without a miracle,— and I can't have the impudence to expect a miracle—

*(When the friar is halfway up, the ladder breaks, and falls down.)*
*(Noise within, Where! Where! Thieves follow.)*

—Oh! they come! they come!—and now at my greatest extremity I cannot pray.—Godso! here's a tree!—I'll try to mount it. *(Gets up the tree.)*

*(Enter the Marquess, and several servants.)*

MARQ. Search well, Boys! leave not a shrub or tuft of grass unexamined—Five pistoles to him who finds one.

SERV. I warrant ye, My Lord! let us alone for ferreting 'em!— Soho! what have we here—A Pox, 'tis a stub of a dead tree— 'thas broke my nose.

*(Another servant looking up in the tree, where the friar is.)*

2 SERV. Oh Rogue! Are ye there? I'll be with ye presently.

*(Friar Andrew, as the fellow gets up, throws his bottle of holy water full in his eyes, and pulls his cowl over his face, and roars out: They both fall from the tree together.)*

—The Devil, the Devil! oh, my eyes are out!

*(The rest cry, The Devil! They drive the Marquess in, who often turns, and cries.)*

MARQ. Let me see him! let me see him!

*(The friar follows 'em, roaring.)*

Scene vi. Changes to the inner part of the house.

*(Several servants enter in confusion,—a great knocking at the door, and cry of Fire, Fire! One of the servants opens the door—Enter Hidewell, men and maids, as from their beds—some crying, Fire, some Murder, Treason, & c. After them—Enter Friar Andrew, driving several servants, who run out, crying, the Devil! the Devil!)*

HIDEW.—Make haste, unlucky devil!—'Twas I cried Fire! opened the door for your deliverance—Fly, and own me for the master of your art for ever.

FRIAR. I cannot stay to thank ye,—But—I yield, I yield. *(Exit running.)*

*(Enter the Governor, in his night-cap, and sword drawn.)*

GOV. *Benedicta Maria!* What! Fire, Murder, and Treason all abroach at once!—a horrible plot!—By the honor of Spain, a terrible one, as I hope to be a Grandee!

*(Enter the Governor's Lady, attended.)*

LADY. Spywell, what can be the meaning of this? My Colonel would not come in such a way.—My Lord! my Deary! the matter,—the cause of this disturbance!

GOV. Here, Sirrah! raise all the guards: Oh Tittup! we're like to be murdered,—drowned, and blown up, nobody knows how, nor which way: A damnable plot! by his Majesty's Mustaches I swear!

LADY. Sure 'tis a false alarm,—The House has been searched by some servants discreeter than the rest,—and they find nothing.

*(Enter Marquess, cutting [hitting?] his servants.)*

MARQ. Villains! Dogs! under the notion of the Devil, these sheep-looked rogues, these dastard whelps, have let the robber of my honor escape; whilst I but just examined if my *wife* was safe, the *wolf,* the *goat* is gone.

GOV. Hey da! my Lord Marquess, are we then alarmed only with a jealous whim of yours? By the peace and pleasure of my life, I'll suffer it no longer.—Any other of my palaces are at your service; but such a wasp shall molest my honey-hive no more.

MARQ. Uncivil Lord! thy palaces, nor all thy wealth should bribe my stay,—Tomorrow I've resolved for my departure.—In the interim, I desire an hour's conference.

GOV. Soon as you please, I am free.

*(Enter a servant, with Hidewell.)*

SERV. My Lord, here we've found a man that nobody knows.

GOV. Ha! who are ye, Sirrah? Your name? From whence d'ye come? Whither d'ye go? What's your business?—Answer me all at once.

HIDEW. I daut I caunt,—but I'll do no more than monny a mon; I will tell ye the truth: Coming to morket with my fruit, d'ye zee, Ich heard the noise of *Fire, Fire! Thieves,* and such-like,—zo che thought good crabtree-stick might walk amongst the rogues; zo Ich have left the fruit with our Margery, and come with main vorce to help ye, d'ye zee.

GOV. An honest lad! and, d'ye hear, you may sell your fruit to my family.

HIDEW. O Lard, O Lard! Ch'am a made mon, and my wife and children: what! zell my fruit to my Lord Governor—made for ever! henceforth I'll scorn my neighbors, and despise my betters.

MAR. I like this fellow because I searched him thoroughly, and found him no go-between.—Here, Sirrah! there's something for ye,—and were I to stay, ye should ha' my custom.

HIDEW. I thank your Honors.

GOV *(to a sentinel).* Let him out. *(Exit Hidew.)*

MARQ. You'll remember, tomorrow morning early.

GOV. Most certainly.

MARQ *(aside).* Then I'll convince this credulous easy man what need there is of watching one's wife:—Good-night. *(Exit.)*

GOV. Farewell; go thy ways, for a troublesome, maggot-pated, jealous-crowned simpleton, as thou art:—Hey boy, Tittup! how is't Tittup? how shall you and I get to sleep again Tittup? ha!

LADY. I know not.

GOV. What, moody, Tittup! *(Sings.)*

I'll rouse ye, and mouse ye, and touse ye,[15] as long as I can,
Till squeaking I make ye confess:
There's heat in a vigorous old man,
When he loves to excess, when he loves to excess.

*(Exeunt.)*

# ACT III.

Scene i. A chamber (in Camillus's lodgings).

*(Enter Camillus and Friar Andrew.)*

CAM. Curst be my disappointing stars, that thus have crossed me! whilst I but aim at Elenora's freedom, she, for my attempts, suffers from her tyrant-husband worse usage.

FRIAR. You may curse your stars, if you please; but for my part, I bless the pretty twinkling gentlemen,—that is, if they had any hand in my deliverance.—I am sure, if I had been caught, my usage would have been bad enough.—I long to know what is become of that hangdog Hidewell.—Oh!—talk of the Devil, and he appears.

*(Enter Hidewell.)*

HIDEW. —Down, on your marrow-bones, Domine, and thank my ingenuity, else your brittle thread had been cut; and you left in a dark way by this time.

FRIAR. Come, come; don't be so triumphant:—for had not my own roaring preaching voice—

HIDEW. Ay, ay; much used to preaching, I believe,—unless it was indulgence to a yielding female.

FRIAR. Well, as I was saying, had not my own almighty voice struck terror through 'em, I had been in Limbo, long before your ingenuity came to my assistance.—Not but you did me a kindness,—and I acknowledge it,—that's enough for a man of my qualifications.

CAM. Oh Hidewell!—all my hopes are ruined, and poor Elenora must remain a slave for ever.

HIDEW. My Lord, you are mistaken,—our expectations now stand fairer; the Governor and Marquess both take me for a very silly honest fellow,—and have ordered I shall have full and free access,—then let me alone for a contrivance.—I'll get the lady for you, and the woman for myself; following the example of all noble knights and trusty squires.

FRIAR. I find you are providing for yourselves: But what must I have for my pains-taking in this affair?

HIDEW. You know, you cannot marry;—I'll give you leave to tempt my damsel, when I have her: D'ye conceive—if she loves spiritual food, I'll not be your hindrance.

CAM. Dear Hidewell! thou shalt go immediately; learn when they remove; fathom their designs; I'll force her from him on the public road.—He forced her from her plighted faith, her vows, and all her wishes: My force is just.

HIDEW. Trust to me, My Lord, and fear not.


*(Enter Colonel Peregrine.)*


COL. My Lord! your humble servant! I ha'n't rested tonight, since I heard of your disappointment, reflecting how my own affair may prove.

CAM. Ah Colonel! our cases are very different,—You hunt but for enjoyment, the huddled raptures of a few tumultuous moments:—But I am in quest of virgin-beauty, made mine by holy vows; constrained by fiends, instead of friends, to break the sacred contract, and follow the *capriccio*[16] of a mad old man.—Virgin did I call her?—By Heaven, I dare believe she is one, at least her mind is such;—and were she in my power, I'd soon convince the world of the justice of my cause.

COL. My Lord! you shall command my sword and interest in Barcelona,—yet you must give me leave to mind my own affairs.—I grant your passion more heroic;—for I should scarce accept the Governor's wife for mine, if he would give her:—but I am amorous and eager, as Love and Beauty can inspire hot and vigorous youth.

FRIAR. By St. Dominic, well said, Old Boy: I'll stick to thee. I hate these whining romantic lovers. Nor would I have trudged to Barcelona, had I thought the Count only fixed on honora—Pshaw, I can get it out,—honorable love.

COL. Since you are so willing, Sir,—I have employment for you.—Can you play the Hector well, pursue with a fiery countenance, swear without intermission, make noise enough, no matter what you say?

FRIAR. I'll try, I'll try,—hum! hum!—by St. Dominic, by St. Patrick, St.—

COL. Hold! hold! what d'ye mean? You must swear by Jupiter, Rhadamanthus, Mars, and those blustering sparks; not such puny passive saints.

FRIAR. Well, Sir,—I shall be soon instructed:—But what must I swear all this for? or like the bullies of the age, must it be all for nothing?

COL. No, no, there is a cause;—Come along with me—and I'll give ye clothes, and full directions.

HIDEW. If I might advise ye, sir, he should not undertake it; he has something in that unlucky phiz shows him unfit, though coveting intrigues: plaguy unfortunate lines, I swear.

FRIAR. Peace, Envy! Screech-owl! Raven! Bat! Devil! When did I ever fail before that night? nor then neither, sirrah, ha!

HIDEW. Rage on, Spite! I say but this.—Have a care, when in all your gallantry, you don't forget, and make a friar-like salutation.

FRIAR. Pox take ye for putting me in mind on't—for I always do a thing I am forbid.

*(Enter a servant.)*

SERV. Please Your Honor, a lady desires to speak with you.

CAM. I'll wait on her.

COL. I'll leave you this apartment free, My Lord, my business being in haste.—Come, Father!

CAM. Farewell: may your desires be fulfilled, or you cured of 'em.

COL. Your servant.

FRIAR. B'w'ye Hidewell! I don't question but to top you in my performance when we meet next.

HIDEW. Heaven help the weak, I say.

*(Exeunt Col. and Friar.)*
*(Enter Orada.)*

CAM. Ha, my dear Orada! What miracle got thee this liberty?

ORA. My Lady was so thoroughly frighted at the noise of the pistols, and the confusion she heard (for you, I suppose) that she has since been ill.—The jealous Marquess could not find in's heart to trust a doctor with her, but sent me for a cordial.

CAM. I hope her sickness has no danger in it.

ORA. No, no; 'tis over now,—scarce enough left for a pretext for my coming.

CAM. But, what hopes? What shall be our next design? Speak comfort, my best friend!

ORA. Faith, I know not well:—Suppose the Marquess were some way informed, you are in Barcelona,—'twould fright him out of his wits;—I'd back it, and persuade him to send Elenora in the night privately, lest you attempt her on the road,—then you may seize the unguarded fair.—Methinks something like this might be done.

CAM. We'll in, and consider farther on't.

HIDEW. Hark ye, *Donna,* if your lady falls to My Lord, you prove my natural perquisite, by the example of a thousand years.

ORO. What means the fellow?

CAM. Despise him not, Orada; he has prodigious parts under that russet coat.

ORA. I care not for him, nor his parts, I shall ne'er examine 'em.

HIDEW. You and I shall be better acquainted for all this.

ORA. Away, Bumpkin!

CAM. I tell ye, he's a beau in disguise.

ORA. I believe so.


CAM. Come to this inner room, Orada, lest we are interrupted.

*(Exeunt.)*

Scene ii. A hall (in the Governor's palace).

*(Enter the Governor, Marquess, and Diego.)*

GOV. A-pox, a-pox! Was this your conference?—If I had guessed at it, the Devil should have conferred with ye for me.

MARQ. I would ha' thanked a friend that forewarned me of an approaching evil.

GOV. Evil! What evil? The evil is my knowing it; if I had not, 't had been none.—Yet how am I convinced you have not abused my Tittup?—By the honor of Spain, I'll fight for Tittup: Guilty or not guilty.—My Lord!—what you have said is a scandalous, contagious, outrageous,—

MARQ. Hold,—if you say one word more, I draw.

GOV. Well, well!—I will have patience,—but if this Colonel doth not come with the sham-plot you have buzzed into my head, by King Philip's beard,—

MARQ. Threaten not; I'll meet you when and where you please, ill-mannered Fool! *(Exit.)*

GOV. Diego! I have borne up,—yet, Egad, to own the truth, I am damnably afraid—there's something in it.—That English Colonel is a plaguy dog; he looks as if he were made to enter all breaches, conquer every way.—I'll try if I can sing after this news. *(Sings.)*

> Lock up a woman, or let her alone;
> Keep her in private, or let her be known:
> 'Tis all one, 'tis e'en all one.

—A scurvy tune, as I hope to be a Grandee.—Nay, if my voice is broke, my heart will quickly follow.—Diego!

DIEG. My Lord!

GOV. I ever found thee faithful;—if the spark does come, follow exactly my directions, and all shall be well yet.

DIEG. Fear not me, My Lord, I'd lose a leg or an arm at any time in Your Honor's service, and never cry, Oh! for't.

GOV. Hark, hark! I think I hear a noise.

*(Cry of Fire here.)*
*(Without, a cry of Murder, and shutting doors.)*
*(Enter Col. Peregrine, his sword drawn, leaning upon his servant.)*

COL. Oh, my noble Lord! I'm ruined, unless your pity save me: in England I, in a duel, killed a gentleman, and his friends have pursued me hither, setting upon me, four at once.

GOV. Alas and welladay! 'tis sad indeed! and you, I warrant, are wounded desperately.

COL. I fear, to death,—oh! oh!

GOV. Ah, the dissembling rogue! it grieves me almost to disappoint him, the smock-faced dog does it so cunningly. *(Aside.)* Diego!

DIEG. Sir.

GOV. Diego, get one of my able surgeons to search the wound.

COL. I thank you, My Lord; my own servant has great skill in surgery, I'll trust him.

GOV. Diego! carry this gentleman to an apartment near the garden, free from noise,—I'll send Tittup to visit ye by and by.

COL. Your Lordship's all goodness. *(Exit.)*

GOV. And thou all treachery,—Oh! the English whining dog—how shall I punish him? By the honor of Spain, he deserves to be utterly disabled,—rendered wholly incapable.—But I'll have mercy in my anger: hang't—I have loved the handsome whipster, and he shall find it.

*(Enter Diego.)*

—So,—have ye disposed of him as I ordered?

DIEG. Yes, My Lord; and whilst I was in the chamber, he groaned as if his heart were breaking,—But I had the curiosity to stay a little at the door, and heard both laugh ready to burst, an't please Your Honor.

GOV. Please me! not much, in faith, Diego; but—let me tell 'em, had they fell into the hands of any other of our nation, their mirth would quickly ha' been spoiled, and their whoring too adod.

*(Enter servants, hauling in Friar Andrew.)*

SERV. My Lord, we have took the ringleader, that pursued the noble English Colonel.

GOV. Good Boys! Good Boys!—Well, Sir,—And what are you?

FRIAR. If you are a man of authority, as by your house and port[17] I guess you are, I charge you, do me justice; for by yonder blue firmament, and all those hated stars, that twinkled at my brother's murder, I'll flay that cursed Colonel.

GOV. Thou hangdog, begot in lewdness, and born in some sink of sin,—Son of a thousand fathers, and maker and contriver of cuckolds without number; I know thee for a pimp: Here, Diego! fasten upon one whisker, whilst I take t'other; if they are fast,

I may alter my opinion—They are reverend whiskers, I confess,—if not, I proclaim thee a pimp.

*(They pull, and the whiskers come off between 'em.)*

FRI. Oh, mercy! mercy! I do own my profession; but good My Lord, forgive me.

GOV. Ay, that I will, but I'll punish thee first,—here,—carry him to the red tower, and let him have two hundred lashes, till all thoughts of concupiscence, either for himself or others, be thoroughly mortified.

FRI. Hear me, My Lord!

GOV. No, away with him.

FRI. You must hear me; I am a priest, I excommunicate ye else.

GOV. A priest, and a pimp! Oh Lord!

FRI. Why? is that such a wonder?

DIEG. Look, My Lord! here hang his beads under his clothes.

FRI. Now, My Lord, you are satisfied the secular arm can't punish me; pray give me a release.

GOV. Hold, hold, not so fast.—Take him, and carry him to the next abbey just as he is, and tell the Fathers what ye know.

FRI. 'Tis well 'tis no worse,—to deal with the tribe, let me alone, they'll judge my frailties by their own.

GOV. Say ye so, Beelzebub, in his own clothing! but I'll be a thorn in thy side, I'll warrant thee, old Father Iniquity.

SERV. My Lord, we'll set the mob upon him, that's worse than all the justices in quorum.

FRI. I'll curse, excommunicate, purgatory ye, hang ye, damn ye. *(Exit forced off.)*

*(Enter Governor's Lady.)*

LADY. My Deary, Spywell tells me our dear Colonel's wounded.

GOV. Oh, most dangerously, Tittup; he had as many holes through him as a Jew's cake.

LADY. Alas, then I fear he's dead.

GOV. No, no; Nature has framed his body for the purpose; a sword passes and repasses like a juggler's ball, and no harm done.

LADY. Cruel Deary! you make a jest on't, but I'll visit and comfort him.

GOV. Hold, hold; his wounds are dressing: You would see him naked, would ye?

LADY. Oh Gad! not for the world.

GOV. Retire to your chamber, I'll send for you when 'tis convenient.

LADY. I will, Dear; but pray take care of him.

GOV. Yes; there shall be care taken of him, I promise ye.—A hopeful young gentleman, by the honor of Spain.—Diego! follow to my closet, there I'll make thee sensible of my design. *(Exeunt.)*

*(Enter the Marchioness Elenora, meeting Orada.*[18]*)*

ELEN. Dear Orada! bring'st thou comfort, or must I remove from Barcelona to wilds and unfrequented deserts, impenetrable castles, and all the melancholy mischiefs sprightly youth can fear?

ORA. I hope not, Madam; the Lord Camillus employs his brain and all his busy instruments for your deliverance.

ELEN. Give me the scheme of his design, that I may guess at the success.

ORA. Madam,—my Lord.—

*(Enter the Marquess.)*

ELEN. Take that—thou impudent performer of my tyrant's will. *(Strikes her.)*

ORA. My Lord, you see what I suffer for your service.

MARQ. But we'll be so reveng'd, Orada; when we have her wholly to ourselves, by Heaven, I'll bring that pampered carcass down: The roses shall wither in her wanton cheeks; her eyes, whose hot beams dart fire, grow dull and languid:—By all my pangs of jealousy, I'd rather clasp a fiend, than doubting sleep by such an angel.

ELEN. And 'tis thy doubts, Old Man, not I, torment thee—Our sex, like water, glides along pleasant and useful; but if grasped by a too violent hand, unseen they slip away, and prove the fruitless labor vain.

MARQ. To waters, waves, and rocks most justly may you be compared;—but I want time to hold an argument.—Prepare this night for your remove,—I am fixed,—your jewels, equipage and all put up.

ELEN. Let my slaves take care of that,—What need have I of jewels, ornaments, or dress, condemned to cells and everlasting solitudes?

*(Enter a servant.)*

SERV. My Lord, a country fellow is very importunate to speak with you.

MARQ. Bring him in,—Mistress, you to your chamber. You hear the man's business is with me.

ELEN. May it prove a vexatious one, I beseech Heaven. *(Exit.)*

*(Enter Hidewell.)*

MARQ. —Oh, my honest fruiterer, what brought you hither?

HIDEW. Why, an't shall please ye,—a marvellous thing has happened since I see ye last,—a parlous contrivance, by th' mess,—as I hope for Margery, I ne'r see the like.

MARQ. The matter, Friend!

HIDEW. Nay, Gadsores, 'tis zo strange, I can't tell whether I was asleep or dreamt, or not.

MARQ. Prithee tell me quickly; what wonder hast thou met with, Fellow?

HIDEW. Zir, I'm but a poor fellow; but, as neighbor Touch has it, I can zee into a millstone, as var as another man.

MARQ. Talk to the purpose, or I shall grow tired:—is it anything concerning me or my honor?

HIDEW. Ay, ay, Zir, you don't know the bottom of this plot.

MARQ. Nor the top on't neither,—dallying Fool, proceed.

HIDEW. Nay, you'll know it soon enough:—Han't you a very handsome wife, buxom and free, as the saying is?

MARQ. Oh the Devil, lies it there? Well! what follows?

HIDEW. Hags, cuckoldom, ch'am afraid, Zir,—for coming out of this hause, there meets me a waundy handsome fellow, Gadsores,—he had the swinginst—what d'ye call't.—

MARQ. Perruque, d'ye mean?

HIDEW. Ay, udslid! our biggest bushel, that's kept on purpose for the masters of the measures to zee, would not,—no, i'facks, ch'um zure—it would not cover it.

MARQ. Did he enquire after my wife?

HIDEW. By my troth he did.—Friend, says he, do you go often to that house?—Mayhap I do,—mayhap I do not, said I, what's that to you? Nay,—no harm, quoth he; and thereupon slipped a piece of gold into my hand.—I must confess that softened me,—and he went on,—Dost thou not know an old jealous, freakish, confounded Marquess lives there? Pray ye now dan't be angry, Sir,—I use but his own words.

MARQ. No, no, go on.

HIDEW. And has he not, quoth he, a young lovely wife?—And then he run on with hard words I could not conceive for above a quarter of an hour, though I was wise enough to pick it out, that he was amour'd on her.

MARQ. Confound him, confound him!

HIDEW. Quoth he,—canst thou convey a letter to her?—why how now, mon, zed I, who dost take me for, a pimp? No, no, ch'am no pimp,—an I war, chou'd ha' better cloas o' my back,—by th' mess, shall do none o' your bawdy messages, not I; Do't yourself, an you wull, for Tim. With that he drew his sword, and I very vairly took up heels, and run away, for ch'am very veard of a naked sword.

MARQ. Couldst thou not discover his name?

HIDEW. His zervants called him—Count—a—Cam—Cam—Cam— ch'am zure 'twas zummot about Cam.

MARQ. (starting) What,—Camillus!

HIDEW. Ay, ay, that's it, that's it, in troth.

MARQ. Oh, I am ruined, blown up, undone! Camillus has his pockets crammed with gold;—he'll bribe the world to take his part:—Then that contract—so firm and sure,—I lose her, and what I value more, her large fortune.—Orada, what shall I do?

ORA. Suppose ye remove my Lady in a litter, without any of your own attendance,—for indeed I fear he'll waylay all the roads.—My Lord, she may be got many leagues this night, and when in safety, you may send back for your equipage.

MARQ. Many leagues! we'll go a thousand,—for I'll be with her, and force her speed.

ORA. (aside). That I suspected.

HIDEW. Zir, Zir., here che may serve ye, for I keep a litter, as well as zell fruit.

MARQ. Oh! thou'rt an honest fellow; and, fear not, you shall be rewarded beyond your wishes.—Come in,—I'll give thee an order for one of my best horses, because my servants shall not suspect 'tis for my self. Orada! get your Lady ready,—'tis now near night, and it shall be done with speed. *(Exit.)*

ORA. Be sure you lame the horse now; for as soon as the litter has lost sight of the Marquess, we return into the city, and towards the morning escape in a felucca already ordered—whilst the disappointed Marquess is hunting the roads in vain.

HIDEW. Madam, I desire none of your directions, I am perfect master of my trade.—I cannot but think how bravely I shall maintain thee, girl; for money comes rolling in.

ORA. Mind your business, and think of fooling afterwards.

*(Exeunt.)*

Scene iv. The Colonel's chamber.

*(The scene draws, and discovers Col. Peregrine upon a bed, and his man by him.)*

COL. I begin to grow damnable weary of nursing up this no wound; I wish the dear angel would but come, and heal the real wound my heart endures.

SERV. Truly, Sir, I should have but little stomach to a mistress, if I were in your circumstances:—What! attempt to cuckold a Spanish Governor in his own house!

COL. Peace, Coward, and see who's coming.

SERV. Sir, Sir, 'tis my Lord Governor.

COL. Well, well.—Oh! oh! oh!

*(Enter Governor and Diego; speaks aside to Diego.)*

GOV. Diego! unobserved secure that sword, hat, and perruque,—I shall have use for't.

DIEG. Yes, My Lord.

COL. Oh, oh, oh!

GOV. How d'ye, Sir?

COL. Oh, very bad,—just, just fainting.

SERV. Please ye to have some cordial, Sir?

COL. A little, if ye will.

GOV. And are not you a damned dissembling handsome toad—

Answer me that now,—answer me that. What! corrupt the wife of my bosom, my darling Tittup! break the laws of hospitality! Well,—thou'rt a desperate fellow, I protest;—design to cuckold one that hopes to be a Grandee of Spain!—Abominable, by St. Jaques! Come, come, get up; your wound's not mortal, I'll engage.

COL. I'm so confounded, I know not what to say.

SERV. Ay, I thought 'twould come to this,—Now shall I be tossed in a blanket, burnt, drowned, hanged!

COL. Be quiet, Rascal, and be damned!

GOV. What, you're out of humor, Sir! I must confess, 'tis a plaguy disappointment. Come, in short, I'll use ye much better than you ought to expect. Go with haste and privacy to your lodgings, and the town shall know nothing of the matter:—Your wig and other accoutrements shall be sent after ye; but I must use 'em first.

COL. My Lord, I beg your pardon for this attempt; you know't has been no more.

GOV. Your good will was not wanting, thanks to your whoring stars.

COL. Though unarmed, I will not stir from hence, if you practise a thousand cruelties upon me, unless I have your promise, that you will not hurt your wife.—I have honor, though the rules are now transgressed. Nor can I leave a lady (whom my love has enticed) to the resentments of a Spanish husband.

GOV. An honorable dog, as I hope to be saved! by all that's sacred, I will not hurt her; only she must remain deprived of that liberty, which, against our country's custom, I had given her.

COL. That I'm sorry for; but cannot ask more.

GOV. But I shall ask you to be gone.—Diego—get one of my closest chairs,[19] and let him be conveyed home, as sick.

COL. Oh, I could tear my flesh.

GOV. No, no, fast and mortify it.

COL. I own you generous, but have not the heart to thank you.

GOV. I tell ye once again—your absence will best express your acknowledgment.

COL. Your servant.

GOV. Oh, your very humble servant, sweet friend in a corner!—Now, Diego! help to equip me.

*(Exit Colonel.)*

DIEG. My Lord!

GOV. The perruque, the perruque block—oh, how the amorous rogue has perfumed it,—the pulvil,[20] essence, and powder o'ercomes me.

DIEG. My Lord, may I presume to tell ye,—your black beard and that white perruque look very disagreeable.

GOV. No matter, the curtains will hide that.—Now go to my wife, and tell her, I am gone to the castle, to see the guards relieved, and shall sup there.—Tell her also, I desire she would visit the wounded Colonel in my absence.—

*(Exit Diego.)*

—Now I shall find if Tittup knew the bottom on't,[21] and were consenting to this roguery. *(Throws himself on the bed.)*

*(Enter his Lady, and Spywell her woman.)*

LADY. Oh, we are happy beyond what we could expect; my husband sups at the castle tonight,—yet I tremble every limb of me:—I swear I love this old Governor, and nothing but this charming Englishman could have tempted me to break my vows.

SPYW. Madam, you walk and talk, you know not where—you are in his chamber. *(Goes towards his bed.)*

LADY. —My Love, my Life, wilt thou not meet me? there is no further need of counterfeiting.

*(Governor leaps up, and snatches her hand.)*

GOV. Ungrateful Tittup!

HIS LADY *(shrieking)*. Ah!

GOV. How couldst thou serve me so?

LADY. Phogh, I knew 'twas you, and did it on purpose to make you jealous.

GOV. A-pies, a-pies, no, no, you did not know 'twas I:—I would be deceived, but cannot.

LADY. Oh, what must I expect?

GOV. Diego!—first turn this baggage out o' doors,—and d'ye hear,

Mistress,—if ye tattle of these affairs, I'll have ye poisoned,— else ye are free and safe.

SPYW. Madam, farewell; I can't excuse myself.

LADY. Now my turn's a coming.

GOV. Ah Tittup! whither, whither art thou fallen?

LADY *(crying)*. No, Deary, not fallen, I was but staggering—and you caught me, Deary.

GOV. For which, I humbly conceive, you wish me hanged, Deary.

LADY. Indeed, indeed, Deary, I'm glad my honor's safe;—I never had an inclination before, and never will again, if you forgive me.

GOV. I'll take care you shall never have another opportunity; your back apartments must be your prison, and an old duenna your companion, till time and age have wrought off your loose desires. No more hoity toity,—no more appearing at windows,— dining at Deary's table, and dancing after it for digestion.—I say, Tittup, all these vanities must be forgotten.

LADY. Oh! stab me first! Let me not be a May-game[22] to all my servants, who by my confinement would guess at my disgrace. You used to swear you loved your Tittup—I never did a fault before, but what a frown might punish—Now let me experience your boasted fondness; and take me to your heart, with kind relenting smiles—else leave me distracted on the earth in endless fears bemoaning my indiscretion, and your cruelty.

GOV *(aside)*. I feel I begin to mollify! *(To her.)* Oh, Tittup, Tittup! Thou hast been a baggage! a very baggage—by the honor of Spain!

LADY. I confess I have been frail—But I will be forgiven, so I will—I'll hang about thy neck; nor leave the dear place till my pardon's signed.

GOV. What! Give you again your freedom to see another Colonel, and be again betrayed?

LADY. No; there is not such another Colonel.

GOV. How, Tittup!

LADY. Not such a tempter; such a seducer, I meant.

GOV. Thou pretty epitome of woman's weakness—I dare not trust thee—Tittup—you must retire.

LADY. Do, lock me up; and next moment you are gone, I'll hang myself in my own garters, so I will.—Can you behold your Tittup hanged? her eyes goggling, her mouth, you have bussed so often, gaping; and her legs dangling three yards above ground?—This is the sight you must expect.

Gov. Oh! I can't bear the thoughts on't—Stand farther off— farther yet—that I may rush upon thee with all the vigor of six- teen, and clasp thee from such a danger—Thou resistless ruler of a doting, fond old fool!—Here—I forgive thee—but if after this, I catch ye staggering, expect no mercy.

LADY. By the new joys your returning kindness brings me, I'll die first!

Gov. The world may blame my conduct; but then—they know not Tittup's charms; the power of her eyes, and pleasure of her arms.—I cannot raise my voice to sing, yet—hum!—No; Gad- zooks, 'twon't do.

LADY. Henceforth

> Good humor shall supply thy want of youth,
> You shall be always kind, I full of truth.

*(Exeunt hugging.)*

Scene v. A hall.

*(Enter Elenora and Orada.)*

ELEN. Do we succeed, my dear Orada?

ORA. Beyond expectation, Madam—within some moments, you are in Camillus's arms.—Hidewell is gone for a well-appointed litter, which wheels but round, whilst Hidewell plays tricks with My Lord; and then carries you to the English Ambassador's.

ELEN. Now my desires are so near fulfilling, I begin to fear 'em— yet I know Camillus is honorable.

ORA. All's honorable. The house is honorable, the Lady honor- able: Fear nothing, but in, and pray for our success—I think I hear my Lord—You must be sure to seem very unwilling.

ELEN. I'll warrant ye. *(Exit.)*

*(Enter the Marquess.)*

MARQ. Is your Lady ready?

ORA. Yes, My Lord. But, Good Lord! what a life have I had with her—I believe she has thrown fifty things at my head—She swears she won't go like a thief in the night.

MARQ. Oh! when the litter comes, we'll do well enough for that—I'll make her go, or leave her dead upon the place.—Dost thou think none of the servants perceive our preparations at this back-door?

ORA. My Lord, there's no danger—'tis so far through the gardens; and now we have these apartments, their people never come at 'em.

*(Enter Hidewell.)*

MARQ. Here comes my trusty fellow. Well! Hast got a litter?

HIDE. Ay; and by th'mess, an able one too—I warn ye, Mon, afore day, we be past whistling after.

ORA. Friend, you never talked to a lord in your life, I suppose.

MARQ. Pho, pho! 'tis all well—Is the horse for me ready too?

HIDE. Just by the litter, My Lord!—My Lord—i'fackens, it saunds rarely.

MARQ. Call Elenora.

ORA. I will venture—but Heavens! how I shall be us'd! *(Exit, and re-enter with Elenora.)*—Nay, Madam, 'tis in vain disputing it; for you must and shall.

HIDE. A vine dame, by th'mess!

ELEN. Commanded by my slave! Monster! whither dost thou intend to have me at this dead hour of night? to death, I hope.

MARQ. To death, if you resist—Orada, haul her along.

ORA. I think I do pull her—I believe her arm will come off.

HIDE. Why law ye, Mistress—dan't be so veard—Ye shall come to no hort—I have had vine vokes in my litter 'vore naw.

ELEN. Away, Fool! leave hauling me—I will go—thou cruel devil!

MARQ. Come, I'll see her in the litter; and then take horse.

*(Exeunt. Re-enter Marquess and Hidewell.)*

MARQ. Sirrah! Sirrah! where's my horse?

HIDE. My Lord! My Lord!

MARQ. Sot! Dunce! my horse!

HIDE. Why a—why a—I tied him to the pales—and tis so waundy dark without, I cannot find him.

MARQ. Fly and search! Bid the litter go softly: I'll o'ertake 'em.

HIDE. I'm gone, I'm gone—*(Comes back.)*—My Lord, must I bring him hither?

MARQ. Eternal Fool! Call to me, and I'll come out.

HIDE *(stopping).* Udsookers! 'ch'am zummat a veard.

MARQ. This fellow will make me mad—Beast! will ye stir!

HIDE. Ch'ave heard vokes talk of ghosts, zo I have, about the park pales.

MARQ. Rascal! I'll make a ghost o' thee if thou dost not go, or direct me where my horse is.

HIDE. I run, I run! *(Exit. The Marquess following him.)*

*(Hidewell crosses the stage running: The Marquess within cries, Where are ye?)*

HIDE. I'll lead him a dance—Here, here! *(Exit.)*

*(Within. Here, here!)*

MARQ. A Pox, where? *(The Marquess entering.)*—Oh! the Devil! I can't wag a step further! I have lost sight of him, and the litter; and am lamed into the bargain—I hope Orada observed my directions for the road—The pass I gave 'em lets 'em through the city gates: If this fool would come once, I should soon overtake 'em.—Numps, Fool! Are ye coming?

HIDEWELL *(within).* O Lard! O Lard! ch'am an undone, Mon! Ch'am an undone, Mon!

MARQ. What's the matter?

*(Enter Hidewell leaning on his stick; as soon as he comes in, he falls down, and roars out.)*

HIDE. Oh! Oh! Oh!

MARQ. What ails the fellow? Where's my horse?

HIDE. A murrain, a plague take your horse—ch'am maimed for ever—For getting up to make haste, he has thrown me, and broke my leg. Oh, my poor wife and children! they must to the parish—Then Margery—how she'll take on! for, to zay truth, I loved her better than my wife—Oh! Oh! Oh!

MARQ. The Devil take thee, and all thy family, for an unlucky dog! I see, I must call up my servants at last. *(Exit.)*

HIDEWELL *(getting up)*. Farewell, sweet Signior! for, by this time, your lady's in safe hands. *(Exit hastily, singing.)*

*(Enter the Marquess.)*

MARQ. Pedro! Olonzo! Valasco!

PEDRO. Did you call, My Lord?

MARQ. Yes. A fellow has broke his leg—You must wake Monsieur Cureclap, my French surgeon—and, Olonzo, give orders to my grooms this moment, to prepare two horses; Valasco shall go with me.

PEDRO. My Lord! What fellow? Where is he? Why, here's nobody!

MARQ *(looking about)*. Gone! Hell and Furies! A plot upon my honor, my life, my wife, my estate! Murder! Murder! Saddle all my horses; get what friends money will purchase; search every road—my estate! my wife! Hell and Damnation!

*(Enter Governor, with a letter in his hand: His lady, Diego, and servants.)*

GOV. So! the cry's up again—but Heaven be thanked, 'tis almost over now—What's the matter, My Lord Marquess?

MARQ. Ruined, undone for ever! My wife's run away!

LADY. How! Run away! That's worse than I, Deary.

GOV. I know not: 'Tis according as you prove, Tittup—A bad wife's better lost than found.

LADY. Unkind Deary.

MARQ. My Lord, burying all animosities, I beg you would assist me now. I shall run mad—my wife, nay more, a great estate, lost! lost!

GOV. My Lord, you must be pacified—I've ill news to tell you—there's a letter sent me from Rome, by the Cardinal Patron of Spain, that you stole a young lady, firmly contracted to a noble Roman count: also His Majesty's order to put the lady in a monastery, till your cause is tried.

MARQ. I'll hang myself! I'll drown myself! I'll bury myself alive! Dogs! Whelps! get me cords, knives, poison, sword, and fire.

GOV. The man's distracted—Diego, after; and persuade him.

LADY. 'Tis a just judgment on him, Deary, for being so jealous.

GOV. Ay, Tittup; when women never give any cause, you know, Tittup.

LADY. Hump!

*(Enter a gentleman.)*

GENT. Sir, my Lord Camillus sends to give you an account, that he expects the Lady Elenora at the English Ambassador's. He hears, by an express, Your Honor has orders from the King relating to her; to which he willingly submits.

GOV. An honest lad, by the honor of Spain—Tell him, Friend, I'll wait on him immediately at the Ambassador's.

LADY. Deary.

*(Exit gentleman.)*

GOV. What now! That begging look's put on for something.

LADY. Let me go with you, and see the Ambassador's lady, and the Marchioness, and—

GOV. —And the English Colonel. Ha! why, Tittup, canst thou look me in the face, and ask this?—By the honor of Spain, I believe this hoity, toity will desire me to admit him for her gallant.

LADY. Truly, Deary, if the Colonel is there, you shall hear me charge him, never to see me more.

GOV. A new way, Tittup! to go into a man's company, to forbid him your sight! Come—thou shalt along! and—*(Sings.)*

> If with horns my kindness thou dost repay,
> I'll punish thee some unknown, uncommon way,
> Nor hear whate'er thy charming tongue can say.

Scene vi. Changes to the English Ambassador's.

*(Camillus meeting Elenora and Orada: Runs and embraces Elenora.)*

CAM. My Elenora! art thou here! do I hold thee fast, thou choicest blessing of my youth!

ELEN. Witness my heart, which strongly beats, how much I'm pleased in my Camillus's arms! But, Oh! I blush, when I remember I am another's wife.

Cam. No more o'that; the Cardinal's my friend, and has promised a divorce[23] immediately—Therefore crown my joys with smiles, and forget past dangers.

Elen. I can say only this: I love ye—

Cam. And not descending angels, with all their heavenly tunes, could charm like that dear sound!—safe in a monastery thou shalt remain, till the dispute is ended. And then—Oh! thou blest charmer—then all my sufferings shall be liberally paid; and longing love revel in feasts of unutterable delight.—Nor art thou forgot, dear Orada, but, whilst I have life, shalt be used like a friend, and mistress of my fortunes.

Orad. I humbly thank Your Honor, and heartily rejoice at my good Lady's happiness.

Cam. Poor Hidewell!—I hope he is in safety.—

*(Enter Hidewell.)*

Hidew. —Yes; and here, at Your Honor's service,—though I have had a broken leg, and two or three other misfortunes,—but all's well now, and I can dance for joy.

Cam. Thou art a witty rogue,—and henceforward shalt ha' no occasion to expose thyself,—I'll provide for thee like a gentleman.

Hidew. I'm your ready slave,—D'ye hear that, Mrs. Scornful? *(To Orada.)* how d'ye like my parts and person now?

Ora. Troth, I've seen so much between my Lady and the Count, that my mouth almost waters.

Hidew. We shall soon agree, I find.

Cam. My dear Elenora, the Ambassador's Lady sends word, her husband is gone for a few days to hunt: she is very ill, but that all things in her house are at your service.

*(A lady enters and whispers Camillus.)*

Elen. Tomorrow I'll wait on her.

*(Enter Colonel Peregrine.)*

Cam. Oh, my dear friend! here's the lovely prize, which so well deserve the pains I have taken.

Col. A charming lady!—My Lord, you are a happy man.

CAM. How goes your affair and what's become of the obliging friar?

COL. Nay, Heaven knows! the story is too long to tell; only this: I found the old Lord generous, and resolve to attempt his wife no more.

CAM. I'm glad on't—in your age you never will repent an uncommitted sin.

ELEN. That Governor's Lady seemed a pretty good-humored creature; therefore, my tyrant, let me see her but once.

(Enter Friar Andrew, his clothes torn, and covered with dirt, and his face scratched.)

CAM. Who have we here! Oh Heavens! Father Andrew!

COL. What! my Hector thus used!

HIDEW. What has befallen thee, oh thou weak brother?

FRI (angrily). What has befallen me! you may behold what has befallen me; dirt, wounds, and disgrace.—The ladies may live in rat-traps, or die o' the pips, for Father Andrew's assistance again.

HIDEW. Look, forward undertaker and wretched performer, there the lady stands, delivered by me!

ELEN. My Lord, is not this the friar brought your first letter, after I was married, whom the Marquess caught and abused?

CAM. The same, Madam.

HIDEW. I said he had unfortunate lines, but he would take no warning.

ELEN. Not to encourage anything that's ill, but because you have suffered in my cause, there's a cordial will revive the heart, and wash out all stains. (Gives him a purse of gold.)

COL. For me you have suffered too; and I beg you would accept of this. (Gives him more.)

FRI. Spite of vows, in this necessity there's no refusing such a favor.

CAM. Come, Father, cheer up yourself, have recourse to your old friend Malaga,—I'll provide for ye, that you shall go through no more dangers.

FRI. By St. Dominic, I had not need; for I have almost lost my life in this.

(Enter a servant.)

Serv. Sir, the Governor of Barcelona is come to wait on ye.

Cam. Godsme—in, Father! you would not see him, I suppose.

Fri. See him! I'd sooner see the Devil:—Well I'll get a pretty wench to wash me without, and good store of Malaga within, and try to forget past sorrows. *(Exit.)*

*(Enter Governor and his Lady, arm in arm.)*

Gov. My Lord, your servant.

Cam. Yours in all obedience.

Gov *(aside).*—Yonder he stands,—the ogling rogue! I thought so.—My Lord Camillus, before I talk to you, pray give me leave for some few words with that gentleman.

Cam. With all my heart.

Gov. Sir!

Col. My Lord!

Gov. Nay, o't'other side, if you please,—Now, Tittup, speak what you promised.

Lady. Colonel Peregrine, my Lord has been so good to forgive me what is past; and I desire, for the future, as you are a gentleman, you would, after this night, never see me more.

Col. Madam, I obey.

Gov. And d'ye hear,—if ye prove a man of honor, about threescore years hence I may leave ye Tittup for a legacy, and abundance of wealth, a world of wealth, by the honor of Spain.—Nay, 'tis worth staying for.

Col. Threescore years hence, quotha!

Gov. Now, my Lord Camillus, to you and the lady. *(They go aside.)*

Hidew. I wish we had some music,—since our success, I can't keep my heels on the ground.

Col. If the company agree to it, I can procure my Lord Ambassador's, and send for my own.

Hidew. I'll motion it presently.

Elen. I freely submit, and will retire to what monastery you appoint. I hope my future conduct will satisfy the world of my innocency.

Cam. And mine, of my faith and constancy.

Col. What say ye now to music and dancing? Hidewell longs.

CAM. With all my soul, this is a jubilee, which I'll keep whilst I've
life.

ELEN. But are we secure?

GOV. Fear not, Madam; my guards surround the house,—and am
not I here?

*(They all sit.)*

*(Songs and dances: Them over, the company comes forward.)*

> CAM. Greatness was the attendant of my birth;
> But love gives me heaven upon earth.
> These comforts my Elenora does impart:
> Joy to my eyes, sweet raptures to my heart.
> GOV. Like you, here stands a happy man;
> And I'll keep my Tittup,—that is, if I can.

# EPILOGUE.

## Spoken by Mrs. Verbruggen.

Our author, by me, puts up her humble prayer,
This farce, this trifle of a play, you'll spare.
I'll try your good nature: But, oh! I fear
You are not like my fond old husband here.
Then, first, my character who will admire?
Some will think it too cold; others, too full of fire.
I dare swear every spark here will say,
Damn it, that cursed baulk[24] has spoiled the play.
Then the ladies my staggering won't allow,
They'll cry, Where's her strict rules of virtue now?

But the ladies are not so ignorant: All know
The difference 'twixt a Spanish husband, and a beau.
With submission our author still appears;
Courts your indulgence, and your judgment fears;
Lives on your smiles, and at your frowns despairs.

## Notes to *The Spanish Wives*

1. Dressed like an officer in charge of a press-gang, who would force seamen into the navy in time of war. England was at war with France (War of the League of Augsburg).
2. Beaus would wear particularly elaborate wigs, whitened with flour.
3. Molest (another ship). Jean Bart, a captain in Louis XIV's navy, seized the ships of the Dutch, allies of England.
4. Clowns performing at Bartholomew Fair, held at the end of August.
5. Pix's first play was a tragedy.
6. Wives in Spain were restricted even more than in England, a point that English writers never tired of making.
7. An exclamation, probably derived from *A pox*.
8. In the seventeenth century, a precontract (formal promise) of marriage had legal force.
9. Wait for my husband to avenge me by a duel.
10. Fleet bringing gold and silver from America.
11. Playing with her arm and gazing into her eyes.
12. Challenge you to a duel.
13. Pale, smooth-faced.
14. Parley.
15. Stir you up and pull you about (affectionately).
16. Capriciousness, arbitrary will.
17. Bearing, manner.
18. Since the Marquess keeps his wife confined, there should presumably be a scene change here to his apartment.
19. A sedan chair with curtains.
20. Perfumed powder for powdering a wig.
21. Understood the situation.
22. Laughing-stock.
23. Actually, an annulment based on her precontract to Camillus. (In real life, such an annulment would have been most unlikely.)
24. The Colonel's disappointment or, more probably, her refusal to gratify him.

# Susanna Centlivre
## (1670?–1723)

THE INFORMATION we have about Susanna Centlivre's early life is based on inauthenticated memoirs,
which show signs of heightening to make her life resemble
that of an adventuress out of Restoration comedy. Her maiden
name is unknown; she may have left home at fifteen to get away
from a hostile stepmother and been picked up by Anthony
Hammond, a Cambridge undergraduate who was to become a minor writer, and may have lived with him at Cambridge, disguised
as a young man, and attended lectures there. She is then supposed
to have lived with another young man, Fox; and she evidently
married Carroll, an army officer who was killed in a duel shortly
afterwards.

It is known that she appeared in London in 1700 as Susanna
Carroll and began to make her way as a writer, contributing fic-
tionalized letters to anthologies and poems to a collection
commemorating the death of John Dryden. (This may have been
edited by Delarivier Manley and included poems by her, Sarah
Egerton, Pix, and Trotter.) Carroll became acquainted with a
number of other writers, including George Farquhar, Tom Brown,
and Richard Steele, as well as the leading actors Anne Oldfield
and Robert Wilks. She is said to have been vivacious and good-
natured, ever ready to oblige her friends.

Although her first three plays (1700, 1702) were not particularly successful, *The Gamester* (1705), a deft comedy that
capitalized on a conspicuous fashionable vice, was a sensational
hit. At first Carroll had presented herself as a female author, but
soon she felt it necessary to conceal her sex and authorship. She
complained in the dedication to *The Platonic Lady* (1707) of "the

186 • SUSANNA CENTLIVRE

carping malice of the vulgar world; who think it a proof of sense to dislike everything that is writ by women." *The Busy Body* (1709), which turned out to be her most successful comedy, narrowly escaped failure when it opened to a thin, apathetic house put off by the rumor that it was "a silly thing wrote by a woman." Nevertheless, she went on to become the most prolific and, after Farquhar's death, the best writer of comedies in England. She produced a total of nineteen plays, most of them intrigue comedies. *The Busy Body* (1709), *The Wonder* (1714), and *A Bold Stroke for a Wife* (1718) enjoyed lasting and well-deserved success; Don Felix in *The Wonder* was one of David Garrick's favorite roles and the one he chose for his farewell performance.

Both before and during her early career as an author, Carroll supported herself in part by acting. She is said to have first attracted Joseph Centlivre, one of Queen Anne's chefs, when acting at Windsor. They married in 1707, after which she apparently led an entirely respectable life. She vigorously promoted Whig politics in poems and plays from 1712 on—one of the reasons why Alexander Pope attacked her in *The Dunciad.*

*A Bold Stroke for a Wife* had a moderately successful run of six nights when it was first performed at Lincoln's Inn Fields, but it did not become really popular until the middle of the eighteenth century.

# A Bold Stroke
# for a Wife

## To His Grace Philip,
## Duke and Marquis of Wharton, Etc.[1]

MY LORD,

It has ever been the custom of poets to shelter productions of this nature under the patronage of the brightest men of their time; and 'tis observed that the Muses always met the kindest reception from persons of the greatest merit. The world will do me justice as to the choice of my patron but will, I fear, blame my rash attempt in daring to address your Grace and offer at a work too difficult for our ablest pens, *viz.*, an encomium on your Grace. I have no plea against such just reflections but the disadvantage of education and the privilege of my sex.

If your Grace discovers a genius so surprising in this dawn of life, what must your riper years produce? Your Grace has already been distinguished in a most peculiar manner, being the first young nobleman that ever was admitted into a House of Peers before he reached the age of one and twenty. But your Grace's judgment and eloquence soon convinced that august assembly that the excelling gifts of nature ought not to be confined to time. We hope the example which Ireland has set will shortly be followed by an English House of Lords and your Grace made a member of that body, to which you will be so conspicuous an ornament.

Your good sense, and real love for your country, taught your Grace to persevere in the principles of your glorious ancestors by adhering to the defender of our religion and laws; and the penetrating wisdom of your Royal Master saw you merited your honors ere he conferred them. It is one of the greatest glories of a monarch to distinguish where to bestow his favors; and the world must do ours justice by owning your Grace's titles most deservedly worn.

It is with the greatest pleasure imaginable the friends of liberty see you pursuing the steps of your noble father. Your courteous, affable temper, free from pride and ostentation, makes your name adored in the country and enables your Grace to carry what point you please. The late Lord Wharton will be still remembered by every lover of his country, which never felt a greater shock than what his death occasioned. Their grief had been inconsolable, if Heaven, out of its wonted beneficence to this favorite isle, had not transmitted all his shining qualities to you and, phoenix-like, raised up one patriot out of the ashes of another.

That your Grace has a high esteem for learning particularly appears by the large progress you have made therein; and your love for the Muses shows a sweetness of temper and generous humanity peculiar to the greatness of your soul; for such virtues reign not in the breast of every man of quality.

Defer no longer then, my Lord, to charm the world with the beauty of your numbers, and show the poet, as you have done the orator. Convince our unthinking Britons by what vile arts France lost her liberty; and teach 'em to avoid their own misfortunes, as well as to weep over Henry IV, who (if it were possible for him to know) would forgive the bold assassin's hand for the honor of having his fall celebrated by your Grace's pen.

To be distinguished by persons of your Grace's character is not only the highest ambition but the greatest reputation to an author; and it is not the least of my vanities to have it known to the public I had your Grace's leave to prefix your name to this comedy.

I wish I were capable to clothe the following scenes in such a dress as might be worthy to appear before your Grace and draw your attention, as much as your Grace's admirable qualifications do that of all mankind; but the Muses, like most females, are least liberal to their own sex.

All I dare say in favor of this piece is that the plot is entirely new and the incidents wholly owing to my own invention, not borrowed from our own or translated from the works of any foreign poet; so that they have at least the charm of novelty to recommend 'em. If they are so lucky in some leisure hour to give your Grace the least diversion, they will answer the utmost ambition of, my Lord,

Your Grace's most obedient,

most devoted, and most humble servant,

SUSANNA CENTLIVRE

# Dramatis Personæ.

## Men.

| | | |
|---|---|---|
| SIR PHILIP MODELOVE, an old beau | | Mr. Knap |
| PERIWINKLE, a kind of a silly virtuoso[2] | All Guardians to Mrs. Lovely | Mr. Spiller |
| TRADELOVE, a change-broker[3] | | Mr. Bullock, Sr. |
| OBADIAH PRIM, a Quaker [hosier] | | Mr. Pack |
| COLONEL FAINWELL, in love with Mrs. Lovely | | Mr. Christopher Bullock |
| FREEMAN, his friend, a merchant | | Mr. Ogden |
| SIMON PURE, a Quaking preacher | | Mr. Griffin |
| MR. SACKBUT, a tavern-keeper | | Mr. Hall |

## Women.

| | |
|---|---|
| MRS.[4] LOVELY, a fortune of thirty thousand pound | Mrs. Bullock |
| MRS. PRIM, wife to Prim the hosier | Mrs. Kent |
| BETTY, servant to Mrs. Lovely | Mrs. Robins |

FOOTMEN, DRAWERS, ETC.

*(Scene: London)*

# PROLOGUE.

## By a Gentleman
## Spoken by Mrs. Thurmond.

Tonight we come upon a bold design,
To try to please without one borrowed line.
Our plot is new, and regularly clear,
And not one single title from Molière.
O'er buried poets we with caution tread,
And parish sextons leave to rob the dead.
For you, bright British fair, in hopes to charm ye,
We bring tonight a lover from the army.
You know the soldiers have the strangest arts,
Such a proportion of prevailing parts,
You'd think that they rid post to women's hearts.
I wonder whence they draw their bold pretense;
We do not choose them sure for our defense:
That plea is both impolitic and wrong,
And only suits such dames as want a tongue.
Is it their eloquence and fine address?
The softness of their language?—Nothing less.
Is it their courage, that they bravely dare
To storm the sex at once?—Egad, 'tis there.
They act by us as in the rough campaign,
Unmindful of repulses, charge again;
They mine and countermine, resolved to win,
And, if a breach is made—they will come in.
You'll think, by what we have of soldiers said,
Our female wit was in the service bred;
But she is to the hardy toil a stranger,

She loves the cloth, indeed, but hates the danger;
Yet to this circle of the brave and gay,
She bid me for her good intentions say,
She hopes you'll not reduce her to half pay.
As for our play, 'tis English humor all;
Then will you let our manufacture fall?
Would you the honor of our nation raise,
Keep English credit up, and English plays.

# ACT I.

## Scene i. A tavern.

*(Colonel Fainwell and Freeman over a bottle.)*

FREEMAN. Come, Colonel, his Majesty's health! You are as melancholy as if you were in love; I wish some of the beauties at Bath ha'n't snapped[5] your heart.

COLONEL. Why faith, Freeman, there is something in't; I have seen a lady at Bath who has kindled such a flame in me that all the waters there can't quench.[6]

FREEMAN. Women, like some poisonous animals, carry their antidote about 'em. Is she not to be had, Colonel?

COLONEL. That's a difficult question to answer; however, I resolve to try. Perhaps you may be able to serve me; you merchants know one another.—The lady told me herself she was under the charge of four persons.

FREEMAN. Odso! 'Tis Mrs. Ann Lovely.

COLONEL. The same; do you know her?

FREEMAN. Know her! Ay—faith, Colonel, your condition is more desperate than you imagine; why she is the talk and pity of the whole town; and it is the opinion of the learned that she must die a maid.

COLONEL. Say you so? That's somewhat odd in this charitable city. She's a woman, I hope.

FREEMAN. For aught I know; but it had been as well for her had nature made her any other part of the creation. The man which keeps this house served her father; he is a very honest fellow and may be of use to you; we'll send for him to take a glass with us. He'll give you the whole history, and 'tis worth your hearing.

COLONEL. But may one trust him?

FREEMAN. With your life; I have obligations enough upon him to make him do anything; I serve him with wine. (*Knocks.*)

COLONEL. Nay, I know him pretty well myself; I once used to frequent a club that was kept here.

*(Enter Drawer.)*

DRAWER. Gentlemen, d'you call?
FREEMAN. Ay, send up your master.
DRAWER. Yes, sir. (*Exit.*)
COLONEL. Do you know any of this lady's guardians, Freeman?
FREEMAN. Yes, I know two of them very well.
COLONEL. What are they?

*(Enter Sackbut.)*

FREEMAN. Here comes one will give you an account of them all—Mr. Sackbut, we sent for you to take a glass with us. 'Tis a maxim among the friends of the bottle that as long as the master is in company one may be sure of good wine.
SACKBUT. Sir, you shall be sure to have as good wine as you send in.—Colonel, your most humble servant; you are welcome to town.
COLONEL. I thank you, Mr. Sackbut.
SACKBUT. I am as glad to see you as I should a hundred ton of French claret custom free. My service to you, sir. (*Drinks.*) You don't look so merry as you used to do; are you not well, Colonel?
FREEMAN. He has got a woman in his head, landlord; can you help him?
SACKBUT. If 'tis in my power, I shan't scruple to serve my friend.
COLONEL. 'Tis one perquisite of your calling.
SACKBUT. Ay, at t'other end of the town, where you officers use, women are good forcers of trade; a well-customed house, a handsome barkeeper, with clean, obliging drawers, soon get the master an estate; but our citizens seldom do anything but cheat within the walls.⁷—But as to the lady, Colonel, point you at particulars, or have you a good champagne stomach? Are you in full pay, or reduced, Colonel?
COLONEL. Reduced, reduced, landlord.
FREEMAN. To the miserable condition of a lover!
SACKBUT. Pish! That's preferable to half pay; a woman's resolu-

tion may break before the peace; push her home, Colonel; there's no parleying with that sex.

COLONEL. Were the lady her own mistress I have some reasons to believe I should soon command in chief.

FREEMAN. You know Mrs. Lovely, Mr. Sackbut?

SACKBUT. Know her! Ay, poor Nancy; I have carried her to school many a frosty morning. Alas, if she's the woman, I pity you, Colonel. Her father, my old master, was the most whimsical, out-of-the-way tempered man I ever heard of, as you will guess by his last will and testament. This was his only child. I have heard him wish her dead a thousand times.

COLONEL. Why so?

SACKBUT. He hated posterity, you must know, and wished the world were to expire with himself. He used to swear if she had been a boy, he would have qualified him for the opera.[8]

FREEMAN. 'Tis a very unnatural resolution in a father.

SACKBUT. He died worth thirty thousand pounds, which he left to this daughter provided she married with the consent of her guardians. But that she might be sure never to do so, he left her in the care of four men, as opposite to each other as light and darkness. Each has his quarterly rule, and three months in a year she is obliged to be subject to each of their humors, and they are pretty different, I assure you. She is just come from Bath.

COLONEL. 'Twas there I saw her.

SACKBUT. Ay, sir, the last quarter was her beau guardian's. She appears in all public places during his reign.

COLONEL. She visited a lady who boarded in the same house with me. I liked her person and found an opportunity to tell her so. She replied she had no objection to mine, but if I could not reconcile contradictions, I must not think of her, for that she was condemned to the caprice of four persons who never yet agreed in any one thing, and she was obliged to please them all.

SACKBUT. 'Tis most true, sir; I'll give you a short description of the men and leave you to judge of the poor lady's condition. One is a kind of a virtuoso, a silly, half-witted fellow but positive and surly; fond of nothing but what is antique and foreign, and wears his clothes of the fashion of the last century; dotes upon travelers and believes Sir John Mandeville more than the Bible.[9]

COLONEL. That must be a rare old fellow!

SACKBUT. Another is a changebroker, a fellow that will outlie the devil for the advantage of stock and cheat his father that got him in a bargain. He is a great stickler for trade and hates everything that wears a sword.

FREEMAN. He is a great admirer of the Dutch management and swears they understand trade better than any nation under the sun.

SACKBUT. The third is an old beau that has May in his fancy and dress but December in his face and his heels; he admires nothing but new fashions, and those must be French; loves operas, balls, masquerades, and is always the most tawdry[10] of the whole company on a birthday.

COLONEL. These are pretty opposite to one another, truly. And the fourth, what is he, landlord?

SACKBUT. A very rigid Quaker, whose quarter begun this day. I saw Mrs. Lovely go in not above two hours ago. Sir Philip set her down. What think you now, Colonel; is not the poor lady to be pitied?

COLONEL. Ay, and rescued too, landlord.

FREEMAN. In my opinion, that's impossible.

COLONEL. There is nothing impossible to a lover. What would not a man attempt for a fine woman and thirty thousand pounds? Besides, my honor is at stake; I promised to deliver her, and she bade me win her and take her.

SACKBUT. That's fair, faith.

FREEMAN. If it depended upon knight-errantry, I should not doubt your setting free the damsel; but to have avarice, impertinence, hypocrisy, and pride at once to deal with requires more cunning than generally attends a man of honor.

COLONEL. My fancy tells me I shall come off with glory; I resolve to try, however.—Do you know all the guardians, Mr. Sackbut?

SACKBUT. Very well, sir; they all use my house.

COLONEL. And will you assist me, if occasion be?

SACKBUT. In everything I can, Colonel.

FREEMAN. I'll answer for him; and whatever I can serve you in, you may depend on. I know Mr. Periwinkle and Mr. Tradelove; the latter has a very great opinion of my interest abroad. I happened to have a letter from a correspondent two hours before the news arrived of the French king's death; I communicated it to him; upon which he bought up all the stock he could, and what with that and some wagers he laid he told me he had got to the tune of five hundred pounds; so that I am much in his good graces.

COLONEL. I don't know but you may be of service to me, Freeman.

FREEMAN. If I can, command me, Colonel.

COLONEL. Is it not possible to find a suit of clothes ready-made at some of these sale shops, fit to rig out a beau, think you, Mr. Sackbut?

SACKBUT. O hang 'em, no, Colonel; they keep nothing ready-made that a gentleman would be seen in. But I can fit you with a suit of clothes, if you'd make a figure—velvet and gold brocade— they were pawned to me by a French count who had been stripped at play and wanted money to carry him home; he promised to send for them, but I have heard nothing from him.

FREEMAN. He has not fed upon frogs long enough yet to recover his loss, ha, ha.

COLONEL. Ha, ha; well, those clothes will do, Mr. Sackbut, though we must have three or four fellows in tawdry liveries. Those can be procured, I hope.

FREEMAN. Egad, I have a brother come from the West Indies that can match you; [11] and, for expedition sake, you shall have his servants. There's a black, a tawny-moor, and a Frenchman. They don't speak one word of English, so can make no mistake.

COLONEL. Excellent. Egad, I shall look like an Indian prince. First I'll attack my beau guardian. Where lives he?

SACKBUT. Faith, somewhere about St. James's; though to say in what street, I cannot. But any chairman[12] will tell you where Sir Philip Modelove lives.

FREEMAN. O, you'll find him in the Park at eleven every day; at least I never passed through at that hour without seeing him there. But what do you intend?

COLONEL. To address him in his own way and find what he designs to do with the lady.

FREEMAN. And what then?

COLONEL. Nay, that I can't tell, but I shall take my measures accordingly.

SACKBUT. Well, 'tis a mad undertaking, in my mind; but here's to your success, Colonel. (*Drinks.*)

COLONEL. 'Tis something out of the way, I confess; but fortune may chance to smile, and I succeed. Come, landlord, let me see those clothes.—Freeman, I shall expect you'll leave word with Mr. Sackbut where one may find you upon occasion; and send my equipage of India[13] immediately, do you hear?

FREEMAN. Immediately. (*Exit.*)

COLONEL. Bold was the man who ventured first to sea,
But the first vent'ring lovers bolder were.
The path of love's a dark and dangerous way,
Without a landmark, or one friendly star,
And he that runs the risk, deserves the fair. (*Exit with Sackbut.*)


Scene ii. Prim's house.

*(Enter Mrs. Lovely and her maid Betty.)*

BETTY. Bless me, madam! Why do you fret and tease yourself so? This is giving them the advantage with a witness.

MRS. LOVELY. Must I be condemned all my life to the preposterous humors of other people; and pointed at by every boy in town?—O! I could tear my flesh, and curse the hour I was born. Is it not monstrously ridiculous that they should desire to impose their Quaking dress[14] upon me at these years? When I was a child, no matter what they made me wear; but now—

BETTY. I would resolve against it, madam; I'd see 'em hanged before I'd put on the pinched cap again.

MRS. LOVELY. Then I must never expect one moment's ease; she has rung such a peal in my ears already that I shan't have the right use of them this month—what can I do?

BETTY. What can you not do, if you will but give your mind to it? Marry, madam.

MRS. LOVELY. What! And have my fortune go to build churches and hospitals?

BETTY. Why, let it go. If the Colonel loves you, as he pretends, he'll marry you without a fortune, madam; and I assure you, a Colonel's lady is no despicable thing; a Colonel's post will maintain you like a gentlewoman, madam.

MRS. LOVELY. So you would advise me to give up my own fortune and throw myself upon the Colonel's.

BETTY. I would advise you to make yourself easy, madam.

MRS. LOVELY. That's not the way, I am sure. No, no, girl, there are certain ingredients to be mingled with matrimony, without which I may as well change for the worse as for the better. When the woman has fortune enough to make the man happy, if he has either honor or good manners, he'll make her easy. Love makes but a slovenly figure in that house where poverty keeps the door.

BETTY. And so you resolve to die a maid, do you, madam?

MRS. LOVELY. Or have it in my power to make the man I love master of my fortune.

BETTY. Then you don't like the Colonel so well as I thought you did, madam, or you would not take such a resolution.

MRS. LOVELY. It is because I do like him, Betty, that I take such a resolution.

BETTY. Why, do you expect, madam, the Colonel can work miracles? Is it possible for him to marry you with the consent of all your guardians?

MRS. LOVELY. Or he must not marry me at all, and so I told him; and he did not seem displeased with the news. He promised to set me free, and I, on that condition, promised to make him master of that freedom.

BETTY. Well, I have read of enchanted castles, ladies delivered from the chains of magic, giants killed, and monsters overcome; so that I shall be the less surprised if the Colonel should conjure you out of the power of your guardians. If he does, I am sure he deserves your fortune.

MRS. LOVELY. And shall have it, girl, if it were ten times as much; for I'll ingenuously confess to thee that I do like the Colonel above all men I ever saw. There's something so *jantée* in a soldier, a kind of a *je ne sais quoi*[15] air that makes 'em more agreeable than the rest of mankind. They command regard, as who should say, "We are your defenders; we preserve your beauties from the insults of rude unpolished foes and ought to be preferred before those lazy indolent mortals who, by dropping into their fathers' estate, set up their coaches and think to rattle themselves into our affections."

BETTY. Nay, madam, I confess that the army has engrossed all the prettiest fellows. A laced coat and feather have irresistible charms.

MRS. LOVELY. But the Colonel has all the beauties of the mind, as well as person.—O all ye powers that favor happy lovers, grant

he may be mine! Thou god of love, if thou be'st aught but
name, assist my Fainwell.

Point all thy darts to aid my love's design,
And make his plots as prevalent as thine.

# ACT II.

## Scene i. The Park.

*(Enter Colonel, finely dressed, three footmen after him.)*

COLONEL. So, now if I can but meet this beau—egad, methinks I
cut a smart figure and have as much of the tawdry air as any
Italian count or French marquis of 'em all. Sure I shall know
this knight again—ha, yonder he sits, making love to a mask,[16]
i'faith. I'll walk up the Mall and come down by him. *(Exit.)*

*(Scene draws[17] and discovers Sir Philip upon a bench with a
woman, masked.)*

SIR PHILIP. Well, but, my dear, are you really constant to your
keeper?
WOMAN. Yes, really sir —Hey day, who comes yonder? He cuts a
mighty figure.
SIR PHILIP. Ha! A stranger by his equipage keeping so close at his
heels—he has the appearance of a man of quality—positively
French by his dancing air.
WOMAN. He crosses as if he meant to sit down here.
SIR PHILIP. He has a mind to make love to thee, child.

*(Enter Colonel and seats himself upon the bench by Sir Philip.)*

WOMAN. It will be to no purpose if he does.
SIR PHILIP. Are you resolved to be cruel then?
COLONEL. You must be very cruel, indeed, if you can deny any-
thing to so fine a gentleman, madam. *(Takes out his watch.)*
WOMAN. I never mind the outside of a man.
COLONEL. And I'm afraid thou art no judge of the inside.
SIR PHILIP. I am positively of your mind, sir, for creatures of her
function seldom penetrate beyond the pocket.

WOMAN *(aside)*. Creatures of your composition have, indeed, generally more in their pockets than in their heads.

SIR PHILIP *(pulling out his watch)*. Pray, what says your watch? Mine is down.

COLONEL. I want thirty-six minutes of twelve, sir. *(Puts up his watch and takes out his snuffbox.)*

SIR PHILIP. May I presume, sir?

COLONEL. Sir, you honor me. *(Presenting the box.)*

SIR PHILIP *(aside)*. He speaks good English, though he must be a foreigner.—*(Aloud.)* This snuff is extremely good and the box prodigious fine; the work is French, I presume, sir.

COLONEL. I bought it in Paris, sir; I do think the workmanship pretty neat.

SIR PHILIP. Neat, 'tis exquisitely fine, sir. Pray, sir, if I may take the liberty of inquiring, what country is so happy to claim the birth of the finest gentleman in the universe? France, I presume.

COLONEL. Then you don't think me an Englishman?

SIR PHILIP. No, upon my soul don't I.

COLONEL. I am sorry for't.

SIR PHILIP. Impossible you should wish to be an Englishman! Pardon me, sir, this island could not produce a person of such alertness.

COLONEL. As this mirror shows you, sir—*(Puts up a pocket glass to Sir Philip's face.)*

WOMAN *(aside)*. Coxcombs; I'm sick to hear 'em praise one another. One seldom gets anything by such animals, not even a dinner, unless one can dine upon soup and celery. *(Exit.)*

SIR PHILIP. O Ged, sir!—*(Calls after her.)* Will you leave us, madam? Ha, ha.

COLONEL. She fears 'twill be only losing time to stay here, ha, ha.—I know not how to distinguish you, sir, but your mien and address speak you *Right Honorable*.

SIR PHILIP. Thus great souls judge of others by themselves. I am only adorned with knighthood, that's all, I assure you, sir; my name is Sir Philip Modelove.

COLONEL. Of French extraction?

SIR PHILIP. My father was French.

COLONEL. One may plainly perceive it. There is a certain gaiety peculiar to my nation (for I will own myself a Frenchman), which distinguishes us everywhere. A person of your figure would be a vast addition to a coronet.

Sir Philip. I must own I had the offer of a barony about five years ago, but I abhorred the fatigue which must have attended it. I could never yet bring myself to join with either party.

Colonel. You are perfectly in the right, Sir Philip; a fine person should not embark himself in the slovenly concern of politics. Dress and pleasure are objects proper for the soul of a fine gentleman.

Sir Philip. And love—

Colonel. O, that's included under the article of pleasure.

Sir Philip. *Parbleu, il est un homme d'esprit;*[18] I must embrace you. *(Rises and embraces.)* Your sentiments are so agreeable to mine that we appear to have but one soul, for our ideas and conceptions are the same.

Colonel *(aside).* I should be sorry for that.— *(Aloud.)* You do me too much honor, Sir Philip.

Sir Philip. Your vivacity and *jantée* mien assured me at first sight there was nothing of this foggy island in your composition. May I crave your name, sir?

Colonel. My name is La Fainwell, sir, at your service.

Sir Philip. The La Fainwells are French, I know; though the name is become very numerous in Great Britain of late years. I was sure you was French the moment I laid my eyes upon you; I could not come into the supposition of your being an Englishman. This island produces few such ornaments.

Colonel. Pardon me, Sir Philip, this island has two things superior to all nations under the sun.

Sir Philip. Ay? What are they?

Colonel. The ladies and the laws.

Sir Philip. The laws indeed do claim a preference of other nations, but by my soul, there are fine women everywhere. I must own I have felt their power in all countries.

Colonel. There are some finished beauties, I confess, in France, Italy, Germany, nay, even in Holland; *mais sont bien rares.* But *les belles Anglaises!*[19] O, Sir Philip, where find we such women? Such symmetry of shape! Such elegancy of dress! Such regularity of features! Such sweetness of temper! Such commanding eyes! And such bewitching smiles?

Sir Philip. *Ah! Parbleu vous êtes attrapé.*

COLONEL. *Non, je vous assure, chevalier,* but I declare there is no amusement so agreeable to my *goût* as the conversation of a fine woman. I could never be prevailed upon to enter into what the vulgar calls the pleasure of the bottle.

SIR PHILIP. My own taste, *positivement.* A ball or a masquerade is certainly preferable to all the productions of the vineyard.

COLONEL. Infinitely. I hope the people of quality in England will support that branch of pleasure which was imported with their peace and since naturalized by the ingenious Mr. Heidegger.[20]

SIR PHILIP. The ladies assure me it will become part of the constitution, upon which I subscribed an hundred guineas; it will be of great service to the public, at least to the company of surgeons and the City in general.[21]

COLONEL. Ha, ha, it may help to ennoble the blood of the City. Are you married, Sir Philip?

SIR PHILIP. No, nor do I believe I ever shall enter into that honorable state; I have an absolute tender[22] for the whole sex.

COLONEL *(aside).* That's more than they have for you, I dare swear.

SIR PHILIP. And I have the honor to be very well with the ladies, I can assure you, sir, and I won't affront a million of fine women to make one happy.

COLONEL. Nay, marriage is really reducing a man's taste to a kind of half pleasure, but then it carries the blessing of peace along with it; one goes to sleep without fear and wakes without pain.

SIR PHILIP. There is something of that in't; a wife is a very good dish for an English stomach—but gross feeding for nicer palates, ha, ha, ha.

COLONEL. I find I was very much mistaken. I imagined you had been married to that young lady which I saw in the chariot with you this morning in Gracechurch Street.

SIR PHILIP. Who, Nancy Lovely? I am a piece of a guardian to that lady, you must know; her father, I thank him, joined me with three of the most preposterous old fellows, that, upon my soul, I'm in pain for the poor girl. She must certainly lead apes,[23] as the saying is. Ha, ha.

COLONEL. That's pity, Sir Philip; if the lady would give me leave, I would endeavor to avert that curse.

SIR PHILIP. As to the lady, she'd gladly be rid of us at any rate, I believe; but here's the mischief: he who marries Miss Lovely must have the consent of us all four, or not a penny of her portion. For my part, I shall never approve of any but a man of figure, and the rest are not only averse to cleanliness but have each a peculiar taste to gratify. For my part, I declare, I would prefer you to all men I ever saw.

COLONEL. And I her to all women.

SIR PHILIP. I assure you, Mr. Fainwell, I am for marrying her, for I hate the trouble of a guardian, especially among such wretches, but resolve never to agree to the choice of any one of them, and I fancy they'll be even with me, for they never came into any proposal of mine yet.

COLONEL. I wish I had your leave to try them, Sir Philip.

SIR PHILIP. With all my soul, sir, I can refuse a person of your appearance nothing.

COLONEL. Sir, I am infinitely obliged to you.

SIR PHILIP. But do you really like matrimony?

COLONEL. I believe I could with that lady, sir.

SIR PHILIP. The only point in which we differ; but you are master of so many qualifications that I can excuse one fault, for I must think it a fault in a fine gentleman, and that you are such, I'll give it under my hand.

COLONEL. I wish you'd give me your consent to marry Mrs. Lovely under your hand, Sir Philip.

SIR PHILIP. I'll do't, if you'll step into St. James's Coffee House, where we may have pen and ink; though I can't foresee what advantage my consent will be to you without you could find a way to get the rest of the guardians, but I'll introduce you; however, she is now at a Quaker's where I carried her this morning, when you saw us in Gracechurch Street. I assure you she has an odd *ragoût* of guardians, as you will find when you hear the characters, which I'll endeavor to give you as we go along.—*(Calls the Servants.)* Hey, Pierre, Jacques, Renno, where are you all, scoundrels? Order the chariot to St. James's Coffee House.

COLONEL. *Le noir, le brun, le blanc—morbleu, où sont ces coquins-là? Allons, monsieur le chevalier.*[24]

SIR PHILIP. Ah, *pardonnez-moi, monsieur. (Offers to follow him.)*

COLONEL *(refusing to go first)*. Not one step, upon my soul, Sir Philip.

SIR PHILIP. The best bred man in Europe, positively. *(Exeunt.)*

Scene ii. Obadiah Prim's house

*(Enter Mrs. Lovely, followed by Mrs. Prim.)*

MRS. PRIM. Then thou wilt not obey me; and thou dost really think those fallals becometh thee?

MRS. LOVELY. I do, indeed.

MRS. PRIM. Now will I be judged by all sober people, if I don't look more like a modest woman than thou dost, Ann.

MRS. LOVELY. More like a hypocrite, you mean, Mrs. Prim.

MRS. PRIM. Ah, Ann, Ann, that wicked Philip Modelove will undo thee. Satan so fills thy heart with pride during the three months of his guardianship that thou becomest a stumbling block to the upright.

MRS. LOVELY. Pray, who are they? Are the pinched cap and formal hood the emblems of sanctity? Does your virtue consist in your dress, Mrs. Prim?

MRS. PRIM. It doth not consist in cut hair, spotted face, and bare necks. O, the wickedness of this generation! The primitive women knew not the abomination of hooped petticoats.

MRS. LOVELY. No, nor the abomination of cant neither. Don't tell me, Mrs. Prim, don't. I know you have as much pride, vanity, self-conceit, and ambition among you, couched under that formal habit and sanctified countenance, as the proudest of us all; but the world begins to see your prudery.

MRS. PRIM. Prudery! What, do they invent new words as well as new fashions? Ah, poor fantastic age, I pity thee—poor deluded Ann. Which dost thou think most resemblest the saint and which the sinner, thy dress or mine? Thy naked bosom allureth the eye of the bystander, encourageth the frailty of human nature, and corrupteth the soul with evil longings.

MRS. LOVELY. And pray, who corrupted your son Tobias with evil longings? Your maid Tabitha wore a handkerchief, and yet he made the saint a sinner.

MRS. PRIM. Well, well, spit thy malice. I confess Satan did buffet my son Tobias and my servant Tabitha; the evil spirit was at that time too strong, and they both became subject to its workings, not from any outward provocation but from an inward call. He was not tainted with the rottenness of the fashions, nor did his eyes take in the drunkenness of beauty.

MRS. LOVELY. No! That's plainly to be seen.

MRS. PRIM. Tabitha is one of the faithful; he fell not with a stranger.

MRS. LOVELY. So! Then you hold wenching no crime, provided it be within the pale of your own tribe? You are an excellent casuist, truly.

*(Enter Obadiah Prim.)*

PRIM. Not stripped of thy vanity yet, Ann! —Why dost not thou make her put it off, Sarah?

MRS. PRIM. She will not do it.

PRIM. Verily, thy naked breasts troubleth my outward man; I pray thee hide 'em, Ann. Put on a handkerchief, Ann Lovely.

MRS. LOVELY. I hate handkerchiefs when 'tis not cold weather, Mr Prim.

MRS. PRIM. I have seen thee wear a handkerchief—nay, and a mask to boot—in the middle of July.

MRS. LOVELY. Ay, to keep the sun from scorching me.

PRIM. If thou couldst not bear the sunbeams, how dost thou think man should bear thy beams? Those breasts inflame desire; let them be hid, I say.

MRS. LOVELY. Let me be quiet, I say. Must I be tormented thus forever? Sure no woman's condition ever equaled mine; foppery, folly, avarice, and hypocrisy are by turns my constant companions, and I must vary shapes as often as a player. I cannot think my father meant this tyranny. No, you usurp an authority which he never intended you should take.

PRIM. Hark thee, dost thou call good counsel tyranny? Do I or my wife tyrannize when we desire thee in all love to put off thy tempting attire and veil thy provokers to sin?

MRS. LOVELY. Deliver me, good Heaven! Or I shall go distracted. *(Walks about.)*

MRS. PRIM. So! Now thy pinners are tossed and thy breasts pulled up. Verily, they were seen enough before; fie upon the filthy tailor who made them stays.[25]

MRS. LOVELY. I wish I were in my grave! Kill me rather than treat me thus.

PRIM. Kill thee! Ha, ha, thou think'st thou are acting some lewd play, sure—kill thee! Art thou prepared for death, Ann Lovely?

No, no, thou wouldst rather have a husband, Ann. Thou wantest a gilt coach with six lazy fellows behind to flaunt it in the Ring[26] of vanity, among the princes and rulers of the land who pamper themselves with the fatness thereof. But I will take care that none shall squander away thy father's estate; thou shalt marry none such, Ann.

Mrs. Lovely. Would you marry me to one of your own canting sex?[27]

Prim. Yea, verily, none else shall ever get my consent, I do assure thee, Ann.

Mrs. Lovely. And I do assure thee, Obadiah, that I will as soon turn papist and die in a convent.

Mrs. Prim. O wickedness!

Mrs. Lovely. O stupidity!

Prim. O blindness of heart!

Mrs. Lovely (aside to Prim). Thou blinder of the world, don't provoke me, lest I betray your sanctity and leave your wife to judge of your purity. What were the emotions of your spirit when you squeezed Mary by the hand last night in the pantry, when she told you you bussed so filthily? Ah, you had no aversion to naked bosoms when you begged her to show you a little, little, little bit of her delicious bubby. Don't you remember those words, Mr. Prim?

Mrs. Prim. What does she say, Obadiah?

Prim. She talketh unintelligibly, Sarah— (Aside.) Which way did she hear this? This should not have reached the ears of the wicked ones; verily, it troubleth me.

(Enter Servant.)

Servant. Philip Modelove, whom they call Sir Philip, is below and such another with him; shall I send them up?

Prim. Yea.

(Exit Servant.)
(Enter Sir Philip and Colonel.)

Sir Philip. How dost thou do, Friend Prim?—(To Mrs. Prim.) Odso, my she-friend here too! What, you are documenting Miss

Nancy, reading her a lecture upon the pinched coif, I warrant ye.

MRS. PRIM. I am sure thou never readest her any lecture that was good—*(Aside.)* My flesh riseth so at these wicked ones that prudence adviseth me to withdraw from their sight. *(Exit.)*

COLONEL *(aside).* O, that I could find means to speak to her. How charming she appears. I wish I could get this letter into her hand.

SIR PHILIP. Well, Miss Cocky, I hope thou has got the better of them.

MRS. LOVELY. The difficulties of my life are not to be surmounted, Sir Philip.—*(Aside.)* I hate the impertinence of him as much as the stupidity of the other.

PRIM. Verily, Philip, thou wilt spoil this maiden.

SIR PHILIP. I find we still differ in opinion; but that we may none of us spoil her, prithee, Prim, let us consent to marry her. I have sent for our brother guardians to meet me here about that very thing.—Madam, will you give me leave to recommend a husband to you? Here's a gentleman which, in my mind, you can have no objection to. *(Presents the Colonel to her; she looks another way.)*

MRS. LOVELY *(aside).* Heaven deliver me from the formal and the fantastic fool.

COLONEL. A fine woman, a fine horse, and fine equipage are the finest things in the universe. And if I am so happy to possess you, madam, I shall become the envy of mankind, as much as you outshine your whole sex. *(As he takes her hand to kiss it, he endeavors to put the letter into it; she lets it drop; Prim takes it up.)*

MRS. LOVELY. I have no ambition to appear conspicuously ridiculous, sir. *(Turning from him.)*

COLONEL. So falls the hopes of Fainwell.

MRS. LOVELY *(aside).* Ha! Fainwell! 'Tis he. What have I done? Prim has the letter, and all will be discovered.

PRIM. Friend, I know not thy name, so cannot call thee by it; but thou seest thy letter is unwelcome to the maiden; she will not read it.

MRS. LOVELY. Nor shall you. *(Snatches the letter.)* I'll tear it in a thousand pieces and scatter it, as I will the hopes of all those that any of you shall recommend to me. *(Tears the letter.)*

SIR PHILIP. Ha! Right woman, faith.

COLONEL *(aside).* Excellent woman.

PRIM. Friend, thy garb savoreth too much of the vanity of the age for my approbation; nothing that resembleth Philip Modelove shall I love, mark that. Therefore, Friend Philip, bring no more of thy own apes under my roof.

SIR PHILIP. I am so entirely a stranger to the monsters of thy breed that I shall bring none of them, I am sure.

COLONEL *(aside)*. I am likely to have a pretty task by that time I have gone through them all; but she's a city worth taking, and egad, I'll carry on the siege. If I can but blow up the outworks, I fancy I am pretty secure of the town.

*(Enter Servant.)*

SERVANT *(to Sir Philip)*. Toby Periwinkle and Thomas Tradelove demandeth to see thee.

SIR PHILIP. Bid them come up.

*(Exit Servant.)*

MRS. LOVELY *(aside)*. Deliver me from such an inundation of noise and nonsense. O, Fainwell! Whatever thy contrivance is, prosper it Heaven—but O, I fear thou never canst redeem me. *(Exit.)*

SIR PHILIP. *Sic transit gloria mundi!*

*(Enter Mr. Periwinkle and Tradelove.)*

*(Aside to the Colonel.)* These are my brother guardians, Mr. Fainwell; prithee observe the creatures.

TRADELOVE. Well, Sir Philip, I obey your summons.

PERIWINKLE. Pray, what have you to offer for the good of Mrs. Lovely, Sir Philip?

SIR PHILIP. First, I desire to know what you intend to do with that lady. Must she be sent to the Indies for a venture, or live to be an old maid and then entered amongst your curiosities and shown for a monster, Mr. Periwinkle?

COLONEL *(aside)*. Humph, curiosities. That must be the virtuoso.

PERIWINKLE. Why, what would you do with her?

SIR PHILIP. I would recommend this gentleman to her for a husband, sir, a person whom I have picked out from the whole race of mankind.

PRIM. I would advise thee to shuffle him again with the rest of mankind, for I like him not.

COLONEL. Pray, sir, without offense to your formality, what may be your objections?

PRIM. Thy person; thy manners; thy dress; thy acquaintance—thy everything, friend.

SIR PHILIP. You are most particularly obliging, friend, ha, ha.

TRADELOVE. What business do you follow, pray sir?

COLONEL (aside). Humph, by that question he must be the broker.—(Aloud.) Business, sir! The business of a gentleman.

TRADELOVE. That is as much as to say you dress fine, feed high, lie with every woman you like, and pay your surgeon's bills[28] better than your tailor's or your butcher's.

COLONEL. The court is much obliged to you, sir, for your character of a gentleman.

TRADELOVE. The court, sir! What would the court do without us citizens?

SIR PHILIP. Without your wives and daughters, you mean, Mr. Tradelove?

PERIWINKLE. Have you ever traveled, sir?

COLONEL (aside). That question must not be answered now.—(Aloud.) In books I have, sir.

PERIWINKLE. In books? That's fine traveling indeed! —Sir Philip, when you present a person I like, he shall have my consent to marry Mrs. Lovely; till when, your servant. (Exit.)

COLONEL (aside). I'll make you like me before I have done with you, or I am mistaken.

TRADELOVE. And when you can convince me that a beau is more useful to my country than a merchant, you shall have mine; till then, you must excuse me. (Exit.)

COLONEL (aside). So much for trade. I'll fit you too.

SIR PHILIP. In my opinion, this is very inhumane treatment as to the lady, Mr. Prim.

PRIM. Thy opinion and mine happens to differ as much as our occupations, friend. Business requireth my presence and folly thine, and so I must bid thee farewell. (Exit.)

SIR PHILIP. Here's breeding for you, Mr. Fainwell. Gad take me, I'd give half my estate to see these rascals bit.[29]

COLONEL (aside). I hope to bite you all, if my plots hit.

# ACT III.

## Scene i. The tavern.

*(Sackbut and the Colonel in an Egyptian dress.)*

SACKBUT. A lucky beginning, Colonel. You have got the old beau's consent.

COLONEL. Ay, he's a reasonable creature; but the other three will require some pains. Shall I pass upon him, think you? Egad, in my mind I look as antique as if I had been preserved in the ark.

SACKBUT. Pass upon him! Ay, ay, as roundly as white wine dashed with sack does for mountain and sherry,[30] if you have but assurance enough.

COLONEL. I have no apprehension from that quarter; assurance is the cockade of a soldier.

SACKBUT. Ay, but the assurance of a soldier differs much from that of a traveler. Can you lie with a good grace?

COLONEL. As heartily, when my mistress is the prize, as I would meet the foe when my country called and king commanded; so don't you fear that part; if he don't know me again, I'm safe. I hope he'll come.

SACKBUT. I wish all my debts would come as sure. I told him you had been a great traveler, had many valuable curiosities, and was a person of a most singular taste; he seemed transported and begged me to keep you till he came.

COLONEL. Ay, ay, he need not fear my running away. Let's have a bottle of sack, landlord; our ancestors drank sack.

SACKBUT. You shall have it.

COLONEL. And whereabouts is the trap door you mentioned?

SACKBUT. There's the conveyance, sir. *(Exit.)*

COLONEL. Now, if I should cheat all these roguish guardians and carry off my mistress in triumph, it would be what the French call a *grand coup d'éclat*[31]—odso! Here comes Periwinkle. Ah,

214 • <small>Susanna Centlivre</small>

deuce take this beard; pray Jupiter it does not give me the slip and spoil all.

*(Enter Sackbut with wine, and Periwinkle following.)*

SACKBUT. Sir, this gentleman, hearing you have been a great traveler and a person of fine speculation, begs leave to take a glass with you; he is a man of a curious taste himself.

COLONEL. The gentleman has it in his face and garb. —Sir, you are welcome.

PERIWINKLE. Sir, I honor a traveler and men of your inquiring disposition. The oddness of your habit pleases me extremely; 'tis very antique, and for that I like it.

COLONEL. It is very antique, sir. This habit once belonged to the famous Claudius Ptolemeus, who lived in the year a hundred and thirty-five.[32]

SACKBUT *(aside)*. If he keeps up to the sample, he shall lie with the devil for a bean-stack, and win it every straw.[33]

PERIWINKLE. A hundred and thirty-five! Why, that's prodigious now—well, certainly 'tis the finest thing in the world to be a traveler.

COLONEL. For my part, I value none of the modern fashions of a fig leaf.

PERIWINKLE. No more do I, sir; I had rather be the jest of a fool than his favorite. I am laughed at here for my singularity. This coat, you must know, sir, was formerly worn by that ingenious and very learned person John Tradescant.[34]

COLONEL. John Tradescant! Let me embrace you, sir. John Tradescant was my uncle, by mother side; and I thank you for the honor you do his memory; he was a very curious man indeed.

PERIWINKLE. Your uncle, sir! Nay then, 'tis no wonder that your taste is so refined; why, you have it in your blood—my humble service to you, sir. To the immortal memory of John Tradescant, your never-to-be-forgotten uncle. *(Drinks.)*

COLONEL. Give me a glass, landlord.

PERIWINKLE. I find you are primitive even in your wine. Canary was the drink of our wise forefathers; 'tis balsamic and saves the charge of apothecaries' cordials. —O, that I had lived in your uncle's days! Or rather, that he were now alive. O, how proud he'd be of such a nephew.

SACKBUT *(aside)*. O pox! That would have spoiled the jest.

PERIWINKLE. A person of your curiosity must have collected many rarities.

COLONEL. I have some, sir, which are not yet come ashore, as an Egyptian's idol.

PERIWINKLE. Pray, what might that be?

COLONEL. It is, sir, a kind of an ape which they formerly worshipped in that country. I took it from the breast of a female mummy.

PERIWINKLE. Ha, ha, our women retain part of their idolatry to this day, for many an ape lies on a lady's breast, ha, ha.

SACKBUT *(aside)*. A smart old thief.

COLONEL. Two tusks of an hippopotamus, two pair of Chinese nutcrackers, and one Egyptian mummy.

PERIWINKLE. Pray, sir, have you never a crocodile?

COLONEL. Humph, the boatswain brought one with design to show it, but touching at Rotterdam and hearing it was no rarity in England, he sold it to a Dutch poet.[35]

SACKBUT. The devil's in that nation; it rivals us in everything.

PERIWINKLE. I should have been very glad to have seen a living crocodile.

COLONEL. My genius led me to things more worthy my regard. Sir, I have seen the utmost limits of this globular world; I have seen the sun rise and set; know in what degree of heat he is at noon to the breadth of a hair, and what quantity of combustibles he burns in a day, how much of it turns to ashes and how much to cinders.[36]

PERIWINKLE. To cinders? You amaze me, sir; I never heard that the sun consumed anything. Descartes tells us—

COLONEL. Descartes, with the rest of his brethren, both ancient and modern, knew nothing of the matter. I tell you, sir, that nature admits an annual decay, though imperceptible to vulgar eyes. Sometimes his rays destroy below, sometimes above. You have heard of blazing comets, I suppose?

PERIWINKLE. Yes, yes, I remember to have seen one; and our astrologers tell us of another which shall happen very quickly.

COLONEL. Those comets are little islands bordering on the sun, which at certain times are set on fire by that luminous body's moving over them perpendicular, which will one day occasion a general conflagration.

SACKBUT *(aside)*. One need not scruple the Colonel's capacity, faith.

PERIWINKLE. This is marvelous strange. These cinders are what I never read of in any of our learned dissertations.

COLONEL *(aside)*. I don't know how the devil you should.

SACKBUT *(aside)*. He has it at his fingers' ends; one would swear he had learned to lie at school, he does it so cleverly.

PERIWINKLE. Well, you travelers see strange things. Pray, sir, have you any of those cinders?

COLONEL. I have, among my other curiosities.

PERIWINKLE. O, what have I lost for want of traveling! Pray, what have you else?

COLONEL. Several things worth your attention. I have a muff made of the feathers of those geese that saved the Roman Capitol.[37]

PERIWINKLE. Is't possible?

SACKBUT *(aside)*. Yes, if you are such a goose to believe him.

COLONEL. I have an Indian leaf which, open, will cover an acre of land, yet folds up into so little a compass you may put it into your snuffbox.

SACKBUT *(aside)*. Humph! That's a thunderer.

PERIWINKLE. Amazing!

COLONEL. Ah, mine is but a little one; I have seen some of them that would cover one of the Caribbean Islands.

PERIWINKLE. Well, if I don't travel before I die, I shan't rest in my grave. Pray, what do the Indians with them?

COLONEL. Sir, they use them in their wars for tents, the old women for riding hoods, the young for fans and umbrellas.

SACKBUT *(aside)*. He has a fruitful invention.

PERIWINKLE. I admire[38] our East India Company imports none of them; they would certainly find their account in them.

COLONEL *(aside)*. Right, if they could find the leaves.—*(Aloud.)* Look ye, sir, do you see this little vial?

PERIWINKLE. Pray you, what is it?

COLONEL. This is called *poluflosboio*.[39]

PERIWINKLE. *Poluflosboio!* It has a rumbling sound.

COLONEL. Right, sir, it proceeds from a rumbling nature. This water was part of those waves which bore Cleopatra's vessel when she sailed to meet Anthony.

PERIWINKLE. Well, of all that ever traveled, none had a taste like you.

COLONEL. But here's the wonder of the world: this, sir, is called *zona,* or *moros musphonon;*[40] the virtues of this is inestimable.

PERIWINKLE. *Moros musphonon!* What in the name of wisdom can that be? To me it seems a plain belt.

COLONEL. This girdle has carried me all the world over.

PERIWINKLE. You have carried it, you mean.

COLONEL. I mean as I say, sir. Whenever I am girded with this, I am invisible; and, by turning this little screw, can be in the court of the Great Mogul, the Grand Signior, and King George[41] in as little time as your cook can poach an egg.

PERIWINKLE. You must pardon me, sir; I can't believe it.

COLONEL. If my landlord pleases, he shall try the experiment immediately.

SACKBUT. I thank you kindly, sir, but I have no inclination to ride post to the devil.

COLONEL. No, no, you shan't stir a foot; I'll only make you invisible.

SACKBUT. But if you could not make me visible again—

PERIWINKLE. Come, try it upon me, sir; I am not afraid of the devil, nor all his tricks. 'Sbud, I'll stand 'em all.

COLONEL. There, sir, put it on.—Come, landlord, you and I must face the east.

*(They turn about).*

—Is it on, sir?

PERIWINKLE. 'Tis on.

*(They turn about again.)*

SACKBUT. Heaven protect me! Where is he?

PERIWINKLE. Why here just where I was.

SACKBUT. Where, where, in the name of virtue? Ah, poor Mr. Periwinkle! —Egad, look to't, you had best, sir, and let him be seen again, or I shall have you burnt for a wizard.

COLONEL. Have patience, good landlord.

PERIWINKLE. But really, don't you see me now?

Sackbut. No more than I see my grandmother that died forty years ago.

Periwinkle. Are you sure you don't lie? Methinks I stand just where I did, and see you as plain as I did before.

Sackbut. Ah, I wish I could see you once again!

Colonel. Take off the girdle, sir.

*(He takes it off.)*

Sackbut. Ah, sir, I am glad to see you with all my heart. *(Embraces him.)*

Periwinkle. This is very odd; certainly there must be some trick in't—pray, sir, will you do me the favor to put it on yourself?

Colonel. With all my heart.

Periwinkle. But first I'll secure the door.

Colonel. You know how to turn the screw, Mr. Sackbut.

Sackbut. Yes, yes—come, Mr. Periwinkle, we must turn full east.

*(They turn; the Colonel sinks down a trap door.)*

Colonel. 'Tis done; now turn.

*(They turn.)*

Periwinkle. Ha! Mercy upon me! My flesh creeps upon my bones—this must be a conjurer, Mr. Sackbut.

Sackbut. He is the devil, I think.

Periwinkle. O! Mr. Sackbut, why do you name the devil, when perhaps he may be at your elbow.

Sackbut. At my elbow! Marry, Heaven forbid.

Colonel *(below)*. Are you satisfied, sir?

Periwinkle. Yes, sir, yes—how hollow his voice sounds!

Sackbut. Yours seemed just the same. Faith, I wish this girdle were mine; I'd sell wine no more. Hark ye, Mr. Periwinkle *(Takes him aside till the Colonel rises again.)*, if he would sell this girdle, you might travel with great expedition.

Colonel. But it is not to be parted with for money.

Periwinkle. I am sorry for't, sir, because I think it the greatest curiosity I ever heard of.

Colonel. By the advice of a learned physiognomist in Grand

Cairo, who consulted the lines in my face, I returned to England, where, he told me, I should find a rarity in the keeping of four men, which I was born to possess for the benefit of mankind, and the first of the four that gave me his consent, I should present him with this girdle. Till I have found this jewel, I shall not part with the girdle.

PERIWINKLE. What can that rarity be? Did he not name it to you?

COLONEL. Yes, sir; he called it a chaste, beautiful, unaffected woman.

PERIWINKLE. Pish! Women are no rarities. I never had any great taste that way. I married, indeed, to please a father, and I got a girl to please my wife; but she and the child (thank Heaven) died together. Women are the very gewgaws of the creation, playthings for boys which, when they write man, they ought to throw aside.

SACKBUT *(aside)*. A fine lecture to be read to a circle of ladies.

PERIWINKLE. What woman is there, dressed in all the pride and foppery of the times, can boast of such a foretop as the cockatoo?

COLONEL *(aside)*. I must humor him.— *(Aloud.)* Such a skin as the lizard?

PERIWINKLE. Such a shining breast as the hummingbird?

COLONEL. Such a shape as the antelope?

PERIWINKLE. Or, in all the artful mixture of their various dresses, have they half the beauty of one box of butterflies?

COLONEL. No, that must be allowed—for my part, if it were not for the benefit of mankind, I'd have nothing to do with them, for they are as indifferent to me as a sparrow or a flesh fly.

PERIWINKLE. Pray, sir, what benefit is the world to reap from this lady?

COLONEL. Why, sir, she is to bear me a son, who shall restore the art of embalming and the old Roman manner of burying their dead; and, for the benefit of posterity, he is to discover the longitude, so long sought for in vain.[42]

PERIWINKLE. Od! These are very valuable things, Mr. Sackbut.

SACKBUT *(aside)*. He hits it off admirably and t'other swallows it like sack and sugar.— *(To Periwinkle.)* Certainly this lady must be your ward, Mr. Periwinkle, by her being under the care of four persons.

PERIWINKLE. By the description it should.— *(Aside.)* Egad, if I could get that girdle, I'd ride with the sun, and make the tour of the whole world in four and twenty hours.—*(To the Colonel.)* And are you to give that girdle to the first of the four guardians that shall give his consent to marry that lady, say you, sir?

COLONEL. I am so ordered, when I can find him.

PERIWINKLE. I fancy I know the very woman. Her name is Ann Lovely.

COLONEL. Excellent! He said, indeed, that the first letter of her name was *L.*

PERIWINKLE. Did he really? Well, that's prodigiously amazing, that a person in Grand Cairo should know anything of my ward.

COLONEL. Your ward?

PERIWINKLE. To be plain with you, sir, I am one of those four guardians.

COLONEL. Are you indeed, sir? I am transported to find the man who is to possess this *moros musphonon* is a person of so curious a taste. Here is a writing drawn up by that famous Egyptian, which, if you will please to sign, you must turn your face full north, and the girdle is yours.

PERIWINKLE. If I live till this boy is born, I'll be embalmed and sent to the Royal Society when I die.

COLONEL. That you shall most certainly.


*(Enter Drawer.)*


DRAWER. Here's Mr. Staytape, the tailor, inquires for you, Colonel.

SACKBUT. Who do you speak to, you son of a whore?

PERIWINKLE *(aside)*. Ha! Colonel!

COLONEL *(aside)*. Confound the blundering dog.

DRAWER. Why, to Colonel—

SACKBUT. Get you out, you rascal. *(Kicks him out, and exit after him.)*

DRAWER *(leaving)*. What the devil is the matter?

COLONEL *(aside)*. This dog has ruined all my scheme, I see by Periwinkle's looks.

PERIWINKLE. How finely I should have been choused.[43] Colonel, you'll pardon me that I did not give you your title before; it was pure ignorance, faith it was. Pray—hem, hem—pray, Colonel, what post had this learned Egyptian in your regiment?

COLONEL *(aside)*. A pox of your sneer.— *(Aloud.)* I don't understand you, sir.

PERIWINKLE. No? That's strange. I understand you, Colonel—an Egyptian of Grand Cairo! Ha, ha, ha. I am sorry such a well-invented tale should do you no more service. We old fellows can see as far into a millstone as him that picks it.[44] I am not to be tricked out of my trust; mark that.

COLONEL *(aside)*. The devil! I must carry it off; I wish I were fairly out.— *(Aloud.)* Look ye, sir, you may make what jest you please, but the stars will be obeyed, sir, and, depend upon it, I shall have the lady, and you none of the girdle.— *(Aside.)* Now for Freeman's part of the plot. *(Exit unseen by Periwinkle.)*

PERIWINKLE. The stars! Ha, ha, no star has favored you, it seems. The girdle! Ha, ha, ha, none of your legerdemain tricks can pass upon me. Why, what a pack of trumpery has this rogue picked up. His *pagod, poluflosboios,* his *zonas, moros musphonons,* and the devil knows what. But I'll take care—ha, gone? Ay, 'twas time to sneak off.— *(Calls out.)* Soho, the house!

*(Enter Sackbut.)*

Where is this trickster? Send for a constable; I'll have this rascal before the Lord Mayor. I'll Grand Cairo him, with a pox to him. I believe you had a hand in putting this imposture upon me, Sackbut.

SACKBUT. Who, I, Mr. Periwinkle? I scorn it; I perceived he was a cheat and left the room on purpose to send for a constable to apprehend him, and endeavored to stop him when he went out; but the rogue made but one step from the stairs to the door, called a coach, leapt into it, and drove away like the devil, as Mr. Freeman can witness, who is at the bar and desires to speak with you. He is this minute come to town.

PERIWINKLE. Send him in.

*(Exit Sackbut.)*

What a scheme this rogue had laid. How I should have been laughed at, had it succeeded.

*(Enter Freeman, booted and spurred.)*

Mr. Freeman, your dress commands your welcome to town; what will you drink? I had like to have been imposed upon here by the veriest rascal.

FREEMAN. I am sorry to hear it. The dog flew for't; he had not 'scaped me, if I had been aware of him; Sackbut struck at him but missed his blow, or he had done his business for him.

PERIWINKLE. I believe you never heard of such a contrivance, Mr. Freeman, as this fellow had found out.

FREEMAN. Mr. Sackbut has told me the whole story, Mr. Periwinkle. But now I have something to tell you of much more importance to yourself. I happened to lie one night at Coventry, and knowing your uncle, Sir Toby Periwinkle, I paid him a visit and to my great surprise found him dying.

PERIWINKLE. Dying!

FREEMAN. Dying, in all appearance; the servants weeping, the room in darkness. The apothecary, shaking his head, told me the doctors had given him over, and then there is small hopes, you know.

PERIWINKLE. I hope he has made his will. He always told me he would make me his heir.

FREEMAN. I have heard you say as much and therefore resolved to give you notice. I should think it would not be amiss if you went down tomorrow morning.

PERIWINKLE. It is a long journey, and the roads very bad.

FREEMAN. But he has a great estate, and the land very good. Think upon that.

PERIWINKLE. Why, that's true, as you say. I'll think upon it. In the meantime, I give you many thanks for your civility, Mr. Freeman, and should be glad of your company to dine with me.

FREEMAN. I am obliged to be at Jonathan's Coffee House at two, and it is now half an hour after one; if I dispatch my business, I'll wait on you. I know your hour.

PERIWINKLE. You shall be very welcome, Mr. Freeman; and so, your humble servant. *(Exit.)*

*(Re-enter Colonel and Sackbut.)*

FREEMAN. Ha, ha, ha, I have done your business, Colonel; he has swallowed the bait.

COLONEL. I overheard all, though I am a little in the dark. I am to personate a highwayman, I suppose. That's a project I am not fond of; for though I may fright him out of his consent, he may fright me out of my life when he discovers me, as he certainly must in the end.

FREEMAN. No, no, I have a plot for you without danger; but first we must manage Tradelove. Has the tailor brought your clothes?

SACKBUT. Yes, pox take the thief.

COLONEL. Pox take your drawer for a jolt-headed rogue.

FREEMAN. Well, well, no matter; I warrant we have him yet, but now you must put on the Dutch merchant.

COLONEL. The deuce of this trading plot. I wish he had been an old soldier, that I might have attacked him in my own way: heard him fight over all the battles of the Civil War—but for trade, by Jupiter, I shall never do it.

SACKBUT. Never fear, Colonel, Mr. Freeman will instruct you.

FREEMAN. You'll see what others do; the coffee house will instruct you.

COLONEL. I must venture, however. But I have a farther plot in my head upon Tradelove which you must assist me in, Freeman; you are in credit with him I heard you say.

FREEMAN. I am, and will scruple nothing to serve you, Colonel.

COLONEL. Come along then. Now for the Dutchman—honest Ptolemy, by your leave,

Now must bob wig and business come in play,
And a fair thirty thousand pounder leads the way.

# ACT IV.

Scene i. Jonathan's Coffee House in Exchange Alley. Crowd of people with rolls of paper and parchment in their hands; a bar and Coffee Boys waiting.

*(Enter Tradelove and Stockjobbers, with rolls of paper and parchment.)*

FIRST STOCKJOBBER. South Sea at seven-eighths![45] Who buys?

SECOND STOCKJOBBER. South Sea bonds due at Michaelmas, 1718! Class Lottery tickets!

THIRD STOCKJOBBER. East India bonds?

FOURTH STOCKJOBBER. What, all sellers and no buyers? Gentlemen, I'll buy a thousand pound for Tuesday next at three-fourths.

[A] COFFEE BOY. Fresh coffee, gentlemen, fresh coffee?

TRADELOVE. Hark ye, Gabriel, you'll pay the difference of that Stock we transacted for t'other day.

GABRIEL. Ay, Mr. Tradelove, here's a note for the money, upon Sword Blade Company. *(Gives him a note.)*

[A] COFFEE BOY. Bohea tea, gentlemen?

*(Enter a Man.)*

MAN. Is Mr. Smuggle here?

FIRST COFFEE BOY. Mr. Smuggle's not here, sir; you'll find him at the books.[46]

SECOND STOCKJOBBER. Ho! Here comes two sparks from the other end of the town; what news bring they?

*(Enter two Gentlemen.)*

TRADELOVE. I would fain bite that spark in the brown coat; he comes very often into the Alley but never employs a broker.

*(Enter Colonel and Freeman.)*

SECOND STOCKJOBBER. Who does anything in the Civil List Lottery?[47] Or Caco?—Zounds, where are all the Jews this afternoon?—*(To Third Stockjobber.)* Are you a bull or a bear today, Abraham?

THIRD STOCKJOBBER. A bull, faith—but I have a good put for next week.

TRADELOVE. Mr. Freeman, your servant. *(Points to the Colonel.)* Who is that gentleman?

FREEMAN. A Dutch merchant, just come to England; but hark ye, Mr. Tradelove—I have a piece of news will get you as much as the French king's death did, if you are expeditious.[48]

TRADELOVE. Say you so, sir! Pray, what is it?

FREEMAN *(showing him a letter)*. Read there; I received it just now from one that belongs to the emperor's minister.

TRADELOVE *(reads [aloud])*. "Sir, As I have many obligations to you, I cannot miss any opportunity to show my gratitude; this moment, my lord has received a private express that the Spaniards have raised their siege from before Cagliari;[49] if this prove any advantage to you, it will answer both the ends and wishes of, sir, your most obliged humble servant, Henricus Dusseldorp." "Postscript. In two or three hours the news will be public." *(Aside to Freeman.)* May one depend upon this, Mr. Freeman?

FREEMAN. You may—I never knew this person send me a false piece of news in my life.

TRADELOVE *(aside to Freeman)*. Sir, I am much obliged to you; egad, 'tis rare news.—*(Aloud.)* Who sells South Sea for next week?

STOCKJOBBERS *(all together)*. I sell; I, I, I, I, I sell.

FIRST STOCKJOBBER. I'll sell five thousand pounds for next week at five-eighths.

SECOND STOCKJOBBER. I'll sell ten thousand at five-eighths for the same time.

TRADELOVE. Nay, nay, hold, hold, not all together, gentlemen; I'll be no bull; I'll buy no more than I can take. Will you sell ten thousand pound at a half, for any day next week except Saturday?

FIRST STOCKJOBBER. I'll sell it you, Mr. Tradelove.

*(Freeman whispers to one of the Gentlemen.)*

Gentleman *(aloud)*. The Spaniards raised the siege of Cagliari! I don't believe one word of it.

Second Gentleman. Raised the siege! As much as you have raised the Monument.[50]

Freeman. 'Tis raised, I assure you, sir.

Second Gentleman. What will you lay on't?

Freeman. What you please.

First Gentleman. Why, I have a brother upon the spot in the emperor's service; I am certain if there were any such thing, I should have had a letter.

A Stockjobber. How's this? The siege of Cagliari raised—I wish it may be true; 'twill make business stir and stocks rise.

First Stockjobber. Tradelove's a cunning fat bear; if this news proves true, I shall repent I sold him the ten thousand pounds.—*(To Freeman.)* Pray, sir, what assurance have you that the siege is raised?

Freeman. There is come an express to the emperor's minister.

Second Stockjobber. I'll know that presently. *(Exit.)*

First Gentleman. Let it come where it will; I'll hold you fifty pounds 'tis false.

Freeman. 'Tis done.

Second Gentleman. I'll lay you a brace of hundreds upon the same.

Freeman. I'll take you.

Fourth Stockjobber. Egad, I'll hold twenty pieces 'tis not raised, sir.

Freeman. Done with you, too.

Tradelove. I'll lay any man a brace of thousands the siege is raised.

Freeman *(aside to Tradelove)*. The Dutch merchant is your man to take in.

Tradelove. Does not he know the news?

Freeman *(to Tradelove)*. Not a syllable; if he did, he would bet a hundred thousand pound as soon as one penny. He's plaguy rich and a mighty man at wagers.

Tradelove. Say you so—egad, I'll bite him if possible.—*(To the Colonel.)* Are you from Holland, sir?

Colonel. Ya, mynheer.

TRADELOVE. Had you the news before you came away?

COLONEL. Wat believe you, mynheer?

TRADELOVE. What do I believe? Why, I believe that the Spaniards have actually raised the siege of Cagliari.

COLONEL. What duyvel's niews is dat? 'Tis niet waer, mynheer— 'tis no true, sir.

TRADELOVE. 'Tis so true, mynheer, that I'll lay you two thousand pounds upon it.—*(Aside to Freeman.)* You are sure the letter may be depended upon, Mr. Freeman?

FREEMAN *(aside to Tradelove)*. Do you think I would venture my money if I were not sure of the truth of it?

COLONEL. Two duysend pond, mynheer; 'tis gedaen. Dis gentleman sal hold de gelt.[51] *(Gives Freeman money.)*

FREEMAN. With all my heart. This binds the wager.

TRADELOVE. You have certainly lost, mynheer; the siege is raised indeed.

COLONEL. Ik gelove't niet, Mynheer Freeman; ik sal ye dubbled houden, if you please.

FREEMAN. I am let into the secret, therefore won't win your money.

TRADELOVE *(aside)*. Ha, ha, ha! I have snapped[52] the Dutchman, faith, ha, ha. This is no ill day's work— *(Aloud.)* Pray, may I crave your name, mynheer?

COLONEL. Myn naem, mynheer? Myn naem is Jan van Timtamtirelereletta Heer van Fainwell.

TRADELOVE. Zounds, 'tis a damned long name; I shall never remember it. Mynheer van Tim—Tim—Tim—what the devil is it?

FREEMAN. O, never heed; I know the gentleman and will pass my word for twice the sum.

TRADELOVE. That's enough.

COLONEL *(aside)*. You'll hear of me sooner than you'll wish, old gentleman, I fancy. —You'll come to Sackbut's, Freeman?

FREEMAN *(aside to the Colonel)*. Immediately.


*(Exit Colonel.)*


FIRST MAN. Humphry Hump here?

SECOND (COFFEE) BOY. Mr. Humphry Hump is not here; you'll find him upon the Dutch Walk.

228 • Susanna Centlivre

TRADELOVE. Mr. Freeman, I give you many thanks for your kindness.

FREEMAN *(aside)*. I fear you'll repent when you know all.

TRADELOVE. Will you dine with me?

FREEMAN. I am engaged at Sackbut's; adieu. *(Exit.)*

TRADELOVE. Sir, your humble servant. —Now I'll see what I can do upon Change with my news. *(Exit.)*


Scene ii. The tavern.

*(Enter Freeman and Colonel.)*

FREEMAN. Ha, ha, ha! The old fellow swallowed that bait as greedily as a gudgeon.

COLONEL. I have him, faith, ha, ha, ha. His two thousand pound's secure; if he would keep his money, he must part with the lady, ha, ha.—What came of your two friends? They performed their part very well; you should have brought 'em to take a glass with us.

FREEMAN. No matter; we'll drink a bottle together another time. I did not care to bring them hither; there's no necessity to trust them with the main secret, you know, Colonel.

COLONEL. Nay, that's right, Freeman.

*(Enter Sackbut.)*

SACKBUT. Joy, joy, Colonel; the luckiest accident in the world!

COLONEL. What say'st thou?

SACKBUT. This letter does your business.

COLONEL *(reads [aloud])*. "To Obadiah Prim, hosier, near the building called the Monument, in London."

FREEMAN. A letter to Prim.— *(To Sackbut.)* How came you by it?

SACKBUT. Looking over the letters our postwoman brought, as I always do to see what letters are directed to my house (for she can't read, you must know), I spied this, to Prim, so paid for't among the rest; I have given the old jade a pint of wine on purpose to delay time, till you see if the letter will be of any service; then I'll seal it up again and tell her I took it by mistake. I have read it and fancy you'll like the project—read, read, Colonel.

COLONEL *(reads [aloud])*. "Friend Prim, There is arrived from

Pennsylvania one Simon Pure, a leader of the faithful, who hath sojourned with us eleven days and hath been of great comfort to the Brethren. He intendeth for the quarterly meeting in London; I have recommended him to thy house; I pray thee entreat[53] him kindly, and let thy wife cherish him, for he's of weakly constitution. He will depart from us the third day; which is all from thy friend in the faith, Aminadab Holdfast." Ha, ha, excellent. I understand you, landlord, I am to personate this Simon Pure, am I not?

SACKBUT. Don't you like the hint?

COLONEL. Admirably well.

FREEMAN. 'Tis the best contrivance in the world, if the right Simon gets not there before you.

COLONEL. No, no, the Quakers never ride post;[54] he can't be here before tomorrow at soonest. Do you send and buy me a Quaker's dress, Mr. Sackbut; and suppose, Freeman, you should wait at the Bristol coach, that if you see any such person, you might contrive to give me notice.

FREEMAN. I will. —The country dress and boots, are they ready?

SACKBUT. Yes, yes, everything, sir.

FREEMAN. Bring 'em in then.

*(Exit Sackbut.)*

Thou must dispatch Periwinkle first. Remember, his uncle, Sir Toby Periwinkle, is an old bachelor of seventy-five, that he has seven hundred a year, most in abbey land; that he was once in love with your mother, and shrewdly suspected by some to be your father—that you have been thirty years his steward and ten years his gentleman; remember to improve these hints.

COLONEL. Never fear; let me alone for that. But what's the steward's name?

FREEMAN. His name is Pillage.

COLONEL. Enough.

*(Enter Sackbut with clothes.)*

Now for the country put.[55] *(Dresses.)*

FREEMAN. Egad, landlord, thou deservest to have the first night's lodging with the lady for thy fidelity. —What say you, Colonel, shall we settle a club here, you'll make one?[56]

COLONEL. Make one? I'll bring a set of honest officers that will spend their money as freely to their king's health, as they would their blood in his service.

SACKBUT. I thank you, Colonel. *(Bell rings.)* —Here, here. *(Exit Sackbut.)*

COLONEL. So now for my boots. *(Puts on boots.)* Shall I find you here, Freeman, when I come back?

FREEMAN. Yes, or I'll leave word with Sackbut where he may send for me. Have you the writings? The will and everything?

COLONEL. All, all.

*(Enter Sackbut.)*

SACKBUT. Zounds, Mr. Freeman, yonder is Tradelove in the damned'st passion in the world. He swears you are in the house; he says you told him you was to dine here.

FREEMAN. I did so, ha, ha, ha. He has found himself bit already.

COLONEL. The devil! He must not see me in this dress.

SACKBUT *(to Freeman).* I told him I expected you here but you were not come yet.

FREEMAN. Very well. Make you haste out, Colonel, and let me alone to deal with him. —Where is he?

SACKBUT. In the King's Head.

COLONEL. You remember what I told you?

FREEMAN. Ay, ay, very well, landlord; let him know I am come in—and now, Mr. Pillage, success attend you.

*(Exit Sackbut.)*

COLONEL. Mr. Proteus, rather.—

From changing shape and imitating Jove,[57]
I draw the happy omens of my love.
I'm not the first young brother of the blade
Who made his fortune in a masquerade. *(Exit Colonel.)*

*(Enter Tradelove.)*

FREEMAN. Zounds, Mr. Tradelove, we're bit, it seems.

TRADELOVE. Bit, do you call it, Mr. Freeman; I am ruined—pox on your news.

FREEMAN. Pox on the rascal that sent it me.

TRADELOVE. Sent it you! Why, Gabriel Skinflint has been at the minister's and spoke with him, and he has assured him 'tis every syllable false; he received no such express.

FREEMAN. I know it. I this minute parted with my friend, who protested he never sent me any such letter. Some roguish stock-jobber has done it on purpose to make me lose my money; that's certain; I wish I knew who he was; I'd make him repent it. I have lost three hundred pounds by it.

TRADELOVE. What signifies your three hundred pounds to what I have lost? There's two thousand pounds to that Dutchman with the cursed long name, besides the stock I bought; the devil! I could tear my flesh. I must never show my face upon Change more, for, by my soul, I can't pay it.

FREEMAN. I am heartily sorry for't. What can I serve you in? Shall I speak to the Dutch merchant and try to get you time for the payment?

TRADELOVE. Time! Adsheart, I shall never be able to look up again.

FREEMAN. I am very much concerned that I was the occasion and wish I could be an instrument of retrieving your misfortune; for my own, I value it not. —Adso! A thought comes into my head that, well improved, may be of service.

TRADELOVE. Ah, there's no thought can be of any service to me without paying the money, or running away.

FREEMAN. How do you know? What do you think of my proposing Mrs. Lovely to him? He is a single man, and I heard him say he had a mind to marry an English woman; nay, more than that, he said somebody told him you had a pretty ward. He wished you had betted her instead of your money.

TRADELOVE. Ay, but he'd be hanged before he'd take her instead of the money; the Dutch are too covetous for that; besides, he did not know that there were three more of us, I suppose.

FREEMAN. So much the better; you may venture to give him your consent, if he'll forgive you the wager. It is not your business to tell him that your consent will signify nothing.

TRADELOVE. That's right, as you say; but will he do it, think you?

Freeman. I can't tell that; but I'll try what I can do with him. He has promised me to meet me here an hour hence; I'll feel his pulse and let you know. If I find it feasible, I'll send for you; if not, you are at liberty to take what measures you please.

Tradelove. You must extol her beauty, double her portion, and tell him I have the entire disposal of her, and that she can't marry without my consent—and that I am a covetous rogue and will never part with her without a valuable consideration.

Freeman. Ay, ay, let me alone for a lie at a pinch.

Tradelove. Egad, if you can bring this to bear, Mr. Freeman, I'll make you whole again; I'll pay the three hundred pounds you lost, with all my soul.

Freeman. Well, I'll use my best endeavors. Where will you be?

Tradelove. At home; pray Heaven you prosper. If I were but the sole trustee now, I should not fear it. Who the devil would be a guardian,

> If when cash runs low, our coffers t'enlarge,
> We can't, like other stocks, transfer our charge? *(Exit.)*

Freeman. Ha, ha, ha, he has it! *(Exit.)*

Scene iii. Periwinkle's house.

*(Enter Periwinkle on one side and Footman on t'other.)*

Footman. A gentleman from Coventry inquires for you, sir.

Periwinkle. From my uncle, I warrant you; bring him up.

*(Exit Footman.)*

This will save me the trouble as well as the expenses of a journey.

*(Enter Colonel.)*

Colonel. Is your name Periwinkle, sir?

Periwinkle. It is, sir.

Colonel. I am sorry for the message I bring. My old master, whom I served these forty years, claims the sorrow due from a faithful servant to an indulgent master. *(Weeps.)*

PERIWINKLE. By this I understand, sir, my uncle, Sir Toby Periwinkle, is dead.

COLONEL. He is, sir, and he has left you heir to seven hundred a
year, in as good abbey land as ever paid Peter pence to Rome.[58]
I wish you long to enjoy it, but my tears will flow when I think
of my benefactor. *(Weeps.)* Ah, he was a good man; he has not
left many of his fellows. The poor laments him sorely.

PERIWINKLE. I pray, sir, what office bore you?

COLONEL. I was his steward, sir.

PERIWINKLE. I have heard him mention you with much respect;
your name is—

COLONEL. Pillage, sir.

PERIWINKLE. Ay, Pillage. I do remember he called you Pillage. Pray,
Mr. Pillage, when did my uncle die?

COLONEL. Monday last at four in the morning. About two, he
signed this will and gave it into my hands and strictly charged
me to leave Coventry the moment he expired, and deliver it to
you with what speed I could. I have obeyed him, sir, and there
is the will. *(Gives it to Periwinkle.)*

PERIWINKLE. 'Tis very well; I'll lodge it in the Commons.[59]

COLONEL. There are two things which he forgot to insert but
charged me to tell you that he desired you'd perform them as
readily as if you had found them written in the will, which is to
remove his corpse and bury him by his father in St. Paul-
Covent-Garden, and to give all his servants mourning.

PERIWINKLE *(aside)*. That will be a considerable charge; a pox of
all modern fashions.— *(Aloud.)* Well, it shall be done, Mr. Pillage; I will agree with one of death's fashion mongers, called an
undertaker, to go down and bring up the body.

COLONEL. I hope, sir, I shall have the honor to serve you in the
same station I did your worthy uncle; I have not many years to
stay behind him and would gladly spend them in the family
where I was brought up. *(Weeps.)* He was a kind and tender
master to me.

PERIWINKLE. Pray, don't grieve, Mr. Pillage; you shall hold your
place and everything else which you held under my uncle. You
make me weep to see you so concerned. *(Weeps.)* He lived to a
good old age, and we are all mortal.

COLONEL. We are so, sir, and therefore I must beg you to sign this
lease. You'll find Sir Toby has ta'en particular notice of it in his

will. I could not get it time enough from the lawyer, or he had signed it before he died. *(Gives him a paper.)*

PERIWINKLE. A lease for what?

COLONEL. I rented a hundred a year of Sir Toby upon lease, which lease expires at Lady Day next, and I desire to renew it for twenty years; that's all, sir.

PERIWINKLE. Let me see. *(Looks over the lease.)*

COLONEL *(aside)*. Matters go swimmingly, if nothing intervene.

PERIWINKLE. Very well, let's see what he says in his will about it. *(Lays the lease upon the table and looks on the will.)*

COLONEL *(aside)*. He's very wary, yet I fancy I shall be too cunning for him.

PERIWINKLE. Ho, here it is—"the farm lying . . . now in possession of Samuel Pillage . . . suffer him to renew his lease . . . at the same rent. . . ." Very well, Mr. Pillage, I see my uncle does mention it, and I'll perform his will. Give me the lease. *(Colonel gives it him; he looks upon it and lays it upon the table.)* Pray you, step to the door and call for a pen and ink, Mr. Pillage.

COLONEL. I have pen and ink in my pocket, sir. *(Pulls out an ink-horn.)* I never go without that.

PERIWINKLE. I think it belongs to your profession. *(He looks upon the pen while the Colonel changes the lease and lays down the contract.)* I doubt this is but a sorry pen, though it may serve to write my name. *(Writes.)*

COLONEL *(aside)*. Little does he think what he signs.

PERIWINKLE. There is your lease, Mr. Pillage. *(Gives him the paper.)* Now I must desire you to make what haste you can down to Coventry and take care of everything, and I'll send down the undertaker for the body; do you attend it up, and whatever charge you are at, I will repay you.

COLONEL *(aside)*. You have paid me already, I thank you, sir.

PERIWINKLE. Will you dine with me?

COLONEL. I would rather not; there are some of my neighbors which I met as I came alone, who leaves the town this afternoon, they told me, and I should be glad of their company down.

PERIWINKLE. Well, well, I won't detain you.

COLONEL *(aside)*. I don't care how soon I am out.

PERIWINKLE. I will give orders about mourning.

COLONEL *(aside)*. You will have cause to mourn, when you know your estate imaginary only.

> You'll find your hopes and cares alike are vain.
> In spite of all the caution you have ta'en.
> Fortune rewards the faithful lover's pain. *(Exit.)*

PERIWINKLE. Seven hundred a year! I wish he had died seventeen years ago. What a valuable collection of rarities might I have had by this time! I might have traveled over all the known parts of the globe and made my own closet rival the Vatican at Rome. —Odso, I have a good mind to begin my travels now. Let me see—I am but sixty. My father, grandfather, and great-grandfather reached ninety odd. I have almost forty years good. —Let me consider—what will seven hundred a year amount to—in—ay, in thirty years; I'll say but thirty. Thirty times seven is seven times thirty—that is—just twenty-one thousand pound. 'Tis a great deal of money. I may very well reserve sixteen hundred of it for a collection of such rarities as will make my name famous to posterity. I would not die like other mortals, forgotten in a year or two, as my uncle will be—no.

> With nature's curious works I'll raise my fame,
> That men, till doomsday, may repeat my name. *(Exit.)*

### Scene iv. A tavern.

*(Freeman and Tradelove over a bottle.)*

TRADELOVE. Come, Mr. Freeman, here's Mynheer Jan van Tim—Tam—Tam—I shall never think of that Dutchman's name.

FREEMAN. Mynheer Jan van Timtamtirelireletta Heer van Fainwell.

TRADELOVE. Ay, Heer van Fainwell; I never heard such a confounded name in my life. Here's his health, I say. *(Drinks.)*

FREEMAN. With all my heart.

TRADELOVE. Faith, I never expected to have found so generous a thing in a Dutchman.

FREEMAN. O, he has nothing of the Hollander in his temper, except an antipathy to monarchy. As soon as I told him your circumstances, he replied he would not be the ruin of any man for the world and immediately made this proposal himself: "Let him take what time he will for the payment," said he, "or if he'll give me his ward, I'll forgive him the debt."

TRADELOVE. Well, Mr. Freeman, I can but thank you. Egad, you have made a man of me again; and if ever I lay a wager more, may I rot in a jail.

FREEMAN. I assure you, Mr. Tradelove, I was very much concerned because I was the occasion—though very innocently, I protest.

TRADELOVE. I dare swear you was, Mr. Freeman.

*(Enter a Fiddler [with his Wife].)*

FIDDLER. Please to have a lesson of music or a song, gentlemen?

FREEMAN. A song, ay, with all our hearts; have you ever a merry one?

FIDDLER. Yes, sir, my wife and I can give you a merry dialogue.

*(Here is the song.)*

TRADELOVE. 'Tis very pretty, faith.

FREEMAN. There's something for you to drink, friend; go, lose no time.

FIDDLER. I thank you, sir. *(Exeunt.)*

*(Enter Drawer and Colonel, dressed for the Dutch Merchant.)*

COLONEL. Ha. Mynheer Tradelove, ik ben sorry voor your troubles—maer ik sal you easy maeken; ik wil de gelt niet hebben.[60]

TRADELOVE. I shall forever acknowledge the obligation, sir.

FREEMAN. But you understand upon what condition, Mr. Tradelove: Mrs. Lovely.

COLONEL. Ya, de juffrow sal al te regt setten, mynheer.

TRADELOVE. With all my heart, mynheer, you shall have my consent to marry her freely.

FREEMAN. Well then, as I am a party concerned between you, Mynheer Jan van Timtamtirelireletta Heer van Fainwell shall give you a discharge of your wager under his own hand, and you shall give him your consent to marry Mrs. Lovely under yours. That is the way to avoid all manner of disputes hereafter.

COLONEL. Ya, waeragtig.

TRADELOVE. Ay, ay, so it is, Mr. Freeman; I'll give it under mine this minute. *(Sits down to write.)*

COLONEL. And so sal ik. *(Sits down to write.)*

FREEMAN. Soho, the house!

*(Enter Drawer.)*

Bid your master come up.— *(Aside.)* I'll see there be witness enough to the bargain.

*(Exit Drawer.)*
*(Enter Sackbut.)*

SACKBUT. Do you call, gentlemen?

FREEMAN. Ay, Mr. Sackbut, we shall want your hand here.

TRADELOVE. There, mynheer, there's my consent as amply as you can desire; but you must insert your own name, for I know not how to spell it; I have left a blank for it. *(Gives the Colonel a paper.)*

COLONEL. Ya, ik sal dat well doen.

FREEMAN. Now, Mr. Sackbut, you and I will witness it. *(They write.)*

COLONEL. Daer, Mynheer Tradelove, is your discharge. *(Gives him a paper.)*

TRADELOVE. Be pleased to witness this receipt too, gentlemen.

*(Freeman and Sackbut put their hands.)*

FREEMAN. Ay, ay, that we will.

COLONEL. Well, mynheer, ye most meer doen; ye most myn voorspraek to de juffrow syn.[61]

FREEMAN. He means you must recommend him to the lady.

TRADELOVE. That I will, and to the rest of my brother guardians.

COLONEL. Wat voor den duyvel, heb you meer guardians?

TRADELOVE. Only three, mynheer.

COLONEL. Wat, donder heb ye myn betrocken, mynheer? Had ik that gewoeten, ik soude eaven met you geweest syn.

SACKBUT. But Mr. Tradelove is the principal, and he can do a great deal with the rest, sir.

FREEMAN. And he shall use his interest, I promise you, mynheer.

TRADELOVE. I will say all that ever I can think on to recommend you, mynheer; and if you please, I'll introduce you to the lady.

COLONEL. Well, dat is waer. Maer ye must first spreken of myn to de juffrow, and to de oudere, gentlemen.

FREEMAN. Ay, that's the best way, and then I and the Heer van Fainwell will meet you there.

TRADELOVE. I will go this moment, upon honor. Your most obedient humble servant.— *(Aside.)* My speaking will do you little good, mynheer, ha, ha; we have bit you, faith, ha ha; my debt's discharged, and for the man,
>    He's my consent—to get her if he can. *(Exit.)*

COLONEL. Ha, ha, ha, this was a masterpiece of contrivance, Freeman.

FREEMAN. He hugs himself with his supposed good fortune and little thinks the luck's of our side. But come, pursue the fickle goddess[62] while she's in the mood. Now for the Quaker.

COLONEL. That's the hardest task.
>    Of all the counterfeits performed by man,
>    A soldier makes the simplest Puritan. *(Exit.)*

# ACT V.

## Scene i. Prim's house.

*(Enter Mrs. Prim and Mrs. Lovely in Quaker's dress, meeting.)*

MRS. PRIM. So now I like thee, Ann. Art thou not better without thy monstrous hoop coat and patches? If Heaven should make thee so many black spots upon thy face, would it not fright thee, Ann?

MRS. LOVELY. If it should turn your inside outward and show all the spots of your hypocrisy, 'twould fright me worse.

MRS. PRIM. My hypocrisy! I scorn thy words, Ann; I lay no baits.

MRS. LOVELY. If you did, you'd catch no fish.

MRS. PRIM. Well, well, make thy jests, but I'd have thee to know, Ann, that I could have catched as many fish (as thou call'st them) in my time as ever thou didst with all thy fool traps about thee. If admirers be thy aim, thou wilt have more of them in this dress than thy other. The men, take my word for't, are most desirous to see what we are most careful to conceal.

MRS. LOVELY. Is that the reason of your formality, Mrs. Prim? Truth will out. I ever thought, indeed, there was more design than godliness in the pinched cap.

MRS. PRIM. Go, thou art corrupted with reading lewd plays and filthy romances, good for nothing but to lead youth into the high road of fornication. Ah! I wish thou art not already too familiar with the wicked ones.

MRS. LOVELY. Too familiar with the wicked ones! Pray, no more of those freedoms, madam; I am familiar with none so wicked as yourself. How dare you talk thus to me. You, you, you unworthy woman, you— *(Bursts into tears.)*

*(Enter Tradelove.)*

Tradelove. What, in tears, Nancy?—What have you done to her, Mrs. Prim, to make her weep?

Mrs. Lovely. Done to me! I admire I keep my senses among you. But I will rid myself of your tyranny if there be either law or justice to be had. I'll force you to give me up my liberty.

Mrs. Prim. Thou hast more need to weep for thy sins, Ann—yea, for thy manifold sins.

Mrs. Lovely. Don't think that I'll be still the fool which you have made me. No, I'll wear what I please, go when and where I please, and keep what company I think fit, and not what you shall direct—I will.

Tradelove. For my part, I do think all this very reasonable, Mrs. Lovely. 'Tis fit you should have your liberty, and for that very purpose I am come.

(Enter Mr. Periwinkle and Obadiah Prim with a letter in his hand.)

Periwinkle. I have bought some black stockings of your husband, Mrs. Prim, but he tells me the glover's trade belongs to you; therefore, I pray you look me out five or six dozen of mourning gloves, such as are given at funerals, and send them to my house.

Prim. My friend Periwinkle has got a good windfall today—seven hundred a year.

Mrs. Prim. I wish thee joy of it, neighbor.

Tradelove. What, is Sir Toby dead then?

Periwinkle. He is. —You'll take care, Mrs. Prim?

Mrs. Prim. Yea, I will, neighbor.

Prim (to Mrs. Prim). This letter recommendeth a speaker; 'tis from Aminadab Holdfast of Bristol; peradventure he will be here this night; therefore, Sarah, do thou take care for his reception. (Gives her the letter.)

Mrs. Prim. I will obey thee. (Exit.)

Prim. What are thou in the dumps for, Ann?

Tradelove. We must marry her, Mr. Prim.

Prim. Why truly, if we could find a husband worth having, I should be as glad to see her married as thou wouldst, neighbor.

Periwinkle. Well said; there are but few worth having.

Tradelove. I can recommend you a man now that I think you can none of you have an objection to.

*(Enter Sir Philip Modelove.)*

PERIWINKLE. You recommend! Nay, whenever she marries, I'll recommend the husband.

SIR PHILIP. What must it be, a whale or a rhinoceros, Mr. Periwinkle, ha, ha, ha? —Mr. Tradelove, I have a bill upon you *(Gives him a paper.),*[63] and have been seeking for you all over the town.

TRADELOVE. I'll accept it, Sir Philip, and pay it when due.

PERIWINKLE. He shall be none of the fops at your end of the town with full perukes and empty skulls, nor yet none of your trading gentry, who puzzle the heralds to find arms for their coaches. No, he shall be a man famous for travels, solidity, and curiosity—one who has searched into the profundity of nature. When Heaven shall direct such a one, he shall have my consent, because it may turn to the benefit of mankind.

MRS. LOVELY. The benefit of mankind! What, would you anatomize me?

SIR PHILIP. Ay, ay, madam, he would dissect you.

TRADELOVE. Or pore over you through a microscope to see how your blood circulates from the crown of your head to the sole of your foot, ha, ha! But I have a husband for you, a man that knows how to improve your fortune; one that trades to the four corners of the globe.

MRS. LOVELY. And would send me for a venture, perhaps.

TRADELOVE. One that will dress you in all the pride of Europe, Asia, Africa, and America—a Dutch merchant, my girl.

SIR PHILIP. A Dutchman! Ha, ha, there's a husband for a fine lady—ya juffrow, will you met myn slapen[64]—ha, ha. He'll learn you to talk the language of the hogs, madam, ha, ha.

TRADELOVE. He'll learn you that one merchant is of more service to a nation than fifty coxcombs. The Dutch know the trading interest to be of more benefit to the state than the landed.

SIR PHILIP. But what is either interest to a lady?

TRADELOVE. 'Tis the merchant makes the belle. How would the ladies sparkle in the box without the merchant? The Indian diamonds! The French brocade! The Italian fan! The Flanders lace! The fine Dutch holland! How would they vent their scandal over their tea tables? And where would you beaus have champagne to toast your mistress, were it not for the merchant?

PRIM. Verily, neighbor Tradelove, thou dost waste thy breath
about nothing. All that thou hast said tendeth only to debauch
youth and fill their heads with the price and luxury of this
world. The merchant is a very great friend to Satan and sendeth
as many to his dominions as the pope.

PERIWINKLE. Right, I say knowledge makes the man.

PRIM. Yea, but not thy kind of knowledge. It is the knowledge of
truth. Search thou for the light within and not for baubles,
friend.

MRS. LOVELY. Ah, study your country's good, Mr. Periwinkle, and
not her insects; rid you of your home-bred monsters before you
fetch any from abroad. I dare swear you have maggots enough
in your own brain to stock all the virtuosos in Europe with butterflies.

SIR PHILIP. By my soul, Miss Nancy's a wit.

PRIM. That is more than she can say by thee, friend. Look ye, it
is in vain to talk; when I meet a man worthy of her, she shall
have my leave to marry him.

MRS. LOVELY. Provided he be one of the faithful.— *(Aside.)* Was
there ever such a swarm of caterpillars to blast the hopes of a
woman?— *(Aloud.)* Know this: that you contend in vain. I'll
have no husband of your choosing, nor shall you lord it over
me long. I'll try the power of an English senate—orphans have
been redressed and wills set aside, and none did ever deserve
their pity more.— *(Aside.)* O Fainwell! Where are thy promises
to free me from these vermin? Alas, the task was more difficult
than he imagined!

> A harder task than what the poets tell
> Of yore, the fair Andromeda befell;
> She but one monster feared, I've four to fear,
> And see no Perseus, no deliv'rer near. *(Exit.)*

*(Enter Servant and whispers to Prim.)*

SERVANT. One Simon Pure inquireth for thee. *(Exit.)*

PERIWINKLE. The woman is mad. *(Exit.)*

SIR PHILIP. So are you all, in my opinion. *(Exit.)*

PRIM. Friend Tradelove, business requireth my presence.